I

Plays: 1

Progress, Fashion, Grace, Gaucho

Progress. 'Abrasive, bitter (not at all sweet), tightly written and heartbreakingly funny. It dispassionately examines the condition of contemporary urban solitude, the individual desperately trying to keep loneliness at bay ... searing, exact and poignant ... a play in a hundred.' *Observer*

Fashion: 'Compelling, dyspeptic ... sparky and tendentious ... very good indeed. Its subject, the relationship between advertising and politics, the selling of politicians like so many new brands of soap powder, is a fascinating one, and it is a real pleasure to encounter a show that puts a large number of articulate, maliciously drawn characters on stage and lets them argue both provocatively and entertainingly.' *Daily Telegraph*
'The finest play Lucie has written.' *Independent*

Grace: 'Doug Lucie is a writer with his ear to the ground and in *Grace* he has written a first-rate comedy not just about big-business evangelism but about a one-woman resistance to the Americanisation of Britain ... What makes this a thundering good play is that like its obvious prototype, *The Cherry Orchard*, it uses the sale of an estate as a social metaphor ... A buoyantly satirical evening.' *Guardian*

Gaucho, based on the career of Howard Marks, the Balliol drugs baron: 'Moss is a huge dramatic creation, the most interesting semi-fictional anti-hero since Hare and Brenton's Lambert LeRoux, a tragic waste of potential who in some other time and culture might have been a guerrilla leader or a national hero ... Lucie likes language, argument ... he speaks for a wounded, guilty generation ... absorbing.' *Time Out*

Doug Lucie was born in Chessington in 1953. He was Resident Playwright with the Oxford Playhouse Company from 1979–80 and worked as a Visiting Playwright to the University of Iowa, USA, in 1981. His plays include *John Clare's Mad, Nuncle* (Edinburgh, 1975), *Rough Trade* (Oxford Playhouse, 1977), *We Love You* (Roundhouse, 1978), *Oh Well* (Oxford Playhouse, 1978), *The New Garbo* (Hull Truck and King's Head, London 1978), *Heroes* (Edinburgh and New End Theatre, London, 1979), *Fear of the Dark* (read by the RSC at the Royal Court Theatre Upstairs, 1980), *Poison* (Edinburgh Festival, 1980), *Strangers in the Night* (New End, 1981), *Hard Feelings* (Oxford Playhouse tour, 1982; Bush Theatre, London, 1983; BBC TV 1984), *Progress* (Bush, 1984; winner of the *Plays and Players* Most Promising Playwright award), *Key to the World* (Paines Plough, Leicester Haymarket and Lyric Theatre Studio, Hammersmith, 1984), *A Class of his Own* (BBC TV, 1984), *Force* and *Hypocrisy* (Young Vic Studio, 1986), *Fashion* (RSC, Stratford, 1987; winner of the *Time Out* award), *Doing the Business* (Royal Court, London, 1990), *Grace* (Hampstead Theatre, 1992), *Gaucho* (Hampstead Theatre, 1994) and *The Shallow End* (Royal Court, 1997).

METHUEN DRAMA CONTEMPORARY DRAMATISTS

This collection first published in Great Britain 1998
by Methuen Drama

Progress first published by Methuen in 1985
Copyright © 1985 Doug Lucie
Fashion first published by Methuen in 1987
Copyright © 1987, 1991 Doug Lucie
Grace first published by Nick Hern Books Ltd in 1993
Copyright © 1993 Doug Lucie
Gaucho first published in this edition in 1998
Copyright © 1998 Doug Lucie

This collection copyright © 1998 Doug Lucie
Introduction copyright © 1998 Doug Lucie

The author has asserted his moral rights

ISBN 0-413-71690-2

A CIP catalogue record for this book
is available from the British Library

Typeset by Deltatype Ltd, Birkenhead, Merseyside

DOUG LUCIE

Plays: 1

Progress
Fashion
Grace
Gaucho

introduced by the author

Methuen Drama

Contents

Doug Lucie:
A Chronology

1975 *John Clare's Mad, Nuncle* performed at the Edinburgh
Festival.

1977 *Rough Trade* performed at the Oxford Playhouse.

1978 *We Love You* performed downstairs at the Round
House Theatre, London.
Oh Well performed at the Oxford Playhouse and *The
New Garbo* performed at Hull Truck and then at the
King's Head Theatre, London.

1979 *Heroes* performed at the Edinburgh Festival.

1980 *Poison* performed at the Edinburgh Festival, *Heroes*
revived at the New End Theatre, London.

1981 *Strangers in the Night* performed at the New End
Theatre.

1982 *Hard Feelings* performed on an Oxford Playhouse tour,
then at the Bush Theatre, London.

1984 *Progress* performed at the Bush Theatre, *Key to the
World* toured by Paine's Plough.

1987 *Fashion* performed by the Royal Shakespeare
Company, Stratford and London.

1990 *Doing the Business* performed at the Royal Court
Theatre, London.

1992 *Grace* performed at Hampstead Theatre, London.

1994 *Gaucho* performed at Hampstead Theatre.

1997 *The Shallow End* performed at the Royal Court
Theatre.

Introduction

The longer I have been writing plays, the more I have realised that control of the plays belongs to the characters. This is not to say that I don't have a strong idea of what I want to say, it simply means that however strongly I feel about the subject, once I begin writing, the direction of the play is only partly determined by my hand. Ultimately, the truth of the play lies in the truth of the characters, and this involves giving them an autonomy which is unique, I think, to drama. The most valuable lesson I learned early in my career, thanks to my long-time friend and collaborator Mike Bradwell, is that a script is only a beginning. It can be difficult at first to accept the loss of control over something which has been with you for what seems an eternity, but later, you come to the rehearsal process eager for the moment or moments where what you are trying to say is suddenly illuminated; where your intuitive mumblings are transformed into a vivid, living language. Only in the theatre does the writer get the opportunity to see his work investigated, explored, ripped apart and reassembled. Other media very rarely have either the time or the will to work this way, being economically constrained and ideologically repressed by market forces.

It is, of course, a truism to say in 1997 that we are at the mercy of market forces. The armies of accountants and marketing people, sponsorship, theatres which can no longer produce new plays, the candle-end cuts designed to give us all ulcers and remind us of the triviality of what we do compared with, say, selling knick-knacks and designer sandwiches to sleep-walking tourists make many people, myself included, pessimistic about the long-term future of the theatre in this country. Part of this is probably inevitable, though not irreversible. On the other hand, we must be aware that a market-forces-led, global communications culture will very quickly extinguish what it deems to be 'difficult' or 'boring' or even 'élitist', all words which are consistently applied to the theatre by its enemies. And they are not going to go away until they have taken over or closed down the few remaining spaces where intelligence, passion and spontaneous creativity still mean something. Meanwhile, an audience taught the safety of ironic detachment, meaningless self-reference and fear of any emotion other than fear, finds the human relationship of live theatre embarrassing. And as entertainment increasingly becomes merely a transaction between buyer and seller, these consumers will find our 'product' as alien to their needs as 'Supermarket Sweep' is to mine.

Our hope must be that the values of live theatre will not only be kept alive in our performing spaces, but that they will permeate the mainstream worlds of TV and Film, to remind audiences that as individuals and communities, we have a soul which needs nourishment if it is not to wither and die.

The plays in this volume are a testament to the many dedicated and talented people who have collaborated in their production. To those people, my thanks.

Doug Lucie
August 1997

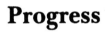

Progress

Characters

Ronee, *33 years old. She is an administrator of a South London Community and Arts Centre. A tough, articulate woman.*

Will, *34 years old. Ronee's husband. He is a Current Affairs researcher at Channel 4. Very much Ronee's male equivalent, though he is slightly in awe of her.*

Oliver, *31 years old. A crafts stallholder. He is small and very talkative, particularly when drunk.*

Martin, *29 years old. He is supposedly Oliver's bisexual live-in companion. He is witty and superficially callous.*

Bruce, *32 years old. A barman. He cultivates a quiet, rather macho image. He is shy, with a stammer.*

Ange, *20 years old. A young wife staying with Ronee and Will, having left her husband after he beat her. Shy and reserved, though with a tough streak.*

Lenny, *21 years old. Ange's husband. He is a car mechanic, conventionally inarticulate, but with animal cunning and an evil sense of humour.*

Mark, *32 years old. He is Ronee's and Will's tenant, a journalist on the Daily Express. Outspoken, a constant stream of fairly tasteless jokes being his trademark. He is already going to seed, but regards himself as irresistible.*

Progress was first presented at the Bush Theatre, London on 2 July, 1984, with the following cast:

Ronee	Lindsay Duncan
Will	Gregory Floy
Oliver	David Bamber
Martin	Kevin Elyot
Bruce	Struan Rodger
Ange	Sharon Maiden
Lenny	Perry Fenwick
Mark	David Cardy

Directed by David Hayman
Designed by Geoff Rose

Act One

Scene One

Monday morning, 10 a.m.

Ronee *is at the table eating muesli and fruit for breakfast.* **Will** *is standing in his dressing gown, rubbing his hair with a towel. She's leafing through the* Guardian *while on the stereo a tape recording of* **Oliver** *'s voice plays.*

Oliver . . . To see him like that. Terrible, just terrible. (*Beat.*) And he denies it, y'know? He can hardly stand up. And he looks me in the eye and says, 'Ollie, on my mother's grave, I haven't touched a drop.' (**Will** *goes off.*) And when I point out that Gran was cremated and therefore doesn't have a grave . . . (*Pause.*) And the next thing. 'All right, Ollie, I admit it. I might have had one or two'. One or two. The amount of vodka he gets through, he's single-handedly keeping the Russian economy afloat. And then it's tears. He breaks down. Y'know? Your own father grovelling around on the floor, begging you to forgive him. I mean, Christ, it hurts. (*Pause. The sound of a drink being poured.*) And, like, my kid brother, it cracks him up completely. He drinks himself senseless. It gets the whole family. My mother doesn't speak to any of us, hardly, any more.

Ronee Clever girl.

Oliver And that's the point. It's her I feel most sorry for. Thirty-five years married to the guy, and he turns out a jerk. What can you say? Tough luck, Mum? (*Pause.*) She's in the WI, y'know. She's not exactly a sister, if you know what I mean. (*Pause.*) I hate him for what he's done. But he is my father. (**Will** *enters, partly dressed.*) Can anybody give me any idea what I can do?

Ronee Switch that awful little twerp off, will you?

Oliver I need help.

Will *switches off the tape.*

Ronee How many hours of tape have you got with that drunk going on about his father?

Will It's not always his father. There's also non-aggressive football supporting, coming to terms with a bisexual nature, and the problems of getting your non-patriarchal leg over. (*Beat.*) He does need help though.

Ronee He needs a psychiatrist, not a men's group.

Will Ronee, love, we're trying.

The phone rings.

Ronee I'll say. (*She answers the phone.*) Hello. Oh, hi. Wie geht's? (*Beat.*) Ja, richtig. Das werden fabulos sein. (*Beat.*) 'The Poison Girls.' Feminist Gruppe. (*She laughs.*) Liar. Du verstehst. (*Beat.*) OK. Sechs Uhr. Ja. (*She glances in* **Will**'s *direction. He's leafing through the paper.*) Ich liebe dich. OK. Tschuss. (*She puts the phone down.*)

Will My clipping got in 'Naked Ape'.

Ronee I saw.

Will Spelled my name wrong, though.

Ronee I saw that too.

Will How's Andrea?

Ronee Fine.

Will She hasn't been round for ages. I'd love to see her. Why don't you ask her to dinner some time? (*Pause.*) It'd just be nice, that's all I mean.

Ronee No.

Will It's not very fair. She's not your property.

Ronee I saw her first.

Mark *enters. He looks as if he's been up for hours, though he hasn't.*

Mark Yo. (*He goes straight to* **Ronee** *and points at her nipples, which are showing under her t-shirt.*) Is it cold in here, or are you just glad to see me?

She starts to go.

That was fantastic last night. Best ever. Don't let on to Will, though. Don't want to make him jealous.

She's gone.

Morning, brother.

Will Good morning, Mark. I'm trying to read the paper, so shut up.

Mark That rag? Call that a paper? This is a paper. (*He holds up the* Daily Express.) And I should know. (*He opens it up.*) Oh, yes. I like it. Look at that. (*He spreads the paper out on the table.*) All my own work.

Will *stares at it.*

Will Mark, tell me, what exactly *is* a love nest?

Mark Depends. In this case it's a council house where a dypso has-been DJ lives on the dole with a very tasty social worker.

Will And you don't think maybe he'd like to be left alone?

Mark Bollocks. He loved it. He's making a come-back, see?

Ange *comes in. She's wearing a see-through blouse over which she's about to put on a jumper.* **Mark** *points at her breasts.*

If you're selling those puppies, I'll have the one on the right with the brown nose.

She quickly puts the jumper on.

Spoilt a lovely view.

Will Hi. Make yourself some breakfast if you want.

Ange Ta. (*She goes out to the kitchen.*)

Mark You dirty dog.

Will Mark . . .

Mark I don't suppose she wants to make an old man very happy.

Will Her name is Ange. She's staying here for a few days on account of her husband keeps using her for a sparring partner and she doesn't box. She doesn't need you breathing down her neck.

Mark It's not her neck I want to breathe down.

Will Give it a rest.

Mark Rest? Bloody hell, rest's about right. Last night I picked up this nymphomaniac . . .

Will I don't want to hear.

Mark . . . Went back to her place, I was done in by midnight. And she kept farting non-stop. Had to scrape the duvet off the ceiling.

Then this morning, I woke up, I felt so rough I had to have a wank to get my heart started.

Ronee *appears at the door.*

Ronee See you.

Will What time'll you be back?

Ronee Late. We've got a social tonight.

Will I could drop in . . .

Ronee Women only.

Will Ah.

Mark A woman's place is in the oven, that's what I always say.

Ronee If you could be late with the rent just once, so I could kick you out.

Mark You love it, really.

Ronee Oh, get cancer.

She goes. He shouts after her.

Mark Don't forget to leave the window open. I'll be up that drainpipe. (*A door slams.*) Here, this fella's walking down the street, sees an old mate. He thinks, funny, he looks like a woman. So he says, 'What's happened to you?' Fella says, 'I've done it, I've had the operation.' So this bloke says, 'Didn't it hurt?' Other bloke says, 'No.' He says, 'What, not when they give you tits?' He says, 'No.' He says, 'Not when they, y'know cut it off?' He says, 'No.' Then he says, 'I'll tell you what did hurt, that's when they shrunk my brain and widened my mouth.' (*He laughs.*)

Will Jesus. You should see someone, y'know. Get professional help.

Mark I've got it. Swedish massage in Brewer Street.

Ange *comes in with a bowl of cereal.*

Hello again.

Ange 'Lo.

Mark I'm Mark. I live in the attic.

Ange Oh.

Mark If you ever feel like coming up to see my etchings . . .

Ange Don't think so.

Mark The door's always open.

Will Have a bit of tact, will you?

Mark Most tactful man in Fleet Street, me.

Will This isn't Fleet Street.

Mark Don't you believe it. We get everywhere. (*Beat.*) Talking of which, I'd better get to work. I'm after some woofter pop singer today.

Will God . . .

Mark Horrible little fudge-packer.

Will Just go, will you?

Mark I'm on my bike. (*To* **Ange** *as he goes.*) Hey, don't forget to leave your window open tonight. I'll be straight up that drainpipe.

Will D'you know what time you'll be back?

Mark No idea. Tell you what, if I'm not in bed by twelve, I'll come home.

Will Don't come barging in if I've got people here.

Mark You should let me in. I'm great fun at orgies.

He goes.

Will That was supposed to be a joke.

Ange Eh?

Will Orgies. You look worried. (*Pause.*) Sit down, make yourself at home. (*She does.*) He's all mouth and trousers.

Ange He's creepy.

Will Sitting tenant, I'm afraid. Comes with the house. Our resident damp patch. (*Pause.*) Hey look, while you're here, treat the place like your own. Don't feel . . . inhibited or anything. (*She nods.*) It's rough for you, I know. Anything we can do, just say.

Ange Ta. (*Pause.*) Cup of tea? I made a pot.

Will Yeah, lovely.

She gets up and goes to the kitchen. He stares at her and takes a deep breath and raises his eyebrows, or does something to indicate he finds her attractive.

He goes over to the stereo and turns on the tape quietly. We can't make out what's being said. **Ange** *comes back in with two cups of tea. He takes his tea and sips.*

Great. Worker's tea. Ronee always makes the perfumed stuff. Earl Grey. Me, I'm an unashamed PG Tips man. (*Pause.*) What I call worker's tea. (*He switches off the tape.*)

Ange What's that?

Will It's a tape of the men's group that meets round here. (*She looks blank.*) We talk about things . . . Try to understand and come to terms with sexism, relationships, that kind of stuff. We're trying to change our attitudes by being open and supportive without resorting to traditional, hierarchical structures. (*Beat.*) Trying to prove that not all men are monsters.

Ange Oh.

Will Y'know, like your husband.

Pause.

Ange He's just a rotten git.

Will Yeah, well . . . (*Pause.*) I can never understand a man hitting a woman. I don't mean that in a sexist way, chivalry, all that crap. I mean, it seems such a pointless thing to do. So negative.

Ange Well, I did hit him with the frying pan.

Pause.

Will Why?

Ange Tried to put my head through the window, didn't he?

Will When it was shut?

Ange 'Course.

Will Not very nice.

Ange No. He's a rotten git.

Will Then he hit you, did he?

Ange Yeah.

Will Poor kid. (*Pause.*) This is great tea. You can come again. (*Pause.*) Well, I better stroll into work, I suppose. (*He puts on his socks, shoes and jacket.*) D'you work?

Ange Only down the Centre.

Will Right. Ronee told me.

Ange Lenny don't like the idea of me going to work.

Will Bit prehistoric, your Lenny. Drags you around by the hair as well, does he? (*She shrugs.*) Maybe he should join our group.

Ange He's got his mates. He goes out on the piss with them. Right rotten lot, they are. Do some rotten things. (*Pause.*) D'you know what they done? Last year?

Will Shock me.

Ange They went camping down Cornwall. Before we was married, this is. And they was at this disco, and they got Bobby – he's the nice one, that's why they call him Bobby, out of Dallas – and they stripped him naked, nude, y'know, and they handcuffed him to this girl in the disco. And Bobby and this girl had to go all the way back to the campsite to get the key. And they wouldn't let her go. They never done nothing to her, but they kept here there. And they all thought it was dead funny. Then her boyfriend came and got her, but he couldn't do nothing 'cause there's like eight of them. I mean, and they thought it was dead funny.

Will Sad, very sad. (*He's dressed: t-shirt, jeans, Kickers.*) Right. Well, look, I'll see you tonight. Help yourself to food and anything else. Ronee gave you a key, did she?

Ange Yeah.

Will OK. I'll see you later. Take care.

He goes. She looks round the room, ending up at the stereo. She turns on the tape, picks up the two cups and goes to the kitchen as **Will***'s voice plays on the tape:*

Basically, what we're talking about, I suppose, is understanding our own maleness.

Fade.

Scene Two

Monday lunchtime.

Ange *comes into the room with a sandwich and a cup of tea. Radio One is playing on the stereo. She sits on the sofa and flips through a copy of* Spare Rib. *The doorbell rings. She looks up. It rings again. She gets up and goes* *through to the front door. Pause.* **Lenny** *appears.* **Ange** *follows him in, and turns off the radio.*

Ange I never said you could come in.

Lenny I'm in now, ain't I?

Ange This ain't your house.

Lenny Ain't yours, neither. (*Pause.*) Bit tasty, this, innit?

Ange What you want?

Lenny Come to look at the drains, ain't I? What the fuck d'you think I want?

Ange Don't start swearing.

Pause.

Lenny Don't I get a cup of tea?

Ange No. (*Pause.*) How'd you know I was here?

Lenny I asked down the Centre. (*Pause. He takes a piece of paper out of his pocket and gives it to her.*) Here.

Ange What is it?

Lenny Open it up. Find out.

She does.

Ange Oh, God . . .

Lenny Read it, then.

Ange Don't want to.

Lenny Why not?

Ange 'Cause I don't.

Pause.

Lenny I wrote it for you.

Ange I didn't think you wrote it for the milkman.

Lenny Read it.

Ange I've read your poems before.

Lenny It's a different one though, innit? It's a new one. Go on.

She gives it a cursory reading.

Ange Yeah. Lovely.

Lenny You never read it.

Ange I did.

Lenny You never. Takes longer than that. Read it properly.

Ange I have read it properly.

Pause.

Lenny Rotten cow.

Pause. She reads it again.

Ange There.

Lenny Like it?

Ange Dunno.

Lenny What d'you mean? Dunno?

Ange I mean, I dunno.

Lenny Don't be stupid. Either you like it or you don't.

Ange I like it.

Lenny Good. (*Pause.*) How come I don't get a cup of tea?

Ange 'Cause you ain't staying.

Lenny Says who?

Ange I do.

He takes a packet of sandwiches out of his overalls pocket.

Lenny I've got to have something to wash me dinner down.

Ange What d'you think you're doing?

Lenny It's me dinner. This is me dinner hour so I'm gonna have me dinner.

Ange Not here you ain't.

He stuffs a sandwich in his mouth.

Lenny Bleedin' well am.

Ange You horrible pig. (*Beat.*) Who made them, then?

Lenny Me mum. (*Beat.*) Egg and cress. Lovely.

Ange You don't like egg.

Lenny I do the way me mum does it.

Ange You can't do nothing with egg, 'cept boil it.

Lenny She mashes it up. With salad cream. Tasty.

Ange Get food poisoning if your mum made it.

Lenny Dead tasty.

He eats. She goes to the kitchen. He looks round the room. He picks up the Spare Rib *and reads it. She comes back in with a cup of tea.*

What the fucking hell d'you call this?

She snatches it off him.

Ange I call it a magazine. What d'you call it?

Lenny Pile o' crap, I call it.

Ange It's nothing to do with you.

Lenny Load o'bollocks. (*Pause.*) Here, Dink and Wobbler had a scrap last night. Down the Duke. Dink bust his finger. (*Beat.*) Pretty good scrap, they reckon.

Pause.

Ange Kids.

Lenny Eh?

Ange Nothing.

Lenny What?!

Ange Kids! You are. Bloody scraps. Bloody stupid nicknames. You're supposed to grow outa that sorta thing when you leave school, y'know.

Pause.

Lenny They're *my* mates.

Ange You can have them.

Pause.

Lenny Right. When you coming back?

Ange You what?

Lenny I got the motor outside. You can dump your gear in it now if you like. Don't matter if I'm a bit late back. (*Pause.*) You ain't making a lot of noise here, doll. (*Pause.*) C'mon. You've usually got enough rabbit for both of us.

Ange 'S not true. I can't say nothing, case you don't like it.

Lenny Only when you're talking crap.

Ange Yeah. Which is most of the time, according to you.

Lenny Well, you ain't exactly Mastermind, are you?

Ange Which university did you go to, then?

Beat.

Lenny I asked you a question. When you coming back?

Ange Dunno.

Lenny Don't know fuck all, you. (*Pause.*) Listen, I ain't got time to muck about. Get your stuff. (*Beat.*) C'mon.

Ange I ain't going nowhere. Not yet.

Beat.

Lenny Ange. 'Case you've forgotten, you're my wife.

Ange 'Case you've forgotten, I ain't a punch-bag.

Lenny You're my wife.

Ange Makes it all right, does it?

Lenny You ain't s'posed to piss off every time we have a bit of a barney.

Ange What *am* I s'posed to do?

Beat.

Lenny What other women do.

Ange What, like Rose?

Lenny Like Rose what?

Ange Your rotten brother breaks her nose and won't even let her go to the hospital, 'case the Old Bill do him for it. I ain't standing for nothing like that.

Lenny When'd I ever break your nose?

Ange Had a bloody good try.

Lenny 'S just a little tap. Anyway, you hit me.

Ange You hit me first.

Pause.

Lenny Look . . . I won't. All right? I won't hit you again.

Ange Pigs might fly.

Lenny I won't. (*Beat.*) I never knew you was gonna leave, did I? Wouldn't have hit you if I did.

Ange What do you expect me to do? (*Pause.*) Eh?

Lenny I dunno. (*Pause.*) Me mum never left me dad when he hit her.

Ange I ain't your mum. And I ain't gonna end up like her, neither.

Lenny What you mean?

Ange You know what I mean. You can end up like your dad if you want, but I ain't ending up like your mum.

Lenny I dunno what you're on about.

Ange Don't you?

Lenny No.

Beat.

Ange Comin' home from work, and if your dinner ain't on the table shouting your head off and kicking the poor bloody dog's what I'm on about. Not letting my mates in the house is what I'm on about. And if they do manage to get past the front bloody door, telling us to shut up 'cause you're watching 'Crossroads' is what I'm bloody on about.

Lenny Well, you sat there jabbering on. Drives me fucking mad.

Ange And you sat there, like bloody God in front of the bloody telly. Drives me mad.

Lenny What's wrong with watching the telly all of a sudden? I work bloody hard all day, I wanna come home and relax.

Ange With your flies undone.

Lenny You what?

Ange You always undo your trousers, soon as you get in that chair.

Beat.

Lenny What's that got to do with anything?

Ange I hate it.

Lenny What? Me undoing me trousers?

Ange Yeah. It's gross. (*He looks puzzled.*) D'you know what I'm talking about?

Lenny I ain't got a fucking clue.

Ange That's it, innit? You ain't. You don't understand nothing I say 'cause you never listen. (*The door slams.*) Oh, Christ, now I'm for it.

Mark (*from the hallway*) Lock up your daughters, 'cause . . . (*He enters and sees* **Lenny**. *Pause.*) How do.

Lenny Wotcher.

Pause.

Ange 'S Lenny. My husband.

Mark Oh, right. Pleased to meet you. (*They shake.*) Thought perhaps you were a burglar. (*Feeble laugh.*) Mark. I live in the attic. (*Beat.*) Uh . . . I forgot my address book. Had to pop back and get it. (*Beat.*) Upstairs.

He goes.

Lenny Who's that then?

Ange I dunno. I just met him this morning. He's a creep.

Lenny Yeah? Looked a bit glad to see you, didn't he?

Ange How should I know?

Pause.

Lenny Where you kipping, then?

Ange You what? Upstairs.

Lenny Yeah, in the attic?

Ange Bloody hell. You're cracked you are. I only met him this morning.

Lenny So what's he doing here now?

Ange He lives here, for God's sake. And he said, 'forgot his address book,' didn't he?

Lenny What, you think I just stepped off the banana boat?

Ange Wish you'd step off a bloody cliff.

Lenny (*standing*) Ange . . .

Mark *reappears.*

Mark Here we are, then. (*He holds up his address book.*)

Lenny Do us another cup of tea, will you?

Ange *goes to the kitchen.*

Mark That's OK. I haven't got time. (*He puts the book in his case.*) You patching things up?

Lenny What's it to you?

Mark Me? Sod all. (*Pause.*) None of my business, pal. I just live here. Tenant, that's all I am. I don't have any say in who comes in and out. That's all down to Will and Ronee. Well, Ronee.

Lenny She the bint from the Centre?

Mark Yeah. Miss Bra Burner of sixty-eight. Mind you, he's no better. Can't say a bloody word round here without getting your head bitten off. Trendy lefties. About as much fun as a plane crash.

Lenny You can always move.

Mark Do us a favour. NW6, highly des. res.? Twenty-five quid a week? I wouldn't move if we had Brezhnev in the basement. Which, for all I know, we might very well have. (**Ange** *comes back in and gives* **Lenny** *his tea.*) Anyway, I've got to go stake out some woofter pop singer. (*They look confused.*) I'm a journalist.

Lenny Yeah?

Mark God's gift to the gutter press. Don't you believe it. So, I'll see you.

Lenny See you.

Mark *goes.*

Journalist, is he?

Ange That's what he said.

Beat.

Lenny This tea's rotten.

Ange Hard luck.

Lenny Trying to poison me, are you?

Ange If you don't want it . . . (*She goes to take it.*)

Lenny Leave off . . .

Ange If it's so bloody rotten . . . (*He snatches it back from her and spills some.*) Oh, you pig. (*She rushes out. He smiles and slowly starts to pour more on the floor. She comes back with a cloth.*) What you doing?

Lenny It's good for the shag pile.

Ange You bloody pig. (*She goes down on all fours and rubs the carpet.*)

Lenny (*laughing*) Fucking look at you.

Ange What's funny?

Lenny Mrs Fucking Mop. Got you skivvying for them, have they? Doing the dishes?

Ange No. Fuck off. (**Lenny** *laughs again. Pause.*) I'll have to shampoo this . . .

He suddenly goes down on his knees behind her and holds her hips tightly. She freezes.

Lenny You coming home?

Pause.

Ange No.

Blackout.

Scene Three

Monday. 7 p.m.

Bruce *is sitting in one of the chairs. He is gripping a wrist strengthener. A door slams off stage.* **Ronee** *enters and puts her bag on the table.*

Ronee Hello, Bruce. (*He raises his hand and gives a half-smile.*) Where's Will?

Bruce Uh . . . probably, I think . . . In the kitchen, maybe.

Ronee He's not cooking, is he?

Bruce Yeah, well . . . He mentioned . . . something, uh, Chinese.

Ronee Delia Smith, eat your heart out.

Bruce Spare . . . ribs in, uh, black bean sauce. I think.

Ronee Sounds ridiculous enough.

She goes out and upstairs.

Bruce Uh, yeah.

He starts clenching again. **Will** *enters.*

Will Did I hear Ronee?

Bruce Yeah.

Will *goes to the door and shouts upstairs.*

Will Ronee?

Ronee (*off*) What?

Will What are you doing?

Ronee (*off*) Getting changed.

Will Oh, right. D'you want some food?

Ronee (*off*) I've eaten.

Will Ribs in black bean sauce.

Ronee (*off*) I've eaten.

Will OK. Sometimes I think my wife doesn't like my cooking. Help yourself to a drink, Bruce.

He goes. **Bruce** *goes to the drinks. He pours a vodka, holds the glass up and downs it in one. He puts the glass down and takes a can of beer. As he sits and opens it,* **Ronee** *enters, changed, and gets her bag. As she goes she calls to* **Will** *in the kitchen:*

Ronee Don't wait up for me.

She goes.

Will (*off*) What? (*He appears.*) What?

Bruce Don't wait . . . up for me. She said.

Will Jesus, she could have waited.

Pause.

Bruce Uh . . . Maybe she . . . needs space . . .

Will (*pouring a glass of wine*) Ollie and Martin are late.

Bruce (*looking at his watch*) Six . . . minutes.

Will Yeah. (*Pause. They are not very comfortable together.*) You had any joy with the flat-hunting?

Bruce I saw a . . . flat at the, uh, Oval?

Will Any good?

Bruce Great.

Will Problem settled, then.

Bruce Uh, no.

Will How come?

Bruce Like . . . Uh, it's got three . . . skinheads squatting in it.

Will Ah. Slight problem.

Bruce Right.

Pause.

Will Is it council?

Bruce Yeah.

Will They'll evict them, won't they?

Bruce Well . . . Yeah, but . . . Really heavy . . . Police and everything . . . Lot of hassle . . .

Will I suppose it would be.

Bruce So, uh . . . I guess something'll . . . Come up.

Will Best of luck.

Bruce (*taking some small bottles out of his bag*): Want some . . . Vitamins?

Will No. Thanks. (**Bruce** *takes some.*) Eat healthy food, you don't need them.

Bruce They're just, y'know . . . A boost.

Will Sure.

Bruce And . . . I don't enjoy it, uh, cooking, a lot . . .

Will I love it, I really do. It's a hobby for me and it liberates Ronee.

Bruce Sort of . . . reversal of, uh, roles . . .

Will Yeah, sort of. (*Beat.*) And it's so bloody easy, y'know. Take this thing I'm knocking up now. When I first read the recipe, I thought, Jesus, stroll on, back to the drawing board. But then I made it a couple of times and now, I can do it from memory. Chop the garlic, ginger, onion, soak the black beans, mix it all together with sherry, soya sauce and water, fry the ribs for five minutes, drain off the oil, put in the black bean mixture, stir fry for half a minute, cover and heat for ten minutes, put in cornflour, water and sugar, stir fry very hot, hey presto. No sweet and sour and a number ninety-three to go, please. This is the genuine article.

Pause.

Bruce I, uh . . . can't . . . wait . . .

Will You'll have to, till Ollie and Martin get here, I'm afraid. Help yourself to drink.

He starts to go.

Bruce I'm OK . . . Thanks.

Pause. **Will** *goes.* **Bruce** *goes to the drinks and pours another vodka and downs it in one. The doorbell rings.*

Will (*off*) Get that, will you, Bruce?

Bruce *goes to the door. As soon as he opens it, we can hear* **Oliver** *talking, very fast, very agitated.*

Oliver Hi, Bruce. Sorry I'm late. Fucking Martin. (*They enter.*) He's not here by the remotest bloody chance, is he? No. 'Course he isn't. Where is he? Your guess is as good as mine, mate. That man is a walking bloody disaster area. I haven't seen any trace of him since last night. Lunch today? No show. Help me out on the stall this afternoon so I can go and see the bank manager? No bloody show. Meet at six in the Dragon? Ha. And where is he? Check missing persons. It's your best bet. I need a drink. (*He pours a huge glass of red wine.*) He could be lying headless in the Thames mud for all I know. I mean, I need this, y'know? I really need this.

Will *enters.*

Will, I'm sorry. Fucking Martin. I'd've been here hours ago, except he didn't show up. I've been hanging on.

Will No bother.

Oliver What does he think he's up to? Ask him. If he ever turns up. You ask him. 'Cause he won't tell me. Might as well talk to the trees for all the information I get out of fucking Martin.

Will Calm down, mate. We've got all night.

Oliver But it's not fair, though, is it? I mean it's not fair to me, it's not fair to you. I'm really going to give him a piece of my mind this time. He's completely buggered up my day. (*Beat.*) I know it's negative but I am bloody furious.

Pause.

Bruce Would you . . . like some vitamins?

Oliver Peace of mind, Bruce, that's all I need. A little bit of mental tranquillity is what I'm after.

Will *pours another glass of wine.*

Bruce But apart from that . . . Mrs Lincoln . . . What did you, uh . . .

Oliver Think of the play.

Bruce Think of . . .

Beat.

Oliver It's the way you tell 'em, Bruce.

Slight discomfort.

Will No point starting without Martin, is there, really?

Oliver Will, I don't know if he's still even in the country, let alone anywhere near the vicinity of North West London. Start if you like.

Will Let's give it a few minutes. (*Beat.*) Hey, I might have something quite interesting for us tonight.

Bruce (*to* **Ollie**) Spare ribs . . . in . . .

Will No, not the food.

Bruce Oh.

Will One of the women from the Centre's been staying here. Her husband's been bashing her about. Ronee brought her back last night. You should see her, poor kid.

Oliver That makes my blood boil. What sort of man does that?

Will Anyway, I thought if she was up to it, we could maybe talk to her.

Oliver I don't know . . .

Will I don't mean give her the third degree. I mean talk. Constructively. Positively. Y'know, show support.

Oliver Probably frighten her to death.

Will Well, obviously, if . . .

Bruce It's the husband . . . we should . . . talk to.

Oliver The thing is, Will, we're supposed to be helping ourselves, right? The group is for us to examine ourselves. (*Beat.*) It's pornography tonight. That's what I've come to talk about. Pornography. I've been working on it all week.

Pause.

Will Sure. OK. Pornography it is.

The doorbell rings. **Will** *goes out.* **Ollie** *pours another drink. Voices outside.* **Will** *and* **Martin** *enter.*

The prodigal returns.

Martin Hi, gang. Sorry I'm late. Will, I could severely molest a G and T, if that's OK.

Will Sure. (*He pours it.*)

Martin Didn't start without me, did you?

Will No.

Martin Good. (**Will** *hands him his drink.*) Thanks. Everybody have a good day?

Will So-so.

Martin Bruce? Good day?

Bruce I . . . saw a film.

Martin Good film?

Bruce Uh . . . No.

Beat.

Martin Ollie? Good day? (*Beat.*) Ollie?

Oliver What?

Martin Did you have a good day? (*Silence.*) You do like to keep us guessing, don't you?

Oliver I had a fucking awful day.

Beat.

Martin Uh-huh.

Pause.

Will What about you?

Martin Me? Well, one day's very much the same as another, really, I tend to find. They all sort of merge. I'm never quite sure where one ends and another begins. So today was . . . another day. Didn't exactly register on the Richter scale or anything.

Oliver God . . .

Martin *looks at him. Pause.*

Will I've still got a couple of things to do in the kitchen. Won't be a minute. (*As he goes, he touches* **Bruce** *on the shoulder.*)

Bruce I want to, uh, see . . . how he does it   . . Chinese . . .

He goes.

Martin My God, how bloody polite. (*Pause.*) OK. Let's have it, Ollie.

Oliver Martin, you've no idea how disappointed, how let down, I feel.

Martin Don't be daft. Of course I have.

Oliver Then how can you . . .? (*Pause.*) What did you do last night?

Martin Oh, I went to a party.

Oliver Whose?

Martin Piers and Molly. You know Piers and . . .

Oliver I don't know Piers and Molly.

Martin I'm sure you do.

Oliver I do not.

Martin I thought you met them at Sandra's that time . . . (*Pause.*) Maybe not.

Oliver No.

Martin I'll invite them round. You'd love Molly, she's a scream.

Oliver Where?

Martin Where is she a scream?

Oliver Where was the party?

Martin Oh. At Piers and Molly's.

Oliver Which is where?

Pause.

Martin Let me get this right. You're asking me these absurd questions because you think what?

Oliver Where were you?

Martin Because you think I was . . . What?

Oliver Where?

Martin I was what?

Oliver Screwing around!

Pause. **Martin** *starts to laugh. He gets up and looks round the room.*

Martin (*opening a cupboard*) No. No one there. (*He looks under the sofa.*) No. The room is empty. Apart from us. (*Beat.*) So. Who's it for? Who are you trying to kid?

Oliver You were going to look after the stall this afternoon.

Martin (*genuine*) Ah, I forgot. Honest.

Oliver Why?

Martin I don't know. (*Beat.*) I'm sorry.

Oliver Martin, believe me, you tear me apart sometimes. (*Pause.*) D'you know what I'm saying?

Martin Yes.

Oliver We've both made a commitment. We've both got to keep it up.

Martin I really did forget. (*Pause.*) So, did you get to the bank?

Oliver How could I?

Pause.

Martin I'll do the stall all day tomorrow. How's that?

Oliver It's something.

Martin Take the day off. Have fun or something.

Oliver Yeah.

Martin Look, don't let's fight.

Oliver OK.

Pause.

Martin Perhaps I ought to let Will and Bruce know we're . . .

Oliver I'll do it. (*He starts to go.*) I need you, mate.

Martin I need you too.

Ollie *goes.* **Martin** *breathes out loudly and gets another drink as* **Bruce** *comes in. They look at each other. Pause.*

All sorted out.

Bruce *nods. He goes to the drinks, pours a vodka and drinks it down in one.* **Martin** *smiles. They look at each other.* **Martin** *throws a glance at the door and turns back. They kiss.* **Bruce** *sits down as* **Will** *and* **Ollie** *come back in.*

Will . . . No, light soya sauce you use more with fish or chicken. In South East Asian food, mainly.

Oliver Oh, I see.

Will Talking of which, did you get to that Malayan place I told you about?

Martin No, not yet.

Will Well, don't forget. You'll thank me.

Martin We could try it tomorrow, couldn't we, Ollie?

Oliver Yeah, why not?

They all settle.

Will OK. Why don't we get started?

Oliver Whose turn is it to chair?

Will (*setting up the tape recorder*) I did it last week.

Oliver So . . . alphabetically . . . It's Bruce's turn.

Martin Will – by the way, how's Ronee?

Will Busy. Very busy.

Martin She's an amazing lady.

Will I know.

Oliver I believe we covered the use of the word 'lady' in our first meeting, didn't we?

Martin Deliberate irony, Ollie.

Oliver Sloppy consciousness, Martin. Very sloppy.

Martin I know. 'Chick, bint, skirt, tart, crumpet, tail, little woman, wifey, bit of stuff'. These words will never again pass my lips.

Oliver Or 'lady'.

Martin You really are becoming a little commissar, you know that?

Oliver It's important. It's what this is all about. What's the point of changing the way we behave if we don't change the way we speak? Y'know?

Martin Right on.

Beat.

Will Tape's running. OK, Bruce.

Bruce Right, Uh . . . Pornography. Shall we . . . do it as normal . . . ?

Martin Beg your pardon?

Bruce I mean . . . Like we . . . Someone start off and . . . Y'know . . .

Oliver I think we should start by talking about our experience of pornography. As men. Be honest about it. OK?

Martin Off you go, Ollie.

Beat.

Oliver OK. I've used pornography. In the past. I'm ashamed to say it, but it's true.

Will Why are you ashamed to say it?

Oliver Because I feel I've exploited fellow human beings. Namely, women. Merely to satisfy selfish male desires. And, I mean, it doesn't stop there does it? Once you've seen one picture of a woman offering herself to you, that's it. The mind automatically makes the connection: all women are like that. Because it appeals to immaturity. We've all got that bit of us that's still four years old, the bit that made us fumble around in bushes and school toilets, finding out what bodies were like. That's the bit of us that's brought into play when we use pornography.

Martin That's the bit of you that's brought into play.

Oliver OK. So, I'm generalising. But isn't it true?

Will I think we should define what we mean by pornography, and what we mean by 'using' pornography.

Oliver All right. I've got us off on the wrong foot.

Martin Again.

Oliver OK. I apologise.

Bruce Doesn't matter.

Will So. Definitions.

Oliver Well, I agree with the feminist argument that all pornography is based on violence against women.

Will Even 'Zipper'?

Oliver Gay porn, obviously, is different. Maybe we can discuss that separately.

Martin Separatism, so soon?

Oliver Try and keep it serious, please, Martin.

Will Look, there are many different types of porn. There's straightforward *Mayfair* crotch shots, there's the gynaecological crotch shot. There's spanking, bondage, SM, TV, lesbianism . . .

Oliver For a male audience . . .

Will Agreed. There's straight couples, groups, animals, paedophiles. All catering to different people, to different needs. So. Do we lump them all together, and say they're all based on violence against women? Or do we try to understand if and how they differ, in content and function? And then explain if and how they may be relevant to our own lives.

Beat.

Oliver Are we supposed to sit here and discuss each variant in sordid bloody detail?

Bruce Well . . . yes . . .

Will *gets up and takes a carrier bag from the cupboard.*

Will They're all in there. I bought a selection.

Oliver God's sake, Will . . .

Will Why not? If we're going to discuss it, we might as well know what we're talking about.

Oliver We do know . . .

Will And most important, if we're going to try to influence other people's rights to use porn, then we most definitely have to know. Otherwise we're just Mary Whitehouse. We must argue from experience, not prejudice.

Pause.

Oliver I find them offensive.

Will So do I. Some of them.

Oliver Then why do we have to look at something we know we find offensive?

Will Some of them, I said. (*Beat.*) I'll get the food on.

He switches off the tape and goes.

Oliver Do you two go along with this?

Martin Why not?

Bruce Sure.

Oliver Bloody absurd. I don't need to look at these.

Martin Seen it all before, eh?

Oliver Piss off.

Martin You're embarrassed, aren't you?

Oliver No.

Martin You can't fool me. (*He looks through the bag.*) Oh . . . My . . . God. He really went to town on this one. What d'you fancy, Ollie? 'Burning Butt' or 'Hot Ass Nurses'?

Oliver (*more to himself*) Lose all sense of dignity. Self respect. Those things, they cheapen your soul.

Martin Do wonders for your other bits, though.

Oliver Fuck off!

He goes out. **Martin** *is a bit shaken by* **Oliver**'*s reaction.*

Martin He's got a stash at the flat y'know. He thinks I don't know. Keeps them at the bottom of a suitcase. (*Beat.*) How do I know? I went through his things.

Bruce What's he . . . into?

Martin Copulating couples. (*He laughs. Pause.*) You know what I don't like about Ollie? He has 'Him' and 'Zipper' on the bookshelf, and he hides the het sex at the bottom of an old suitcase.

Ollie *comes back in.*

OK? Not hyperventilating, or anything?

Oliver (*mock cheerful*) No, no. Just took a deep breath and counted to ten. Works every time. Now then. (*He takes out a magazine.*) 'Lesbian Lasses.' (*He flicks through it.*) Uh huh. Women pretending to cavort together for the benefit of the male viewer. Uh huh. (*Beat. He holds it up for them to see.*) What's missing?

Martin Sorry?

Oliver What all-important object is missing from that picture?

Beat.

Martin Dunno. Toothbrush? (*He and* **Bruce** *laugh.*)

Oliver No. (*Beat.*) Can't spot it? (*Beat.*) The phallus. That's what's missing. Women forced into a faked impersonation of male/female sex. Forced into behaving like men. Two women, and it's all about penetration. All it lacks is the phallus. Which is what the male reader supplies.

The door opens. **Ange**, *her lip now cut and swollen, comes in.* **Ollie** *is still holding the magazine up.*

Jesus . . . (*He puts it in the bag.*) I'm sorry, I wasn't . . .

Ange I was upstairs . . .

Beat.

Oliver Yeah. (*He goes to the door.*) Will? You got a minute?

They look at her. **Will** *appears.*

Will Oh, Ange, hello . . . (*He sees her face.*) Bloody hell. Sit down, c'mon. (*He sits her down.*) When did you do that?

Ange I . . . didn't do it.

Will Your husband, was it? Ange? Was it your husband?

Ange Lenny done it.

Will Here? He came here?

Ange He came round . . . It was his dinner hour . . .

Oliver For Christ's sake, he comes round in his dinner hour to beat his wife up.

Will Yeah, OK, Ollie. Ange, is there something I can get you? That's a nasty cut.

Ange And he . . .

Will What?

Ange After . . .

Will After what?

Ange After he hit me . . . He . . .

Will What did he do after he hit you?

Beat.

Bruce D'you think . . . Maybe he . . . raped her . . . or something?

Oliver No, dear God . . .

Will Is that it, Ange? Did he? Did he rape you? (*She breaks down.*) Someone get a brandy, will you? (**Oliver** *does.*) Here, drink some of this.

Oliver Should be bloody castrated.

Will Someone ring the centre, tell Ronee. Number's by the phone. (**Oliver** *goes to the phone and dials.*)

Oliver We can report him, y'know. To the pigs. Get her seen by a doctor. They can put him away.

Will (*to* **Ange**) Have you been upstairs all this time? Have you? (*She nods.*) You should have come down, you daft kid.

Ange I's frightened.

Will No need to be frightened of us.

Oliver (*into the phone*) Hello, Johnson Place? (*Beat.*) Yeah, can I speak to Ronee? (*Beat.*) Thanks. (*To* **Will**.) They're getting her. (*Beat.*) Hello? Ronee? It's Oliver. From the men's group. I'm at your house. Look, I think you'd better come home. The girl who's staying here –

Will Ange.

Oliver Yeah, Ange. Her husband's beaten her up again, and we think he might have raped her. (*Beat.*) She's in a terrible state, we don't know for sure. (*Beat.*) OK. Good. (*He puts the phone down.*) She's coming straight back.

Will Ronee'll be here soon, Ange. You're going to be all right. (*Beat.*) Oh fuck.

Martin What's the matter?

Will The ribs. They'll be bloody ruined. (*He goes out.*)

Oliver (*next to* **Ange**) It's OK. You'll be OK. (*She pulls away.*) We're your friends. (*She pulls away.*) No one's going to hurt you.

Ange Leave me alone.

Oliver Hey, c'mon. We're friends of Will's.

Martin Ollie . . .

Oliver We can help.

Ange Leave me alone.

Oliver Please.

Martin Ollie.

Oliver What, for Christ's sake?!

Bruce *puts his hand on* **Ollie** *'s shoulder.*

Bruce Best, maybe, leave her alone.

Martin C'mon, Ollie.

Ollie *pulls violently away from* **Bruce**.

Oliver All right, all right.

Will *comes back in.*

Will Food's fucked. Sorry.

Bruce 'S OK.

Martin Look, why don't we go?

Bruce Yeah . . .

Will I think it's best. Sorry and all that . . .

Martin Oh, come on. This is more important than our meeting. (*Pause.*) Ollie?

Oliver Yeah.

They get their things.

Will I'll call you tomorrow, work out another time.

Oliver (*indicating the magazines*) Burn those bastard things, Will.

Beat. They go.

Will (*to* **Ange**, *who has curled up*) 'S OK, mate. Ronee won't be long. (*Beat.*) What d'you want to do? Have a sleep? (*She nods.*) I'll cover you up.

He puts his jacket over her and sits down. She closes her eyes. He goes and gets a drink and sits again.

Ange?

She seems asleep. He takes out one of the magazines and sits facing away from her. She opens her eyes and looks at him.

Fade.

Scene Four

Monday evening, 11 p.m.
Will *is sitting in the same chair reading Mastering the Art of French Cooking.* **Ronee** *comes in and pours two drinks. She takes one and goes out.* **Will** *carries on reading. She comes back, takes the other drink and sits down.* **Will** *puts the book down and looks at her. She's very tense.*

Will Well?

Beat. **Ronee** *doesn't seem able to say what she wants to say.*

Ronee Sod it. There are times . . . (*Beat.*) Yes. He did. And you don't have to be a doctor to see it. 'Injuries consistent with forceful sexual intercourse' is how they describe it in court. (*Beat.*) And she won't do anything about it. She won't report him.

Will For crying out loud . . .

Ronee I know. But she's scared to death of him. And who wouldn't be?

Pause.

Will How is she now?

Ronee She keeps waking up. That's the worst thing. It keeps coming back, apparently. (*Beat.*) It's a bloody good job Andrea's here. She knows all about it. From personal experience. (*Pause.*) She's staying tonight. (*Pause.*) You don't mind sleeping down here, do you?

Will No. (*Meaning yes.*)

Pause.

Ronee (*after a nervous laugh*) I just don't know if Ange could handle it. If she woke up. And saw a man . . .

Will It's OK. It really is.

Pause.

Ronee All in all, this has been a bastard day. Two kids had a fight at the Centre. Girls. Using those Afro combs, y'know. (*Beat.*) I tell you, I despair sometimes.

Will Don't.

Ronee I'm tired. That's all.

Will You sure?

Ronee What d'you mean?

Beat.

Will Are you *just* tired?

Ronee I don't understand.

Will Neither do I. (*Beat.*) Sorry. I didn't mean to lay that on you.

Ronee Forget it. (*Pause.*) I know I've been a bit . . . distant lately. I can't help it. Work and everything . . .

Will And Andrea . . .

Ronee Yes. And Andrea. (*Pause.*) Don't forget you encouraged me. It was actually your idea.

Will It wasn't my idea that you'd have a completely independent affair.

Ronee No, what you wanted was a happy little set-up where you got your kicks whenever you felt like it, without any involvement. And I can't do that. I have to invest a piece of *me* in people I sleep with. I can't just do it and – I dunno – tape record it and play it back. I'm not that detached.

Will I wanted to try something a bit radical. I'm sorry you couldn't handle it.

Ronee There's nothing radical about a harem.

Will Bullshit, Ronee. That's not what I wanted. I wanted to try other ways of keeping a relationship alive.

Ronee Our relationship wasn't dead.

Will And it is now?

Ronee I don't know. (*Beat.*) You're forever meddling with people. You're never content just to be, and let other people be. You have to keep fiddling about, trying new things. And it doesn't work.

Pause.

Will And your little lesbian affair isn't 'fiddling about'? That works, does it?

Ronee Don't say 'little lesbian affair' like that. You were happy enough when we let you in. And yes, it does work. Now that you're not involved, it works. Like a dream.

Pause.

Will This is political lesbianism we're talking about, isn't it? It's nothing to do with sex. You'd prefer to keep sex right out of it. Because sex can be dangerous. You can't always control it. Sometimes it turns wild on you. And you don't go too near things you don't understand, do you? 'O Lord, spare us the unpredictable.' That's your prayer.

Ronee Unpredictable? You? You inflict a few dippy ideas on me and Andrea, a few dusty clichés you've got hanging around from the sixties and that's supposed to indicate a wild, dangerous nature, is it? You: a progressive free spirit? (*Beat.*) Well, the reason we exclude you is that it had become a cliché. There's nothing wild or dangerous about a live sex show, although you might disagree. And that's all we were. You put your penny in the slot, and we'd perform. For you. For your entertainment. We got absolutely nothing from it, except the growing realisation that if you weren't there, then there was maybe something we could find together. For ourselves. Just ourselves. (*Beat.*) You're right. It was unpredictable. It was dangerous. For you. (*Pause.*) You wanted cheap thrills, and you got 'em. But you paid. (*A door slams.*) I'm very tired, Will. I'm sorry.

Mark *puts his head round the door.*

Mark Yo. All right if I come in?

Will Yeah, I want to have a word.

Mark (*coming in*) Christ, have I had a day. I finally collared this fella, this singer, and I said, 'Given that you've denied in print that you're a screaming woofter, how d'you account for the little Filipino back-door boy you've had in your trendy mews flat all night?' And he says 'Are you pulling my plonker! I don't know what you're on about.' At which point, said Filipino bum-bandit tries to make it away out the back. Well, immortalised forever by the process of photographic impression, isn't he? So, man with the golden tonsils cracks up, rings his manager and agrees to exclusive interview in which he admits that he may just have indulged in some male willy-stretching in the dim and murky past, but that's all behind him, 'scuse the pun. And anyway he's thinking of becoming a Christian. (*Beat.*) Mission accomplished. Am I a reptile, or what?

Ronee You're disgusting.

Mark (*smiling*) Mmm. (*Pause. To* **Will**.) Hey, ask me how many feminists it takes to screw in a lightbulb. Go on. Ask me.

Will Get lost, Mark.

Mark Come on. How many feminists does it take? Ask me.

Beat.

Will (*reluctantly*) How many feminists does it take to screw in a . . .

Mark (*mock strident, pointing his finger*) That's not funny! (*He laughs.*) Heard that one today.

Will *stands.*

Will (*to* **Ronee**) I'm going for a walk. Get some chips. You can tell him . . .

Ronee Yeah.

Will *goes.*

Mark Just you and me, eh? Cosy.

Ronee Shut your sexist trap for two seconds, will you?

Mark I love it when you talk dirty.

Ronee Like banging your head against a brick wall . . .

Mark I'm not fussy. Brick wall, chandelier, wardrobe, you name it, I'll bang against it.

Ronee Stop! While I talk to you, I'll be brief. I won't overtax your powers of concentration, I promise. I just want your undivided attention for two seconds, OK?

Mark What are you doing for the rest of your life?

Ronee OK?

Mark Fixed up for breakfast, are you? (*Pause.*) All right.

Beat.

Ronee Did you meet Ange? She stayed last night.

Mark Told you, has she?

Ronee Told me what?

Mark That she finds me irresistible.

Ronee You've met her, then?

Mark I should cocoa. Blood pressure's been up all day. Amongst other things.

Ronee Sometime today her husband came round and . . .

Mark Yeah, I met him.

Ronee When?

Mark Lunchtime. I came back for my address book. Seemed a nice enough fella.

Ronee What was he doing?

Mark Er . . . having a cup of tea.

Beat.

Ronee Well, I presume after you'd gone your nice enough fella beat up and raped his wife.

Mark Get away.

Beat.

Ronee Bloody hell, you're sympathetic . . . Anyway, the thing is, she's in a dreadful state, so: one, be as quiet as you can, and two, don't give her any of your hilarious scatalogical badinage. Cut the sexist crap, all right?

Beat.

Mark Never entered your head, has it, that all this linguistic and ideological purity – don't forget I've got a degree too – is just a little bit arrogant?

Ronee If you weren't so crass I wouldn't have to keep telling you.

Mark And if you didn't keep telling me, then maybe I wouldn't be so crass. (*Beat.*) Think about it.

Beat.

Ronee I've got someone else staying the night, too. A friend of mine. Pinch her bum and she's likely to cut your throat. You think about that.

Mark I don't pinch bums. I admire them.

Ronee Whatever.

Pause. She gets blankets and a pillow from the cupboard and spreads them on the sofa.

Mark Well, really, I'm not that kind of boy. (*No response.*) You wind yourself up any tighter, you're going to snap. (*Beat.*) G'night. And don't forget to leave that window open . . .

He laughs and goes. She takes a deep breath and finishes making up the bed. Then switches out the main light. As she's about to go, the doorbell rings.

Ronee Why didn't you take your keys . . . ?

She goes. We hear talking and suddenly **Lenny** *appears with* **Ronee** *following. He's totally legless.*

Lenny Where you got her? Eh?

Ronee I said out! Now!

Lenny Upstairs, is she? With that bloke? That cunt?

She shuts the door.

Ronee If you go out of this room, it's to go out the front door, OK?

Lenny Listen, you fucking cow, I wanna see Ange.

Ronee You can't. She's not here.

Lenny Fuck off.

Ronee She's where you put her. In the hospital.

Lenny What you talking about? Get fucked. I wanna see my wife. (*Pause. He sees the drinks and takes a bottle of gin and swigs from it.*)

Ronee You've had enough to drink.

Lenny I've only had eleven fucking pints. (*He takes a huge swig. As he drinks, we see him quickly become less and less capable.*)

Ronee If you don't go, I'm calling the police.

Lenny Fucking try it.

Ronee I'm warning you.

Lenny Shove it up your middle class fucking arsehole, fucking bitch. (*He takes a huge swig, then takes a bottle of scotch and drinks from that. He takes his poem out of his pocket.*) Hey, listen. This is what I wrote. Didn't think I could fucking write, did you? Well I can. Listen. 'When I look up at the sky / And the clouds are floating by / I think about you / And the things you do. When the sun comes out / It makes me want to shout / Your name out loud / To the passing crowd. When it starts to rain / I can feel the pain / That's going to come / Now that you're gone.' Yeah. I fucking wrote that.

Ronee Yeah. Very nice . . .

Lenny But I've written another one. 'Cause I reckon that one's fucking stupid. This one's better. (*He reads.*) 'When I get my hands on you / I'm gonna put my fingers round your throat / And squeeze till you go blue. I'm gonna write on your face / With a razor blade / I'm Lenny and I love you. I'm gonna slice your tits / And slash your fanny / And cut your tongue out too. I'm gonna drop you in the river / With your head cut off / And a note saying I love you.'

He takes a swig and stands staring at the floor, completely preoccupied.
Ronee *goes to the phone and picks it up. He moves towards her, and, as she*

puts the phone down, raises his arm to give her a backhander. As his arm comes down, she blocks it karate style and hits him hard in the stomach. He drops, retching, throws up and passes out. Door slams. **Will** *enters, puts the light on, and sees them. He's eating a bag of chips.*

Ronee Will, Lenny. Lenny, Will.

Beat.

Will Hello, Lenny.

Beat.

Ronee Passed out.

Will Mmm. (*Beat.*) Fancy a chip?

Blackout.

Act Two

Scene One

Monday morning, 10 a.m.
A week later. **Ange** *is lying on the sofa.* **Mark** *is at the table reading the paper, eating toast and drinking coffee. They're ignoring each other.* **Ronee** *enters.*

Ronee What bright spark left the hot tap running in the bathroom?

Mark *looks at her then at* **Ange.**

Ange . . .

Ange What?

Ronee Love, try to get it together, will you? Please?

Ange I never left it on.

Ronee Taps don't turn themselves on.

Ange I never.

Ronee OK . . .

Mark *stands with his cup.*

Mark Round the bloody twist.

He goes.

Ronee You going to make it to the Centre today?

Ange Dunno.

Ronee I wish you'd try. (*Pause.*) I'll wait if you want to come now. (**Ange** *shakes her head.*) Look, we'll have a talk. You can't go on like this.

Ange I have talked.

Ronee I know.

Ange Fed up with talking.

Ronee It's for your own good. (*Beat.*) You've got to get back into it. You can't stay here indefinitely.

Ange Why not?

Beat.

Ronee Look, Will and I are having some problems. We need to sort ourselves out. And it's not very easy . . . Y'know.

Ange 'Cause of me.

Ronee No, not because of you.

Ange What about Andrea?

Ronee What do you mean?

Mark *enters with a cup of coffee.*

We'll talk about it later. See you.

She goes.

Mark Give me half an hour, I could sort all your problems out. (*Pause.*) Milking it a bit, don't you think? (*Pause.*) You like it here. I can tell. I wonder why? (*He goes over to her.*) What are you after?

Ange Nothing.

Mark Think I'm stupid, do you?

Ange Yeah.

Mark Be making a silly mistake, you go around thinking that. (*Pause.*) Why don't you come out for a drink with me. (*Beat.*) Take you somewhere a bit classy. Wine bar. Cocktail bar. You'd like that. (*Pause.*) No? (*Pause.*) You've got a fantastic body. (*Beat.*) Look at me. (*She does.*) I mean . . . You could do worse.

Ange You reckon?

Mark Much worse. See I'm not the sort of fella who fiddles about with little girls' minds.

Ange No, I know what you fiddle about with.

Mark I'm good at it, too.

Ange I'll bet.

Pause.

Mark So. Try it?

Ange Up yours.

Mark You should be so lucky. (*Pause. He gets up and goes back to the table.*) I might start exercising my tenants' rights, y'know. You're not exactly my idea of a positive addition to the household, if you know what I mean. I might have to complain.

Ange All the bloody same, ain't you?

Mark Yeah. Deep down. I suppose we are.

Will *enters in his dressing-gown.*

Will Morning.

Mark Morning.

Ange Hello, Will.

Will Ange.

Beat.

Mark Here, media joke. You'll like this one, it's about your lot. How many feminists does it take . . .

Will You've told me.

Mark It's a new one. How many feminists does it take to screw in a lightbulb?

Will I don't know.

Mark Thirty-six. One to screw in the lightbulb and thirty-five to make a documentary of it for Channel Four.

Will That's not funny.

Mark Loosen up, pal.

Ange *gets up.*

Ange D'you want some tea, Will?

Will Thanks.

Mark Do us some coffee.

Ange You know where the kitchen is.

She goes.

Mark Obviously, I don't have your charisma.

Will Obviously.

Pause.

Mark Being a bit naughty, aren't we?

Will Who is?

Beat.

Mark You given her one yet?

Will What are you talking about?

Mark Simple question.

Will From a simple mind. You've got to reduce everything, haven't you? Drag it all down to the gutter. Well, for your information, Ange has been through a pretty rotten experience, and what she needs is support. That's the only thing I've given her. Support. Human warmth. A couple of things you know nothing about.

Mark I know about quite a few things. You'd be surprised.

Will Such as?

Pause.

Mark She's using you as much as you're using her.

Beat.

Will You're a walking insult, you know that? It's not just progressive ideas you can't cope with, it's basic human relationships as well. Just because you think with your prick, you imagine we all do. (*Beat.*) It must be a pretty weird experience, seeing, feeling everything from only that high above the ground. (*He gestures at groin level.*) I'll tell you what, you should trade in that nice company Volvo you drive. You'd be happier swinging through the trees.

Mark Nice one.

Will Well, wouldn't you?

Mark Bollocks. You know your trouble? You can't change your socks without pretending you're changing the world.

Will You just don't understand, do you?

Mark Don't be so piss-arrogant.

Will Don't be so thick.

Ange *comes in with a cup of tea and gives it to* **Will**.

Ange Here y'are.

Will Thanks.

Mark *gets his jacket and case.*

Mark You'll be late for work.

Will Got the morning off.

Mark Yeah. Figures.

He laughs and goes.

Will Has he been giving you a hard time?

Ange Not really.

Will Tell me if he does.

Ange Yeah. (*Beat.*) He said I had a fantastic body.

Will I'm sorry. Look, if he does it again . . .

Ange 'S OK. I don't mind.

Will You should do. Fantastic body. Christ, that's all he can see, isn't it?

Ange Don't worry about it.

Will I can't help it. I just do. (*Pause.*) It just seems to me sometimes, that all that's required is the tiniest amount of thought. If we all, suddenly, one day said, 'Yeah, OK, I'll try it.' All at once. Then . . . And it could happen. It would happen. (*Pause.*) Not like me to be optimistic first thing in the morning. I'd better see a doctor. (*She smiles.*) That's better.

Ange You're funny.

Will I'm not quite sure how to take that.

Ange You think about everything all the time. I never know what you're gonna say next.

Will Me neither.

Ange That's not true. You got an answer for everything.

Will If only. (*Pause.*) Ange. D'you think of me as old?

Ange You what?

Will Do I seem . . . a lot older, to you?

Ange Never thought about it.

Pause.

Will I was in grammar school, fourteen, studying for O-levels the day you were born. All acne and pubertal angst.

Ange Sounds filthy.

Will It probably was.

Pause.

Ange You're only as young as you feel. That's what they say, isn't it?

Will Is it?

Ange Yeah.

Will Well, then . . .

Ange How old do you feel? (*Beat.*)

Will Eighteen . . . Eighty . . . It varies.

Ange Stick with eighteen if I was you.

Will What, never grow up?

Ange No, never.

Will I'll think about it.

Ange No, don't think about it. Just do it.

Pause.

Will You didn't answer my question.

Ange Which one?

Will D'you think I'm old?

Ange I don't think about it.

Will Very diplomatic.

Ange I don't.

Beat.

Will 'Course, the main danger in feeling old, is that you start getting boring about it. Let me know if I'm boring you.

Ange You're not.

Will And you don't have to be polite.

Ange Wouldn't know how.

Will You're not daft.

Ange Ain't got no O-levels.

Will Some of the daftest people I know are graduates. Including me.

Ange Well *you* ain't daft.

Will No?

Ange 'Course not.

Will Shows how little you know me. (*The doorbell rings.*) Who the bloody hell's that?

He goes to the door. We hear muffled voices. **Oliver** *comes in followed by* **Will**.

Oliver I rang your office. They said you wouldn't be in today. Hope you don't mind.

Will No.

Oliver Hi, Ange.

Ange Wotcher.

Will You look bloody terrible, mate.

Oliver I've been up all night.

Will Problems?

Oliver Since when did I have anything else?

Will Martin?

Oliver Oh, yes. Very much. Martin.

Ange Shall I do some tea?

Will Great idea. Ta.

Oliver Coffee for me.

She goes.

I'm sorry, Will. I just don't know who to turn to.

Will Come on, it's OK. (*Beat.*) So what's happening?

Oliver Jesus, where do I start. (*Beat.*) Basically, I haven't seen him for two days. See, I gave him a sort of ultimatum. Yeah. I know. Pretty naff, right? Standing there in my curlers, with the rolling pin. Not exactly progressive, I know. But. Like. I had to do something. I mean, we're falling apart. Our so-called relationship is just about ready for the knacker's yard.

Will It happens.

Oliver Sure, it happens. Happens all the time. All over the world. (*Pause.*) Will, *why?*

Long pause.

Will Lots of reasons, Ollie. Depends on the people.

Pause.

Oliver When my ex-wife left me, I said, right, that's it. I am never again going to get myself stung like that. Never. I don't care what it takes. I'll never again put myself in a position where one person can single-handedly dismantle my life. Y'know? (*Beat.*) You build it up, slowly . . . (*Beat.*) Like the business . . . I mean, I've put everything into that stall. Even started thinking about getting premises. A shop. Yeah. A shop. Hip capitalism. Well, I haven't made or sold a thing all week. I can't. It's just collapsing. I'm paralysed. (*Pause.*) Martin. I thought, it'll never turn out like it did with Marie, my ex-wife. I won't let it. This is different. Martin's a guy, for chrissakes. He won't do that to me. (*Pause.*) Will. We don't have sex. I know we pretend . . . I mean, it's not that we don't want to, it's just . . . It's another complication. And Martin knew that. The ad I put in Time Out, it said, 'Guy wants guy for friendship.' That's all. All. Christ, isn't it enough? Doesn't anybody want to be friends in this world any more?

Pause.

Will Ollie . . . Maybe Martin didn't like the pretence.

Oliver Maybe Martin just wanted to get his rotten little end away. Maybe Martin doesn't give a damn if he fucks our relationship up. (*Pause.*) And maybe Martin didn't like the pretence. Shit. Pretence? Let's not kid ourselves. Lies, Will. What it boils down to. Lies.

Ange *comes in with tea and coffee on a tray and puts it down.*

Ange I'll . . .

Will Yeah.

Oliver Thanks. For the coffee.

Ange 'S OK.

She goes.

Oliver I've realised it too late, haven't I?

Will Maybe.

Oliver Why do I find it so hard to admit the truth? Marie once said to me that, when I died, I'd refuse to lie down and admit it. Why do I find it so hard?

Will We all do, don't we?

Oliver Do you? Even you?

Pause.

Will Yes. (*Pause.*) Look . . . Don't despair. (*Pause.*) Sorry. That's all I can say. If Martin's gone for good, then you'll have to adjust.

Oliver Have you ever been lonely, Will?

Will Yeah . . .

Oliver I mean . . . *Lonely. Alone.* (*Beat.*) I've gone days without talking to another person. Whole days of drinking coffee, pretending to work, drinking a bottle of scotch. All in total silence. God, I hate silence. (*Beat.*) One of the things . . . About Martin: he talks a lot. I like that. I always dry his hair for him when he's had a shower. And we babble. Nothing in particular, y'know. Chat about the weather. You've got split ends, that's a nice shirt . . . (*Pause.*) Sorry. (*Pause.*) It's why I hate the country. The silence. It frightens me. (*Beat.*) Have you ever tried listening to the radio? When you're alone?

Will Sure.

Oliver I don't really mean *when* you're alone, I mean *because* you're alone. Anything to fill the gap. I always do it. And it makes it worse. Well-bred voice, sort of hanging in the middle of the room. I look at the radio, and I think, there's nobody fucking there. (*Pause.*) I remember a rainy afternoon. My mother doing the ironing. The smell of clean shirts. And the radio on.

Pause.

Will He might come back.

Oliver Don't know if I want him back. (*Beat.*) Of course I bloody want him back. He's all I've got.

Will Have you tried to find him?

Oliver Where? I don't know any of his friends. I wouldn't know where to start. I just have to sit and wait.

Will I'd offer to let you stay here, but . . .

Oliver No, no. I want to be there if he comes back.

Will And if he doesn't?

Oliver I suppose I'll just . . . be there.

Pause.

Will You're still coming round tonight, aren't you?

Oliver Yeah. He might turn up.

Will That's what I was thinking. Look on the bright side.

Oliver Yeah. (*Beat.*) Will. You're a good man. Thanks.

Will Any time.

Oliver Say goodbye to Ange for me.

Will Will do.

Oliver See myself out.

He goes. **Ange** *comes in.*

Ange Funny little bloke, inne?

Beat.

Will Yeah. Funny little bloke. (*Beat.*) I don't know what it is, but something about him . . . makes me very angry.

Ange Why?

Will I wish I knew.

Pause.

Ange Have you had some breakfast?

Will Angela. Stop doing things for me.

Ange Have you?

Will Had some muesli when I got up.

Ange Rabbit food. You'll turn into a rabbit. He's like a rabbit. Or a mouse. (*Pause.*) Lenny always has a cooked breakfast. Bacon, sausage, fried slice. And he covers it in HP sauce. Then he goes out. And all day there's this smell . . . Grease . . . all round the flat. I open the windows, keep washing my face, but it just stays there. All day. (*Pause.*) Why ain't you at work then?

Will Basically, I'm skiving.

Ange You'll get the sack.

Will But I'm pretending I'm working. Nobody knows.

Pause.

Ange What you gonna do all day then?

Will Lounge around. Read a book. I dunno. Have a think.

Beat.

Ange You and Ronee . . .

Will What?

Beat.

Ange You having a barney?

Will We don't have barneys. We have orgies of socio-political truth-telling.

Ange Maybe you should have a barney.

Will Maybe you're right.

Pause.

Ange She must be mad . . .

Will Why?

Ange Bloke like you. One in a million. (**Will** *laughs.*) What's funny?

Will I'm not very different.

Ange I think you are.

Will Well, thank you very much.

Ange Don't muck about. I do.

Beat.

Will If only you knew.

Ange What?

Will What a . . . mucky sort of person I am. You'd find I'm the same as anyone else. Worse.

Ange No.

Will *sits and plays with the backgammon set open on the table.*

D'you want a game?

Will Didn't know you played.

Ange Ronee showed me. Not very good though.

Will OK. I'll give you a thrashing.

Ange You good at this, are you?

Will Pretty good. Used to be the strip backgammon king of Sussex University. That's the smutty version. If one of your counters gets taken off, you take off an article of clothing.

Ange Like strip poker.

Will Yeah. Anyway throw for start. (*They throw.*) You go first. (*She throws and moves. He throws and moves. She throws again.*) Oh dear.

She moves two counters, both uncovered. He throws and smiles.

Sorry about that.

He takes one of her counters off. Pause.

Ange We playing the smutty version?

Will If you like.

Blackout.

Scene Two

Monday evening, 6.30 p.m.

Ange *is polishing the table, singing to herself.* **Ronee** *enters, sees her and smiles.*

Ronee Well.

Ange (*very cheery*) Hi.

Ronee What are *you* on?

Ange Come again?

Ronee You been at the gin?

Ange Don't drink. You know that.

Ronee First time I've seen you smile in days.

Ange Not against the law, is it?

Ronee No. Definitely not.

Pause.

Ange I've cleaned upstairs and the kitchen.

Ronee Thanks. You don't have to, y'know.

Ange I wanted to.

Ronee Fine by me. (*Beat.*) God, I think I'll have a drink. (*She pours a sherry.*) Had a finance committee meeting this afternoon. Council want to cut our grant. Not a lot. Just enough. Enough to make running the place an even bigger headache. I've got to try and decide which is more important: amplifier for the music workshop, or a new ping pong table. And they call this creative administration. Pretty soon, y'know, the only activities we'll be putting on will be benefits. Save the Centre. Rock for a new ping pong table. That kind of thing.

Ange Council are stupid. Trouble we had getting our flat. Like the football league, Lenny said. We never had enough points. When the bloke came round, Lenny asked him if we was gonna get relegated to the second division. The bloke laughed and said, far as the council's concerned, we're division four. Yeah. What a pig.

Ronee It's not their fault. Well, not all of them. The orders come from on high. I vos only obeyink orders, jawohl. (**Ange** *laughs.*) Shall we have that talk now?

Pause.

Ange If you like.

Ronee Come and sit down. (**Ange** *sits next to her on the sofa.*) Right.

Ange 'S like being back at school.

Ronee Hey, do me a favour.

Ange Sorry.

Beat.

Ronee First, what are you going to do about Lenny?

Ange Dunno. Shoot him?

Ronee An attractive, if impractical, suggestion. No. Are you intending to go back to him?

Ange You gotta be joking.

Ronee OK. So that's out. It's separation, then. Where are you going to live? (*Pause.*) Ange?

Ange What?

Ronee Where are you going to live?

Ange Dunno.

Ronee Your mum's?

Ange Could do.

Ronee You've got to think about it.

Ange Well, I thought that . . .

The phone rings.

Ronee Shit. Hang on a minute. (*She picks up the phone.*) Hello? (*Beat.*) Oh, hi. (*Pause.*) Ja. Nach zwei Stunde. (*Beat.*) Oh. (*She laughs.*) But my pronunciation's improving. (*Beat. She laughs again.*) Rat. Schwein. (*Beat.*) Ja. Ich werde dich dahin gesehen. (*Beat.*) What? (*Beat.*) I'm trying to say I'll see you there in a couple of hours. (*Beat.*) Well I think it'd be easier if you learned English, so there. (*Beat.*) Ja. OK. Ich liebe dich. Wiedersehen. (*She puts down the phone.*) That woman is totally crazy.

Ange Andrea?

Ronee Well, I don't talk to my mother in German, do I? (**Ange** *shrugs.*) Right, where were we?

Ange Ronee? Can I ask you something?

Ronee Trying to get off the subject?

Ange I want to ask you something.

Ronee Go on then.

Beat.

Ange You and Andrea . . . When you . . .

Ronee And stop it right there. If you were going to ask what I think you were going to ask, the answer is: none of your bloody business.

Ange I was just . . .

Ronee Curious. Well, use your imagination.

Ange I mean, I can't imagine . . .

Ronee So don't. (*Pause.*) Sorry, love. It's just that my relationship with Andrea is private and personal, y'know? I don't like it being . . . spied on.

Ange I wasn't spying . . .

Ronee I know. Just curious. (*Pause.*) I don't think I could describe it, anyway.

Ange But . . . It's different, innit?

Ronee Yes. It's very different.

Ange Better?

Ronee For me, yeah.

Beat.

Ange What about Will? (*Beat.*) Don't you like him?

Ronee We're married.

Ange So am I, and I don't like Lenny.

Ronee They're very similar, Will and Lenny.

Ange Get off.

Ronee Oh, I know, one's a TV researcher, the other's a mechanic; one went to University, the other left school at sixteen. But they're both men. And very similar ones at that.

Ange I think that's horrible. Will's nice.

Pause.

Ronee Will is evil. (*Beat.*) And that's it. No more. There's nothing he'd like more than to think that we were sitting here talking about him. Bit of an egomaniac, is our Will.

Will *enters with* **Bruce**. *They've been mending the car and are both covered in oil. They each have a can of beer and two more unopened.*

Will You called?

Ronee Done it?

Will Not quite. Got to bleed the brakes. Thought we'd have a quick beer. So. Talking about me?

Ronee Pick it up on your radar, did you? Someone, somewhere, says 'Will' and a little bleep appears on the screen?

Will Something like that.

Ronee I was just disabusing Ange of a rather peculiar notion she had. She seems to have been labouring under the misapprehension that you are nice.

Will But you put her straight.

Ronee Of course, dear heart.

Will You're a treasure.

Will *crushes his empty can.*

Ronee I know. (*Beat.*) God, this is all too macho for me. I've got to get changed, anyway. Come on, Ange, we can carry on talking. I intend to get you sorted out. (*She stands.*)

Will Come along, Angela. Walkies.

Ronee Let's leave the boys to their beer and motor cars.

She and **Ange** *go.*

Will Ain't she sweet? (*Beat.*) Never get married, Bruce.

Bruce I . . . won't.

Pause.

Will Hey, listen, mate, thanks for your help. That car's been a pain in the arse since I bought it. I'd never have got it straight if you hadn't come over.

Bruce No problem. I . . . enjoy it.

Beat. **Will**, *as always, is uncomfortable with* **Bruce**.

Will You can take a shower later, if you want.

Bruce 'S OK. You've got some . . . uh . . . Swarfega . . .

Will Yeah. I'll get it . . .

Bruce No, I'll . . . finish this . . . (*He holds up his beer.*)

Will Sure. (*Pause.*) So.

Beat.

Bruce You don't have to . . . talk. If you don't want to.

Will Bit pre-occupied, that's all.

Bruce Ah.

Will Ronee and me. Well, you can probably see . . . We're not . . . I dunno . . .

Bruce Maybe you should split.

Beat.

Will Does it look that bad?

Bruce Doesn't . . . look good.

Will No. (*Pause.*) Rationally . . . you're probably right. But who thinks rationally at times like this? (*Pause.*) Ten years we've been together. Married for six. Very unfashionable, marriage, when we did it. Which is probably why we did it. (*Beat.*) Ten years. (*Beat.*) That . . . is a bloody long time.

Pause.

Bruce I've got a flat.

Will Good news. Where?

Bruce Earl's Court. Sharing.

Will Who with?

Bruce Couple of . . . blokes I know . . .

Will That's you sorted out, then.

Bruce Yeah.

The doorbell rings.

Will I'll get it.

He goes to the door. There are muffled voices. **Martin** *comes in, followed by* **Will**.

Drink?

Martin Yeah. Gin. On its own. (*He glowers at* **Bruce**. **Bruce** *ignores him and sips his beer.*)

Will There you go. (*He hands him his drink.*) Cheers. (**Martin** *drinks most of it down in one go.*) So. You're early.

Beat.

Martin Yeah.

Beat.

Will To what do we owe the pleasure? (*Pause.*) Well, it's OK. Since you're here. Know anything about cars?

Martin No.

Will Oh, well. (*Pause.*) Ollie was round this morning.

Martin Oh, Christ . . .

Will He was . . . in a bit of a bad way.

Martin What else is fucking new?

Will He was worried about you. (*Pause.*) Have you seen him?

Martin No.

Will Not to worry. He'll be here soon. He's usually early. (*Pause.*) Look, Martin . . .

Martin (*to* **Bruce**) What the fuck are you playing at? (*Pause.* **Will** *is baffled.*) Come on. It's only a speech defect. You're not dumb.

Bruce, *very calmly, goes over to* **Martin** *and suddenly grabs the hair on the back of his neck. It is very painful.*

Bruce (*speaking carefully so as not to stammer*) Don't ever speak to me like that. OK? (*He lets go.*)

Will Er . . . I get the feeling there's something I'm missing here. (*Pause.*) But . . . Maybe the penny's dropping.

Pause.

Bruce Can I have another . . . beer?

Will Oh, help yourself.

Bruce *does as* **Martin** *takes a piece of paper out of his pocket.*

Martin I mean, what is this?

Beat.

Will Looks like a piece of paper to me . . .

Martin (*reading*) 'Dear Martin, I've moved. Don't try to find me. Don't come round. Goodbye. Thanks. Bruce.' (*Pause.*) I mean, y'know . . .

Will Sounds like the brush-off to me.

Pause.

Martin Bruce?

Beat.

Bruce Sounds like . . . the brush-off to me, too.

Martin But why?

Bruce I got bored.

Martin You what?!

Will He got bored.

Pause.

Martin Jesus Christ, what have I done?

Will Tell you one thing: you've made a little man very unhappy, for a start.

Martin Please, Will, I think this is between me and Bruce.

Will So go to your place to discuss it. (*Beat.*) Look, Ollie was here in what I can only describe as a mess, this morning. A mess on your account. You appear to be in a mess on Bruce's account. Why don't you and Ollie get your respective messes together and live happily ever after?

Martin Don't patronise me, you sod.

Will I wish there was a way not to. I wish it wasn't inevitable. (*Beat.*) You, and Ollie, what is it you're always on the verge of? Huh? You're always teetering on the brink. The brink of what?

Beat.

Martin The same as you.

Will Cryptic.

Martin You know what I mean.

Will Enlighten me.

Martin What are you going to do when Ronee leaves you?

Beat.

Will Oh, oh, oh, I see what you're driving at.

Martin Not going to teeter on the brink? Huh?

Will (*arch*) I'll burn that bridge when I come to it. Until then, let's remember that it's my private affair.

Martin Oh, so cool.

Will If by that you mean that I don't wank my private life all over other people's boots, then you're dead right. (*Pause.*) It's just occurred to me. We shouldn't be having this discussion. We're not quorate and we haven't got a chairperson.

Bruce *laughs.*

Martin Bruce?

Bruce It was fun. That's . . . all.

Beat.

Martin OK. (*He gets up and starts to pour a drink.*)

Will I'm really going to have to think about setting up a drinks kitty.

Martin *pulls a pound note out of his pocket and throws it in* **Will***'s direction.*

All I meant was – ask.

Martin (*having poured*) May I?

Will Be my guest.

Martin *goes to* **Bruce** *and theatrically throws the drink in his face. Beat.* **Bruce** *starts to laugh, as does* **Will***. As they laugh* **Bruce** *indicates that he's going to the bathroom. He goes, still laughing.*

You definitely get tonight's Joan Crawford award.

Martin *is nearly in tears.*

Think about it. He's only doing what you did to Ollie.

Martin I know. (*Pause.*) Except, Bruce and me . . .

Will Yeah. (*Beat. He goes to the window.*) Beautiful day. (*Beat.*) I've got an idea. Let's have a barbeque.

Martin What, now?

Will I'll have to go and get some mince . . . (*He goes to the door.*) Ronee?

Ronee (*off*) Yeah?

Will What time are you back tonight?

Ronee (*off*) Not late.

Will I've got an idea.

Ronee (*off*) Golly.

Will What about a barbeque in the garden? (*Beat.*) Eh?

Ronee (*off*) Yeah. Great.

Will You back by half nine?

Beat.

Ronee (*off*) I suppose so.

Will OK. Bring Andrea, if you like. (*Beat. He comes back into the room.*) It'll be beautiful out there tonight. Just right.

Ange *appears.*

Ange Need any help?

Will Uh . . . Not really. I've got to get to the shop . . .

Ange I'll go.

Will 'S OK. I want to get out. (*Beat.*) Come with me, if you like.

Ange Yeah.

Will Know anything about barbeques?

Ange What, hot dogs and stuff?

Will I was thinking more in terms of burgers and kebabs.

Ange You can show me.

Will OK. (*Beat.*) See you later.

Martin Yeah.

They start to go as **Bruce** *comes in.*

Will Just going to the shop, Bruce.

Bruce I'll finish the car.

Martin Bruce.

Will *and* **Ange** *go.*

Sorry. I made a fool of myself. (*Beat.*) I'm apologising. Say something.

Bruce What?

Martin I don't know.

Pause.

Bruce The only . . . creatures on this earth worth pitying . . . are animals. 'Cause, like . . . people . . . y'know? People are so stupid. They're . . . happy with all their crap . . . Like . . . They don't want to get any better. (*Beat.*) Politics is a joke. People don't want

to be . . . liberated. I think people . . . like being chained up. Not
real chains . . . Y'know. Keep those for the animals.

Pause.

Martin (*sings gently*) Chains, my baby's got me locked up in
chains. And they ain't the kind . . . that you can see . . .

Pause. The doorbell rings. **Bruce** *goes.* **Oliver** *enters.* **Martin** *sees him
and carries on singing.*

Whoah-oh these chains of love, gotta hold on me.

Beat.

Oliver Are you pissed? (**Martin** *shakes his head.*) What's Bruce
doing?

Martin Mending Will's car.

Pause.

Oliver (*sitting*) Martin . . . (*Beat.*) Where have you been?

Ronee *comes in.*

Ronee Boy scout night again already?

Oliver Hi, Ronee.

Ronee Hi. Look, if you bump into my husband, tell him I'll do
my best to be back in time, will you?

Oliver Sure.

Ronee But, I can't promise.

Oliver OK.

She goes.

In time for what?

Martin It'll be beautiful out there tonight.

Oliver Eh?

Martin We're having a barbeque in the garden. Songs round the
old campfire.

Oliver What for?

Martin Because it's nice.

Pause.

Oliver Where were you?

Martin The truth?

Oliver Please, yeah. The truth. (*Beat.*) I know I haven't been too good at the truth but I need it now. I really do.

Martin I needed time to think. (*Beat.*) About us. (*Beat.*) About me. (*Beat.*) I went and stayed with an old friend. From way back.

Oliver Did you sleep with her?

Martin Did I sleep with her? (*Pause.*) Sorry. Yeah. But it didn't mean anything. Just a way of paying the rent. (*Pause.*) You wanted the truth.

Oliver It's all I ever wanted. (*Pause.*) And . . . Did you think?

Martin Yeah.

Oliver And?

Beat.

Martin What would you like me to say?

Oliver I don't know.

Martin I mean . . .

Beat.

Oliver Are you going to need to go away and think any more?

Martin I might.

Oliver Often?

Pause.

Martin No. I don't think so.

Oliver Honest?

Martin Honest.

Oliver Good. (*Pause.*) Martin. Come back. If you want to. I've changed. No more fussing. No more stupid ultimatums. Just us. Friends. Or more, if you want. (*Beat.*) What I'm saying is: I'll do anything to have you back. (*Beat.*) If you want sex . . .

Martin Ollie . . . Let's just see what happens.

Oliver OK. (*Beat.*) What, you mean you're coming back?

Martin Why not?

Beat.

Oliver It'll be different. I promise.

Martin I believe you. (*They hug.* **Martin** *sings.*) 'Whoa-oh, these chains of love . . . (**Bruce** *appears, wiping his hands on a cloth.*) . . . got a hold on me. Yeah.'

Blackout.

Scene Three

Monday evening, 9.30 p.m.

Lenny *is sitting nervously at the table.* **Ange** *enters from the kitchen.*

Ange I'm busy. What d'you want?

Beat.

Lenny What you doing?

Ange A barbeque. (*He looks away.*) Y'know, kebabs and things.

Lenny I know what a barbeque is.

Pause.

Ange Well?

Beat.

Lenny Y'know Tony? Landlord down the Duke? Yeah? (*She nods.*) I had a long chat with him the other night. (*Pause.*) I tried me dad, but . . . (*Pause.*) Tony says it ain't all my fault. Not all of it. We been stuck in that flat. Bloody rathole. So it ain't all my fault. But . . . (*Pause.*) He was telling me about his first wife. Apparently, she done a bunk when he hit her. (*Beat.*) Eight years ago. Still loves her, he says. (*Pause.*) Well, I was telling him about us and everything and he started having a right go at me. Yeah. (*Long pause.*) See, it's a question of respect. Gotta respect each other, ain't we? That's where we was going wrong. I didn't have no respect for you. (*Pause.*) And the thing is . . . I'd never thought about it.

Ange Lenny, don't go on. I'm not coming back.

Long pause.

Lenny See, I got it all wrong. (*Pause.*) Tony says what we oughta do is: you get a job, if you can, start saving, and try and get a mortgage on a decent place. He reckons this is a good time to be buying your own house. Interest rates and that.

Ange What you talking about? Since when did you know anything about bloody interest rates?

Lenny Since I talked to Tony.

Ange You have half an hour's chat with a bloody alcoholic and suddenly you know all about everything?

Lenny He ain't alcoholic.

Ange Drinks like a fish.

Lenny He helped me out. Advice and that.

Ange So go and live with *him*.

Lenny I don't wanna live with him, I wanna live with you.

Ange Well, that's tough Lenny. I'm staying here. (*Pause.*) 'Cause, d'you know what? You're just an animal, Lenny. 'S all you are. I never knew till I came here. 'Cause you and your family and your mates, the lot of you, you're all just a pack of animals.

Lenny That ain't fair.

Ange Bloody well is. And I'll tell you something else. I'd rather slit me wrists than come anywhere near you again.

Pause.

Lenny Gimme another chance . . .

Ange I won't give you nothing. (**Will** *is listening from the kitchen.*) Why should I? I'm starting again. New place. New people. (*Beat.*) Nice people. (*Beat.*) So go away, Lenny.

Lenny It ain't fair.

Ange My heart bleeds.

Lenny It ain't. I've tried to understand things. And you won't give me a bloody chance.

Will *enters with a tray of cups.*

Will Sorry to break things up, but I'm just about to start cooking. So, if you're . . .

Lenny Please, Ange . . .

Will Time to go, Lenny.

Lenny I wasn't talking to you, cunt.

Will Careful. Or I might have to set my wife on you.

Beat.

Ange Time to go, Lenny.

Beat.

Lenny You know what my dad said? He said you wouldn't have gone if I'd hit you where it didn't show. Said it was just 'cause it was your face got marked. (*Pause.*) Look, you know where I am, if you . . . (*Beat.*) Fuck it. Fuck the lot of you.

He goes.

Will OK?

Ange Good riddance. (*Beat.*) I'll do those.

*He kisses her. She pours wine into the cups. **Will** runs his hand down her back. She turns.*

Don't muck about.

Will This is serious.

She picks up the tray.

Ange I don't wanna spill this.

He runs his hands over her body. She can't move in case she spills the drinks.

Will . . .

Will You've got a . . . fantastic . . . body . . . (*He dissolves into laughter.*)

Ange Daft sod, you're drunk. (*He just laughs.*) Don't laugh at me.

Will I'm not . . .

Ange You are. Don't. I don't like it. (*He composes himself.*) 'S better.

He stares at her.

Will Hey, listen, don't forget . . .

Ange I dunno . . .

Will You promised.

Ange But, she might not . . .

Will Make her. You could make anybody do anything.

Ange Sure. And what about Andrea?

Will She rang. She's coming home alone.

Beat.

Ange I don't know if I can.

Will You can. (*He lifts a cup to her lips.*)

Ange I don't drink.

Will You do tonight.

Beat. She takes a swig. He makes her take a drag of the joint he's smoking.
OK?

Ange OK.

She starts to go as **Oliver**, *already fairly pissed, comes in. He takes a cup from the tray and she goes.*

Oliver Give that woman a medal. (*Beat.*) Do you know, Will? Do you know what women are? What they really are? (*Beat.*) Apart from our sisters in the struggle, of course. Hmm?

Will You're either going to say something dreadfully silly or misogynist.

Oliver What? (*Beat.*) Me? I love women. Love them. The problem is, the problem is, Will . . . They don't love me.

Will Ah. Something dreadfully silly. That's a relief.

Oliver No, no, no, you don't understand. Non comprendo, old sausage. I mean, not *me*. I mean, all of us. Men. You. Me. All of us. (*Pause.*) Is that controversial, or what?

Beat.

Will Vague.

Oliver Oh, granted. You want chapter and verse?

Will No.

Oliver Why not?

Will You're pissed.

Oliver What the hell difference does that make? I'm being honest. I'm going to empty my soul.

Will You're going to bore me rigid, if you're not careful.

Oliver You can't take emotion, that's the trouble. Here I am, speaking from the heart, and all you want to do is shut me up. Well I won't be shut up. (*His voice rises to near tantrum level.*) This anal social life, this English, tight-arsed, clenched-buttock politeness. It should be . . . blown away. I won't shut up. I am a Russian. I am a Papua, New Guinea headhunter. I am alive.

Martin *has entered.*

Martin Oh, shut up, Ollie.

Beat.

Oliver That's all they can say, isn't it. Oh, shut up. (*Beat.*) Shall I compare thee – oh, shut up. Tyger, Tyger, burning bright – put a sock in it, will you? We're British. Stiff upper lip. Arsehole like a vice. Emotion? The occasional fart. Love? One big shit. (*Pause*). There's no poetry in life. No beauty.

The front door opens and **Mark** *enters.*

Mark Yo.

Oliver This man looks like a fascist. Doesn't he? Tell me, are you a fascist? (**Mark** *is bemused.*) Come on, you're English, aren't you? You must be a fascist.

Beat.

Mark What's this? Alternative cabaret?

Oliver Ha. A sense of humour. I like him. What's your name? I don't care if you are a fascist.

Mark Go boil your bum.

Will His name's Mark.

Oliver Mark. Mark. I don't know if I like that. We might have to change it. (*Beat.*) I know. Vladimir. I'll call you Vladimir. OK, Vladimir? Or may I call you Vlad?

Mark Don't be formal. Call me 'sir'.

Oliver Beneath his sarcasm is a soul of pure poetry. I can tell.

Mark *pats him on the face.*

Mark When did they let *him* out?

Will Wait till the valium wears off.

Martin Ollie. Let's grab some food.

Oliver Grab. Grab, grab, grab. Crab. Blab. Stab. Let's stab some food.

Martin Whatever you say.

Ronee *enters.*

Oliver (*to* **Ronee**) Why don't you love me?

He and **Martin** *go.*

Ronee Oh, dear.

Mark Where do you get your friends? Joke shop?

Will (*aware of the joke*). Local Labour Party.

Mark That's what I said.

Will For once, you might have a point.

Ronee If tonight is going to consist of the poison dwarf embarrassing everyone in sight, I might just pass.

Will I think he's got it out of his system.

Bruce *enters.*

Come and get some food.

Ronee OK.

They go.

Mark Hi. I'm Mark. I live here.

Bruce I'm Bruce. (*They shake.*)

Mark You're not crackers like that other bloke, are you?

Bruce Who?

Mark Short-arsed fella with the big mouth.

Bruce No.

Pause. **Bruce** *pours himself a drink.*

Mark Here, d'you hear the one about the two Irish queers? Patrick Fitzmaurice and Maurice Fitzpatrick?

Beat.

Bruce No . . . I didn't.

Beat.

Mark I see.

Bruce What's a queer?

Mark Eh?

Bruce What's a . . . queer?

Beat.

Mark Well, you *have* led a sheltered life. A queer is a poof is a woofter.

Bruce Oh. Like . . . Pakis.

Beat.

Mark Sort of.

Bruce And nig nogs.

Pause.

Mark Except woofters are white.

Ange *comes in with the tray and cups.*

Ange That stupid little git just knocked all the cups over, then collapsed on the rockery. Squashed all the flowers. Bloody nerd. (*She puts the cups out and starts pouring more wine.*)

Mark Shouldn't you be wearing a pinny? And a mob cap?

Ange Tie a knot in it.

Mark Could tie a sheep shank in mine. (*Beat.*) Here, seeing as you won't come upstairs to me, how about I come below stairs to you?

Oliver *appears carrying a couple of squashed flowers.*

Here comes laughing boy again.

Oliver What have I done? Look. Murder. I've killed something of beauty.

Mark Well, you know what they say. A thing of beauty is a boy forever.

Oliver *goes over to him and puts his arm round his neck.*

Oliver Vlad. Oh, Vlad. Is this all that's left to us? Cruelty? Arbitrary killing and cruelty?

Mark Yup.

Oliver It can't be. Where's hope?

Mark In the bath with Faith and Charity.

Ange (*enjoying it*). Don't.

Oliver Look what a precious jewel I've cast away . . .

Mark Terrible.

Oliver *absent-mindedly puts the flowers in his mouth and starts chewing them.*

Ange Oh, he's horrible.

She starts to go. As she passes **Oliver** *he takes a cup. She goes.*

Oliver A toast. To flowers. Everywhere. May they forgive me. (*He drinks.*) Hey, listen . . . (*He starts to laugh.*) . . . Where have . . . Where have all the flowers gone? Eh? (*Beat.*) Squashed them all, haven't I? (*He laughs.*)

Mark Yeah, nice one.

Oliver I like you, Vlad. Let's be friends. Hmm?

Mark You smooth talking man.

Ronee *enters.*

Oliver I mean it. Let's be blood brothers. Cut our arms. Let the blood intermingle. What do you say?

Mark Tell you what, I'll cut my arm if you cut your throat.

Ronee If it's blood you're after, Will's just done some burgers.

Mark Right. (*To* **Oliver**.) Come on, smiler, let's find you some flowers to press.

Oliver They haunt me. Hollyhocks, geraniums, nasturtiums . . .

Mark Pansies?

They leave.

Ronee And hello, Bruce.

Bruce Hi.

Ronee You know what this reminds me of?

Bruce What?

Ronee The bad trips tent at the Isle of Wight festival. (*Beat.*) Actually, life sometimes reminds me . . . (*She waves her hand in the air and smiles.*) Found a flat, I hear.

Bruce That's right.

Ronee Sharing it with a couple of leather queens . . . (**Bruce** *looks worried.*) Come on, just a joke.

Pause.

Bruce One . . . is. The other isn't.

Ronee Ah. (*Beat.*) And you've been a bit naughty, I also hear. (*He shrugs.*) Listen, can I ask you something?

Bruce Sure.

Ronee This might sound odd . . . (*Beat.*) You're not married, or anything?

Bruce Not now.

Beat.

Ronee Do you miss the security? Of a permanent relationship?

Beat.

Bruce I'm . . . not sure. Maybe. I'm not very . . . good with people. They don't stay very long. Sometimes . . . I want them to.

Ronee Martin?

Beat.

Bruce Martin was just a fuck.

Ronee Uh-huh. (*Beat.*) I might leave Will and live with Andrea. She wants me to. (*Beat.*) She's getting understandably pissed off. Having to share me, you see.

Bruce So's Will.

Beat.

Ronee Poor old Will. When we first met, y'know, I was a real wallflower. And he was something of a celebrity. Well, a big fish in a little pool.

Beat.

See, in the last nine, ten years, whatever it is, he hasn't changed. He's just sort of . . . got worse. (*Beat.*) He's like someone drowning. If you try to help, you just get dragged down. (*Beat.*) He tries. The men's group and what have you. But it's such an effort. I mean, you can see it. He's actually going against his nature.

Bruce But he's doing it for you.

Beat.

Ronee Perhaps.

Pause.

Bruce His nature can change.

Ronee I don't know about that.

Bruce He's changed in the time I've known him.

Ronee How?

Bruce He . . . listens now. I mean . . . without offence . . . he's got things into perspective. Like . . .

Ronee He's not such a big-headed bastard.

Bruce Yeah. No offence. (*Pause.*) You mean a lot. I think.

Ronee Is that good or bad?

Bruce It's security. (*Beat.*) Yes, I do . . . miss it.

Ronee So might I.

Pause.

Bruce I think you owe him a chance. (*Pause.*) Really.

Will *enters.*

Will Hey, party poopers. (*He gets a drink.*) What's this? Illicit joint-smoking? The passing-out room? It's not that kind of party. I admit the paper cups may be somewhat reminiscent of a late sixties bring a bottle bash, but I like to think we've progressed.

Beat.

Ronee I think you're enjoying yourself.

Will Darling, I'm having a ball.

Ronee Good. (*She kisses him.*)

Will I'm now over the moon. Official. (**Ange** *comes in.*) Hey,
Bruce. Give us a hand with the fire, will you? It's a bugger to get
re-started if it goes out.

Bruce I don't know . . . much about it . . .

Will Then learn, baby, learn.

They go. **Will** *winks at* **Ange** *as he goes.* **Ronee** *stretches out on the sofa.*

Ronee (*expansive*) Angela. Peel me a grape.

Ange (*uptight*) Eh?

Ronee Get me a glass of wine, angel. A glass. This is nineteen
eighty-three and we're grown-ups now. (**Ange** *pours a glass of wine,
hands it to her and sits on the edge of the sofa.*) Ta. You know, I think I
might have a cigarette. I think I dare. There's some on the table.
(**Ange** *gets them and sits.* **Ronee** *takes one out.* **Ange** *lights it for her.*)
Thanks love. (*She runs her hand down* **Ange***'s face and rests it on her
shoulder.*) Well. Having a good time?

Ange Yeah.

Ronee Good. Against all the odds, so am I. And I intend to have
a better time.

Ange, *misunderstanding, visibly relaxes.*

Ange It's all new to me.

Ronee You'll get used to it. We're all a bit crazy. But then, who
isn't?

Ange Right. (*Beat.*) Ronee. You ain't half been good to me.
Letting me stay and everything. I really want to pay you back.

Ronee You're your old self, that'll do for now.

Ange But I wish there was something . . . (*She leans down and gives
her a friendly kiss, her hand now resting on* **Ronee***'s shoulder.*) There.

Ronee Where? (*She laughs.* **Ange** *kisses her again.*)

Ange There. (*She laughs.*) There. (*She kisses her each time she says
'there'.*) There. There. There. (**Ange** *starts running her hands over*
Ronee*'s body.*)

Ronee Ange . . . (*She breaks away and sits up.*) Break. Cool it. OK?
(*Pause.* **Ange**, *unsure what to do, slowly puts her arm round* **Ronee***'s neck*

and tries to kiss her again. **Ronee** *stands up.*) I don't know what you think you're doing, but whatever it is, don't.

Ange I was . . . (*She is completely shattered.*)

Ronee I know what you was. Where the bloody hell'd you get the idea? . . . (*Beat.*) I mean, just because . . . (*Beat.*) Honestly, Ange . . .

Ange I'm sorry. I thought . . .

Ronee What?

Pause.

Look, forget it. Don't feel you have to pay me back. You don't owe me anything. And you certainly don't want to complicate your life any more than it already is.

Ange That's not it.

Ronee What?

Ange I wasn't trying to pay you back.

Ronee What, just a sudden impulse, was it?

Ange No.

Ronee Then what? (*Pause.*) Come on. (*Pause.*) What put the idea into your head . . . ? (*Beat.*) Oh no. (*Beat.*) Tell me Will had nothing to do with this. (*Beat.*) Ange. Tell me. Will. Tell me. (**Ange** *nods her head.*) Oh, my Christ. I am so stupid. What a fool. What a soft bloody fool. (*She goes to the door.*) Will. (*Beat.*) Will!

Will (*off*) What is it?

Ronee Come here.

Will (*off*) The fire'll go out.

Ronee Too bloody right. (*Shouts.*) It's important.

Will (*off*) OK.

Ronee *comes back into the room.*

Ange Ronee, I want to go home.

Ronee No. Not yet.

Will *enters.* **Ange** *is sitting looking crushed.* **Will** *is smiling. He slowly stops smiling.*

I told Ange that you and Lenny were very similar. I was wrong.

You're worse than Lenny. Much worse. (*Beat.*) What you've done to her is certainly as bad as anything he did. (*Pause.*) That's not to mention what you've done to me. Will, are you so insensitive, so feeble, that you had to do this?

Beat.

Will Er, yes?

Pause.

Ronee Look at him, Ange. Look at him. There's your 'nice' man. There's your open, honest, charming man who can't get his mind past your tits. Whose idea of maturity is to screw everything in sight. (*Beat.*) Talking of which, did you? (*Beat.*) Did you two screw?

Will Yes, this morning . . .

Ronee I don't want to know when, I don't want to see the pictures or . . . read the book or see the bloody film . . . (*Pause.*) Oh, why do I care? (*Beat.*) Will, did you seriously think that if you sent Ange in here to . . . That I would or could possibly go along with it? After everything I've told you? Did you?

Will Obviously.

Ronee How?

Will Why should I change? I've done what you expected. You can't pretend to be disappointed.

Ronee Don't you feel *anything* for anybody else?

Pause.

Will Contempt and lust. Those are my two strongest feelings.

Ronee Why?!

Beat.

Will Because . . . I can't feel anything else. I can't love anybody. I can't even bring myself to like very many people. (*Beat.*) I keep thinking back to ten years ago, when people *did* things. Nobody was expected to do the 'right' thing. We just did them, right or wrong, good or bad, nasty or nice. (*Beat.*) Thing is, I think I preferred them wrong, bad and nasty. Is that a crime?

Ronee It hurts people.

Will So what? (*Pause.*) The problem with you is, you still want love. After everything, after all the disillusion, the naked facts of life, the ugliness, the pointlessness, the kicks in the teeth, the bad scenes in bed, the downright bloody failure . . . You . . . still want love. Well, where is it? Andrea? She got it? Is Andrea a mystical receptacle of all that's good and fair in life? Is she?

Ronee No. She's another human being who wants love. Who wants me.

Will Then you deserve each other.

Ronee Yes! (*Pause.*) Nobody deserves you. Nobody who ever smiled or had a simple thought without wanting to soil somebody else deserves you. Live in the dirt. There are plenty of others there like you. But don't ever expect to find me down there again. I'm going to live knowing that I don't need to cut people to prove they're flesh and blood. Knowing that I don't need to smear their faces in shit to prove that it exists. Knowing, most of all, that I don't need to carve my name on their face to prove that *I* exist.

Beat. Enter **Oliver**.

Will Well, climb every mountain.

Ronee *goes.* **Oliver** *sings, loudly.*

Oliver Ford every stream. Follow every rainbow. *Till you find your dream!!* I have always wanted . . . to perform . . . cunnilingus . . . on Julie Andrews! I admit it.

Will And I have always had a secret desire to roger Judith Chalmers.

Oliver Anna Ford.

Will Valerie Singleton.

Oliver The Queen.

Will The world.

Mark *comes in, followed by* **Martin** *and* **Bruce**, *who leans in the doorway, watching.*

Mark here, has no secret desire whatsoever. Do you, Mark? Because little Mark's desires are always well out in front where they ought to be.

Oliver Vladimir, me old pal, is this right?

Mark I don't know what you're on about.

Oliver We're talking about desire. The turgid electricity in the loins. The dark, insatiable fire in the belly. Fucking.

Mark I dunno.

Oliver Well, that's not a very intelligent remark, is it for chrissakes? I expect better of you, Vlad.

Martin Ollie, do us a favour.

Oliver Certainly. What had you in mind?

Martin Keep it down.

Oliver Keep it down? I have trouble keeping it up. (*Liberal helpings of drink are being poured.*) The one-minute wonder, they used to call me. Oh, yes. Inoutinoutinout? In, mate. That was my lot. Thank you for coming, do call again.

Mark Here, this bloke, right. He's just got out of the nick. Been in for thirty years. And he thinks, 'Christ do I need a fuck.' So he goes off, right, and finds this scabby old whore, throws it on the bed and gives it the shagging of its life. When he's finished, he says, 'That was good. Just one thing, though.' 'What's that?' she says. 'Why was it that every time I give it some thrust, your toes turned up?' 'Next time,' she says, 'remember to take my tights off.' (**Mark**, **Ollie** *and* **Will** *laugh.* **Martin** *looks embarrassed.* **Bruce** *just stares.*)

Oliver Hey, you should join our group. We could do with a few laughs.

Martin Ollie, let's go home.

Oliver And rut like healthy stags.

Martin Let's just go home.

Oliver I . . . am . . . enjoying myself. I am letting it all hang out.

Martin Fab.

Pause.

Oliver (*slurring*) What is it? What's all this? . . . Killjoys . . . Why can't I have fun, for once? Just for once in my life, why can't I fart in church?

Martin Because it's stupid.

Oliver How dare you?! You dare to call me stupid?! Why, I've got more brains in my big toe than you've got in your entire body. I was a socialist when you were in nappies. I'm still a better socialist than you.

Martin What's that got to . . .

Oliver Everything. I am a socialist. I don't kowtow to the ruling class.

Martin What are you talking about?

Oliver Socialism's about truth and love and fucking. It's blood and sperm. What do Tories know about fucking? Nothing. (*In a tantrum.*) I've fucked my way around the world. There's nothing you can tell me. I've fucked socialists, fascists, pigs, my mother, myself. So I know what I'm talking about. *All right?!*

Martin If you say so.

Oliver I do say so! And don't contradict me. (*He hurls his drink in* **Martin**'s *face.*)

Martin For God's sake, Ollie . . .

Oliver God? How the fuck did he get into this? I've fucked God. (*He pours whatever he can lay his hands on over* **Martin**'s *head.*) God is a Nazi. And I don't have anything to do with Nazis. I shit on them. I fuck them. You're a Nazi. You're an anti-semite. Don't tell me you're not, because . . . (*He bawls into his face.*) *I know you bloody are!* (*Pause.*) I'm sorry, but you deserved that.

Pause.

Martin It wasn't a woman. It was Bruce.

He goes.

Oliver (*advancing on* **Bruce**) Ha. So. (*Beat. He stops.*) What?

Pause. He suddenly lunges at **Bruce**, *attempting to throw a punch.* **Bruce** *clocks it and knees him in the stomach. He falls to the ground out of breath and hurt.*

Bruce I won't be . . . coming to the group any more. I don't think I . . . need it.

He goes.

Mark Often like this, is it? (*He picks up* **Oliver** *and dumps him on the sofa.*)

Will Better, usually.

Mark Don't know what I've been missing.

Oliver (*doubled up*) Christ, what happened?

Will Martin went.

Oliver Where?

Will How the fuck should I know?

Oliver Vlad, Vlad, come and live with me.

Mark Sure thing.

Ronee *enters.*

Will Ah. Goodnight, sweet lady.

Ronee Yeah. Ange, get your case. You're coming with me.

Ange *goes upstairs.*

Will Ronee . . .

Ronee Don't, Will. You know where you're going. See it through. You might as well. It's all you've got.

Will It is now.

Beat.

Ronee I'll pick my stuff up tomorrow. And I'll see my solicitor.

Will What's it going to be? Mental cruelty?

Ronee I hadn't thought about it. But yeah, I think mental cruelty would do very nicely.

Will Y'know, deep down, deep inside somewhere . . . I hate you. I think I always have.

Ronee You poor, dried up little man. (*Beat.*) I used to love you.

Ange *reappears.*

Will Yeah. Funny, isn't it?

Ronee Bloody hilarious . . .

She and **Ange** *go.*

Mark Don't forget to leave that window open . . . (*Beat.*) You must be mad. What I wouldn't have done for a piece of your wife.

Will What *I* wouldn't have done . . .

Beat.

Mark Why don't we drop the laughing gnome off and hit the town? Maybe pick up some crumpet.

Will I dunno . . .

Mark Listen. We've never been out for a drink together, you and me. Let's go and get rat-arsed, find some dirty slags and have a bachelor night. Eh?

Beat.

Will Be just like old times. (*Pause.*) No. Not tonight, Josephine.

Oliver (*holding up a flower*) Look what I did. Why did I do that?

Mark 'Cause you're a prick.

Oliver No, no, no, I've got a prick.

Mark I call them as I see them.

He nods to **Will** *and goes.* **Will** *finishes his glass and goes to* **Oliver**, *who is asleep.* **Will** *sighs and goes to the stereo. He switches it on. The tape plays.*

Oliver I need help. ·

Martin Ollie, don't make it so hard on yourself.

Oliver I can't help it. (*Beat.*) I'm sorry everyone, I'm talking too much. I'm sorry. I'll give someone else a chance.

Will It's OK. It's not right to keep it bottled up, Ollie. It's not honest. (*Beat.*) No, I really think we're getting somewhere here. Let's keep going.

Fashion

Fashion was first presented by the Royal Shakespeare Company at The Other Place, Stratford-upon-Avon, on 7 April 1987, with the following cast:

Paul Cash	Brian Cox
Liz Scoular	Stella Gonet
Robin Gingham	Akim Mogaji
Stuart Clarke	Alun Armstrong
Eric Bright	Clive Russell
Howard Lipton	David Howey
Amanda Clarke	Estelle Kohler
Dooley	David O'Hara
Gillian Huntley	Linda Spurrier

Directed by Nick Hamm
Set design by Fotini Dimou
Lighting by Ian Loffhagen
Sound by Mo Weinstock
Fights by Malcolm Ransom

The revised version of *Fashion* reproduced in this volume, was first presented at the Leicester Haymarket in 1989 and the Tricycle Theatre, Kilburn, London in 1990, with the following cast:

Paul Cash	Paul Freeman
Liz Scoular	Karen Lewis
Robin Gingham	Paul Battacharjee
Stuart Clarke	Jim Carter
Eric Bright	Robin Soans
Howard Lipton	Robert East
Amanda Clarke	Gillian Eaton
Dooley	Paul Higgins
Gilliant Huntley	Lorna Heilbron
The Voice of Berkowitz	Linal Haft

Directed by Michael Attenborough
Decor Michael Pavelka
Lighting Bill Bray
Fights Malcolm Ransom

Act One

Scene One

6.40 a.m. A plush office on the top floor of a building in a quiet back street in central London. The set is split level. The lower, office level is hi-tech: desk, sofa, chairs, hi-fi, large video screen. The upper level is a modern kitchen and dining area, with a pine table and chairs. To one side of the set is a glass door leading to the lobby where the reception desk is.

On the sofa, we can just make out a blurred shape. It is **Paul Cash**, *asleep, under a duvet.*

A telephone rings once and the answering machine clicks on. All phone calls are amplified round the office on a speaker. When **Cash** *uses the phone, he has one he can use without needing to use the receiver, so he can hold a conversation almost anywhere in the room.*

The voice on the answering machine tape is that of **Liz Scoular**, **Cash**'s *secretary.*

Liz Hello, Cash Creative Consultancy. There's nobody in the office at the moment, but if you'd like to leave your name and number, we'll get back to you as soon as possible. Thank you for calling.

The tone sounds.

Berkowitz Hi, Cash. Berkowitz. New York. Listen, I just finished with McLeish and Harper, and thank God, the landscape's starting to flatten out at last. They bit on Windfall and the TCC promo, but I have to tell you, Gingham's five-part went down like cold cockroach chilli. You see who we're getting in the sack with here. The Guggenheim Foundation it ain't. Anyhow, two for three's an OK strike rate. And hey, listen, Buckley's still chewing me out over the visit. See what you can do, huh? Dinner at Downing Street is top option, but I know how these things are. It'd sure grease the wheels, anyhow. Oh, yeah, you can reach me at the Boston office after tomorrow a.m. OK? Ciao.

The phone line goes off. **Cash** *slowly gets out of the duvet, naked. He sits for a moment, scratching, stretches, stands up and walks across to the answering machine and presses the button to rewind the tape. On the desk are last night's Chinese takeaway containers. He picks up a spoon and eats some cold Chinese food, then goes to the drinks cabinet and pours a mineral water. The*

*tape has rewound. He switches it on. As it plays, he takes two hand weights
from under the sofa and does lifting exercises and t'ai chi style movement and
breathing. The first call is from* **Howard**.

Howard Hello, Paul. Howard. Ten thirty p.m. Tuesday. Sorry
not to get back to you earlier. Got stuck in a bloody briefing at
Number Ten. Twerp from the *New Statesman*'s got hold of some
defence leak. End of civilisation as we etcetera. Honestly, what a
bunch of tossers. Of course they'll all be rounded up if there's a
nuclear alert, what on earth do they bloody well expect? Still, page
and a half in the *New Statesman*, thirty seconds on Channel Four
News, total audience figures: two lesbians, a dog and Tony Benn.
Anyway, the matter in hand. I have a cautious green light. So see
what you and our dusky chum can magic up for me. OK? And
listen, it's not entirely a matter of public record just yet, so
complete discretion would be appreciated. Right. I'll be popping
in lunchtime as arranged so you can meet the Lincoln candidate
before we take her through the TV training drill. All right? Over
and out.

The tape beeps and goes on to the next call which is from **Eric Bright**.

Eric Paul, it's Eric Bright, returning your call returning my call.
Yes, lunchtime tomorrow would be fine. 'Bye.

The tape beeps and goes on to the next call, which is from **Stuart Clarke**.
He is drunk.

Stuart Cash, you bastard? It's Stuart. Old Clarkie. Listen, you
creep, why can't you return my calls? Eh? I've left you three
bloody messages in a week. So come on. You know I'm the best
director you're going to get. Give me a job. Any job. I'm not
proud. Hovis, Andrex, the wonder of sodding Woolworths. I don't
care. Just employ me, right? We go back a long way, Cash, so
shuffle some of that green folding stuff my way, or I'll come round
there and break your teeth. (*Beat. He belches.*) Oh, and Amanda
sends her love.

*The tape beeps and goes on to the next call, which is from a young Scottish
man.*

Dooley I know you. (**Cash** *stiffens slightly.*) Yeah. I know you all
right. Nancy boy. Nonce. (*Beat.*) Thought it was a secret, didn't
you? Well, it's not. 'Cos I know. (*Beat.*) I'll bet you're trying to put
a face to my voice now, aren't you? A pretty wee face. (*Beat.*) Well,
fret not. You'll get your chance. In the flesh. (*Beat.*) Is it nice up

there in your castle? Eh? Thick carpets? Leather chairs? Money pasted all over the walls? The smell of lovely money? (*Beat.*) I'm coming. I'm going to invade your space. Soon. 'Bye 'bye. Darling. (*He blows a kiss and puts the phone down.*)

The **Berkowitz** *call begins to play back.* **Cash** *saunters over and switches off the answering machine, opens a desk diary, finds a phone number and dials. It rings for a long time. Finally it's answered. It is* **Amanda Clarke**.

Amanda (*half asleep*) Hello?

Cash Amanda, hello, darling.

Amanda What? Paul, is that you?

Cash Yes. (*Beat.*)

Amanda Are you all right?

Cash Fine. (*Beat.*)

Amanda What time is it?

Cash Six-forty.

Amanda Uh huh. (*Beat.*) Well?

Cash Oh, what are you doing for dinner tonight?

Amanda Are you kidding?

Cash No.

Amanda Actually, I'm busy. Maxwell's in town, so my arse has to be well in gear.

Cash Never mind. Let me talk to your husband, will you?

Amanda Stuart?

Cash That's the one. Unless there's something you haven't told me.

Amanda I don't know where he is. Last time I saw him, he was popping out for a drink . . . three days ago . . . oh, hang on, his coat's here. I'll see if I can find him.

Pause, during which **Cash** *takes out an electric razor and starts to shave.* **Amanda** *comes back.*

Hello, Paul?

He switches off the razor.

He's on the sofa with a bottle of Jack Daniels. I've woken him up. What d'you want him for?

Cash I'm just returning his call.

Amanda You bastard. (*Beat.*) I'm going to take a shower, now I'm awake.

Cash Wish I could be there.

Amanda Yeah (*Beat.*) Look, I may give you a ring at lunch, OK?

Cash OK.

Pause, during which **Cash** *starts shaving again.* **Stuart** *comes to the phone.*

Stuart Cash?

Cash *stops shaving.*

Cash Hang on a minute, will you, Stuart? (*He finishes shaving.*) Right. (*Beat.*) How are you?

Stuart For fuck's sake, man, you don't ring me at this time of day to ask how I am.

Cash Never did have much time for the formal niceties, did you?

Stuart Bollocks.

Cash Still the angry young man.

Stuart No, I've matured. I'm now a slightly peeved, middle-aged man. With a terrible fucking hangover. So what is it?

Cash You've been ringing me, Clarke. I don't need this. (*He hangs up, goes over to the duvet and folds it up. The phone rings. He flips the switch on the desk.*) Cash.

Amanda Paul, what are you playing at? You ring at the crack of dawn and hang up . . .

Cash Listen, darling, some of us get up early. That's why some of us are very successful. On the other hand, some of us spend our lives in an alcoholic stupor. Which is why some of us are no-hope ex-movie directors.

Amanda Paul . . .

Cash But, seeing as Stuart's an old friend, and seeing as he's been leaving begging messages on my answering machine, and seeing as I'm screwing his wife behind his back, I thought I might help

him out. Put a bit of work his way. Just like you wanted.
Remember? (*Beat.*) However, when I call him to tell him the good
news about his career prospects, all I get is the usual fucking
mouthful. And so I hang up. (*Beat.*) And I can smell his breath
from here. I thought you said he'd got it under control.

Amanda He had when I last looked.

Cash When was that?

Amanda I don't remember.

Cash Well, you should look more often.

Amanda What? No fear. (*Beat.*) Actually, he had a little bit of
money through, so he went on a bender. (*Beat.*)

Cash Just put him back on, will you?

Amanda OK.

*She goes away from the phone and we hear her call 'Stuart' etc. Suddenly the
lights in the office come on.* **Cash** *doesn't react. We see* **Liz** *going into the
lobby towards the reception desk in her coat. She disappears. She comes back
across by the door, coat in hand, to hang it up.* **Cash** *drops the food container
in the waste bin.* **Stuart** *comes to the phone.*

Stuart Hello.

Cash Let's start again, shall we?

Stuart Yeah. (*Beat.*)

Cash Tell me, Stuart, do you still subjugate your art to your
politics?

Stuart Christ's sake, Cash . . .

Cash What I mean is, do you still refuse to produce work which
you consider to be detrimental to the interests of the proletariat?

Stuart I don't get the chance. I don't produce. Remember?

Cash Well really, Clarkie, a film with an Arab hero is a touch near
the knuckle. A Palestinian Arab hero . . . that's a fucking suicide
note. (*Beat.*) Anyway, I need to know whether you're politically a
little bit more flexible these days.

Stuart Isn't everybody? (*Beat.*) Try me.

Liz *enters with a small bowl, flannel and towel. She puts it on the desk by*
Cash. *They don't acknowledge each other.* **Liz** *goes.* **Cash** *washes and
dries his face through the following conversation.*

Cash What I want to know, Stuart, is if I employ you on a specific campaign, would you allow your personal – sorry, ideological – feelings to interfere with your work?

Stuart Depends.

Cash No. Let's have no grey areas. I want it cut and dried, black and white. Are you a professional director, or a professional liberal?

Stuart I've never been a liberal. You know that.

Cash How very true.

Liz *comes back in with* **Cash***'s clothes for the day. Suit, shirt, tie, socks, underwear. She lays them out on the sofa and goes, taking the duvet.*

Stuart One thing I do know. You've got to be a realist to survive. So, if you want it straight, yeah, I'll do the work, whatever.

Cash Glad to see you've adjusted to the spirit of the time.

Stuart No one said it's going to last for ever. It's not as if we're talking about the thousand-year Reich. I hope.

Liz *comes in and goes up to the kitchen and prepares coffee and orange juice.* **Cash** *opens his diary.*

Cash OK, I want you here this morning. Say ten.

Stuart Oh God . . .

Cash Realism, Stuart . . .

Stuart Yeah. I'll be there. Listen, I think Amanda wants to speak to you. Dinner invite or something.

Cash OK. See you at ten.

Stuart Yeah.

Pause while **Amanda** *comes to the phone.*

Amanda Paul?

Cash Hi.

Amanda Look, I thought, seeing as you'd called, we could arrange . . . (*Beat.*) It's OK, he's gone.

Liz *looks round.*

Amanda (*speaks softly*) So?

Cash He's coming in.

Amanda Thanks. (*Beat.*) I'm sure you can use him. We both know how good he is.

Cash Was, darling.

Amanda You don't lose something that special. (*Beat.*) If you want to meet up tonight, we could always go for a nightcap at the Bluebird.

Cash Sounds good.

Amanda Maybe you deserve a treat. (*Beat.*) Speak to you later.

Cash Bye.

Amanda Bye.

He flips the switch and goes over to his clothes and starts to dress.

Liz Good morning, Mr Cash.

Cash Good morning, Liz.

Liz D'you want toast?

Cash No thanks.

Liz Cereal?

Cash No.

Liz You'll get an ulcer. Or worse. Bowel cancer. That's terrible. And it's really common.

Cash So I hear.

Liz I'll just get you a small bowl, then, shall I?

Cash Why not?

Liz (*doing the cereal*) Don't want you wasting away, do we?

Cash Not much chance of that.

Liz It happens really quickly. Like my dad. He got so skinny you could see the bones. Like one of them concentration camp people. (*She puts the cereal on the desk.*) There. And eat it all up.

Cash Keep me clear till lunch, Liz, Eric Bright should be in mid-morning, and I've got someone coming in at ten.

Liz Right.

Cash And have Robin clear his desk for the day. I'm going to need him.

Liz What about calls?

Cash No domestic. Only New York or Jo'burg. Message if you can. And if Amanda calls this morning while there's anybody with me, definitely take a message.

Liz Uh huh. (*She opens the window blinds. Light floods in.*) It's a beautiful day.

Cash *is dressed. He buttons his jacket and sits at his desk.*

Cash What?

Liz It's a beautiful day. (*Beat.*)

Cash Every day's a beautiful day, Liz. Every day.

She turns and half smiles.

Blackout.

Scene Two

The office, about 9.45 the same morning. It is deserted. Pause. **Robin Gingham** *enters, just arrived for work. He's eating an apple. He goes to the kitchen area and pours a coffee, then comes down to* **Cash**'s *desk and browses through some papers on it.* **Liz** *enters.*

Liz Good morning, Mr Gingham.

He starts slightly.

Robin Oh, hi Liz.

Liz *tidies the papers up.*

State secrets?

Liz *smiles professionally.*

Where's sir?

Liz Popped out.

Robin What? Out of his office? Out of . . . the building? Christ. Have we had the four minute warning, or is his bank on fire?

Liz He's gone to buy a shirt.

Robin The plot thickens.

Liz He spilled coffee down the one he had on.

Robin Ah. (*Beat.*) Liz, do you ever have, like, really silly thoughts?

Liz No.

Robin I thought not.

Liz I'm a secretary.

Beat while he ponders this for a moment. She starts to go. He calls her back.

Robin Liz.

Liz Yes?

Robin Cardinal Richelieu died in 1642. (*Beat.*) Thought you might like to know.

Liz Thank you. Mr Cash wants you to keep yourself free today.

Robin For what?

Liz Work?

Robin Hey, careful, I had a heavy night.

Liz There are people coming in this morning. The Tory Party account, I think.

Robin Ah. Indeed. Work. (*Beat.*) Have we got the account then?

Liz I don't know.

Robin So who's coming in?

Liz I don't know.

Robin What's the only mammal that can't jump? (*Beat.*)

Liz The elephant.

*She turns and goes as **Cash** comes in with his new shirt.*

Cash Rob.

Robin Hi.

Cash (*changing his shirt*) Stan Berkowitz called.

Robin The Beast of the Bronx. What'd he have to say?

Cash They loved Windfall and TCC.

Robin Hacks.

Cash And they found your grand opus . . .

Robin Yuh?

Cash A crock of shit, darling. (*Beat.*) No reason as yet. (*Beat.*) *I* liked it.

Robin Paul, why do we work for these jerks? I mean, that's the third biggie they've nixed.

Cash We'll get there.

Robin Christ, I spent nearly two weeks getting that bastard looking right. And it looks bloody perfect. That promotion's a work of art, for Christ's sake. (*Beat.*)

Cash Rob, I've told you: advertising is the revenge of business on culture. We inform, we entertain, but most of all, we oil the wheels of commerce.

Robin Paul, people are image-sophisticated. They read the messages loud and clear. The most snotty-nosed tower block kid can recognise Russia in a Levi's ad. References stretching back through Le Carre, 'Ipcress', Tarkovsky, 'The Twilight Zone', Dostoevsky, James Dean. Every advert thirty seconds of cinematic purity. Claude Chabrol with Persil in the starring role. People *know*. They're sussed, Paul.

Cash Not so McLeish and Harper. (*Quickly, he doesn't want to have this conversation.*) Look, we've market tested, we've random sampled, we've pinpointed our target group. Now all we have to do is convince the Yanks we can come up with the package to sell to that group. Easy, really. So fuck art. Let's make money.

Beat. **Robin** *smiles.*

Robin Whatever you say.

Cash I'd never have put your idea in if I hadn't believed in it. Honestly.

Robin Yeah. (*Beat.*) I have this fantasy, right? We're filming for a new shampoo, and on the studio floor we've got . . . I dunno . . . Redgrave and Irons, with Menges and Joffe behind the camera, and in the corner, doing a rewrite, there's Stoppard and Shaffer. Don't tell me that wouldn't make money.

Cash Did the British film industry? (*Beat.*) How's the script coming on, by the way?

Robin (*evasive*) How did yours come on?

Cash Got as far as the title page.

Robin I haven't even got that far.

Cash It'll come.

Robin Yours didn't.

Cash I got sidetracked.

Robin Me too. D'you know what I mean? I go back to that nice piece of real estate I call home, and I sit there and I think, right, Robin old son, let's make like Hollywood. Let's do the Putnam shuffle. And I come up with three brilliant ideas, and I pour a nice long writer's drink and I visualise these great movies. They are so good. So I decide I have to tell somebody, go out, get absolutely plastered and end up playing 'Trivial Pursuits' till the sun comes up. I've got visualisation and I've got realisation. It's just the intervening period of creation that's absent.

Cash And I thought you took your *work* home with you.

Robin Bollocks, boss. Ahem, talking of which, what's this Liz tells me about Smith Square?

Cash I'm not absolutely sure yet. I'm just putting some people together, see what happens, see if we can't get a little piece of the action.

Robin Think we'll get it?

Cash How could they resist? We have genius on our side.

Robin Why, thank you.

Cash I meant me.

They exchange a smile.

Anyway, Eric's coming in later. (*He looks at his watch.*) And I've got a director coming in any minute.

Robin Anybody I know?

Cash Could be. So . . . thinking-cap time. I want to see you sparkle.

Robin OK. I'll just make a couple of calls.

Cash Fine.

Robin *goes as* **Liz** *comes in with some letters to be signed.*

Coffee, Liz. (*She goes to the kitchen.*) And can you get on to Rodney, tell him that if Benson keeps stalling we'll have to take him to court.

As he speaks, **Stuart Clarke** *comes into reception. He stands a moment and looks around*

And send him a copy of the figures. Just in case the last set got lost in the post.

Liz I understand Mr Benson has cash flow problems.

Stuart *is thinking about coming into the office.*

Cash This is not an episode of 'Minder', Liz. Mr Benson's chirpy cockney patois will not excuse the fact that he owes me seventeen grand.

Stuart *stands gingerly in the doorway. He takes a deep breath, knocks on the door and strides in very purposefully.*

Stuart Cash, you old bastard.

Cash Stuart.

They greet each other with a warm but tentative handshake.

Long time, long time.

Then **Stuart** *holds out his arms and they embrace, still tentative.*

Cash How are you?

Stuart Great, y'know . . .

Cash Yeah, you've put on weight.

Stuart Idle living.

Cash Couple of games of squash, I'll soon sort you out.

Stuart Make that five card draw and you're on.

Cash Times *have* changed.

Stuart Yeah. They have. (*Beat.*)

Cash Uh, that's Liz. My secretary and saviour.

Stuart Hello, Liz.

Liz Hello.

Cash Is that coffee ready?

Liz Nearly.

Cash (*going to the kitchen*) Strong, black. I'm guessing here . . .

Stuart Spot on.

Cash How's Amanda?

Liz *looks at him.*

Stuart You tell me.

Cash *stiffens.*

I've hardly spoken to her for a month.

Cash Diverging lifestyles . . .

Stuart No, she hates my guts. (*Beat.*) Hey, I have to thank you.

Cash For what?

Stuart For opening my eyes to a new cultural experience.

Liz *has poured the coffee, which* **Cash** *brings down to* **Stuart**. **Liz** *goes.*

Cash I have?

Stuart Yeah. Y'know, before this morning, when you summoned
me here for this dawn rendezvous, I had never seen, that is to say,
I had gone out of my way to avoid seeing, breakfast television.
And now . . . well, what can I say? It's terrifying. Like being
locked in a Barratt home with three hairdressers from
Cockfosters.

Cash Actually, they're terribly chummy. (*Beat.*) I've been on.

Stuart What, on Breakfast TV?

Cash Yes.

Stuart Fuck me. (*Beat.*) The only bugger I recognised was Clare
Rayner, God bless her and all who sail in her, but who in their
right mind wants to discuss breast cancer and Inter-Uterine
Devices at eight o'clock in the morning? Who in their right mind
even wants to be up at that time of day?

Cash The masses?

Stuart Oh them. (*Beat.*)

Cash Here, sit down.

They sit.

Got a lot to catch up on.

Stuart Yeah. (*Beat.*) Sorry about the phone calls.

Cash Not at all. Breath of fresh air.

Stuart No, I was soused.

Cash The way I remember it, you always were.

Stuart No. That was energy. But . . . you get older, the energy flags, the drink talks. (*Beat.*) Cash, I'm up for it. I need to work.

Cash Money problems?

Stuart (*lying*) Not really. I still get a few bob from the old stuff. And Amanda's very good, y'know . . .

Cash Done any work?

Stuart (*laughs*) Home video.

Cash Ah. Let's not talk about that, then.

Stuart Not the hard stuff. Just . . . I dunno, women with no clothes on. Cadbury's Flake without the Flake, if you know what I mean.

Cash Yeah. (*Beat.*) Look, I can't promise on this particular project, it's all up in the air at the moment, but if it doesn't work out, there's other stuff I could consider you for.

Stuart Thanks.

Cash And if it does work out, I'm doing myself a favour. You've been out in the cold for too long now.

Stuart I'm not into a comeback. I just want to work.

Cash I know. (*Beat.*) God, this is funny isn't it? Fifteen, twenty years ago, you were up there. You commanded the heights. People like me . . . well . . .

Stuart You were into money.

Cash I know. The lowest of the low. Completely ruined my sex life. Politics and art were sexy. Money and work were a cold shower. While you were making those movies . . . great movies, I might say . . . and enjoying the fruits thereof, I was on my own, tossing off and dreaming of this.

Stuart And tell me, Mr Cash, when did you *stop* beating your meat? (*Beat.*) Sorry. I'm here for a job. I better shut up.

Cash No. What I mean is . . . things are *very* different now. *This* is sexy.

Stuart You're making me feel old.

Cash No, not old. Old-fashioned.

Stuart Fashions change. Today the miniskirt, tomorrow trouser suits.

Cash Don't underestimate it. The one constant is that it's always there. You were fashionable once. Be grateful. (*Beat.*) Lecture over.

Stuart No, feel free. I seem to remember haranguing you at every available opportunity in the old days.

Cash That's true. You threw me out of the house once.

Stuart God, did I?

Cash Uh huh. Called me a despicable Tory anarchist and shoved me down the steps.

Stuart I remember.

Cash And I shouted: 'Hey, less of the anarchist if you don't mind'.

Stuart I don't remember that.

Cash (*icy*) No. You'd slammed the door by that time. (*Beat.*) I could hear you all laughing inside. Amanda, Maggie, John, Freddy, I think was there . . .

Stuart The three-day week. It was then.

Cash Yeah. Candles.

Stuart One thing about Ted Heath: he knew how to lend atmosphere to a dinner party.

Cash It's more than I did.

Stuart Not true. You provided us with some very entertaining moments.

Cash I *am* glad. (*Beat.*) Anyway, that's all in the past.

Stuart So what's in the present?

Cash Right. I've got a very specific proposition to put to you. It's not definite yet, but if we get it, it's big. If we don't get it, you'll still receive a development fee. Sound OK?

Stuart Why me?

Cash I went down the BFI last week. Had a look at some of your old stuff. Some of that work is incredible. Just the camera work. Brilliant. Incredibly powerful.

Stuart Thank you.

Cash It's true. (*Beat.*) And that's what I need. Something unashamedly manipulative. Emotive.

Stuart In what sort of area? (*Beat.*)

Cash Propaganda. Stuart, I want to make the sort of film that, were he alive today, Goebbels would be making. (*Beat.*)

Stuart I see. And who exactly would be exploiting my talents for this little trip down memory lane? (*Beat.*)

Cash The Conservative Party.

Stuart What?

Cash I've been asked to create a dummy campaign. If they like it, we could be looking at the chance to produce the next series of Tory party political broadcasts.

Beat. **Robin** *comes in.*

Ah, Robin, great. Robin, this is Stuart Clarke. Robin's my chief partner in crime, Stuart. Well, not quite partner yet.

Robin *holds his hand out.* **Stuart** *has stood up. He stares at* **Cash.**

Stuart You absolute fucking toerag. (*Beat.*) You arsehole.

Robin *has withdrawn his hand.*

Yeah. Good game, Cash. I'll be seeing you.

Cash Stuart . . .

Stuart *turns round.*

Stuart Don't mate. Let me go, then you can have your little laugh.

Cash I won't be laughing if you go.

Stuart No?

Cash No. If I wanted to humiliate you, I could do it in a million ways. Sorry, but it's true. I never joke about work.

Stuart *considers his next move.*

Cash Have another coffee.

Cash *nods at Robin, who takes* **Stuart***'s cup to the kitchen and fills it.*

Black.

Robin Hmmm?

Cash The coffee.

Robin *brings* **Stuart** *his coffee.* **Stuart** *takes out a quarter bottle of Scotch and pours some into his cup. He drinks, daring* **Cash** *to say something. He sits again.*

Stuart Right. So what makes you think a socialist director who hasn't made a film in six years is the right person to produce films for the Tory Party?

Cash Simple. I want the best.

Stuart How the fuck d'you expect me to work for the people my whole professional life's been spent trying to expose?

Cash This is work. Not art. Skill. Not passion. (*Beat.*) Look, Stuart, I have a reputation for making things happen. Things people thought were impossible. Come on. Let's do the impossible. (*Beat.*) I happen to find the idea of you making Tory Party broadcasts mind-bogglingly brilliant. (*Beat.*)

Stuart I suppose if I turn this down, I don't get another chance.

Cash That's right, yes. (*Beat.*) It's an interesting team. You won't be the only renegade socialist.

Stuart Oh? Dug up Ramsay MacDonald, have you?

Cash Close.

Stuart Who?

Cash Ex-Labour MP. Now a TV pundit and newspaper columnist . . . (*Beat.*)

Stuart Eric Bright.

Cash On the button.

Stuart Eric sodding Bright. I can't work with that schmuck.

Cash Why not?

Stuart Christ, if we all moved to the right as fast as he did, we'd knock the earth off its axis.

Robin *sighs heavily.*

Stuart Sorry?

Robin Politics is boring.

Stuart Oh, it talks then.

Cash Rather well.

Stuart Does it ever think? Or is *that* too boring?

Robin I don't know what it is, but whenever I encounter a sixties has-been flaunting his political soul, I come over all lethargic.

Stuart This boy of yours any good?

Cash Very.

Stuart He'll have to be if he wants to get away with talking to me like that.

Robin *smirks.* **Stuart** *turns to* **Cash.**

Stuart D'you remember that time . . . God, where was it . . . the Chinese place. That Tory prat. Remember?

Cash Yeah.

Stuart Gave us a lecture on the evils of socialism. Said I should be shot. (*He smiles.*) Looked a bit funny, didn't he, when I broke his nose. (*Beat.*)

Robin Wow. Right on. You break a guy's nose because he has different politics to you. Highly egalitarian.

Stuart No, I broke his nose because he knocked my drink over and refused to buy me another one. See, there's only one thing I hate more than a Tory, and that's a graceless Tory. (*Beat.*)

Cash I want you in on this one Stuart. And I have to tell you, it feels good. (*Beat.*) D'you want a bit of time? Think it over?

Stuart *looks at him glumly and shakes his head.*

Stuart No. No thanks.

Beat. Then he holds out his hand to **Robin,** *smiling.*

Hello, Robin. I understand we're going to be working together.

They shake.

Blackout.

Scene Three

Lunchtime the same day. **Stuart** *is sitting on the sofa, a near-empty bottle of wine on the table, and a half-eaten salad on his lap.* **Liz** *is washing up in the kitchen. She seems half-nervous and half-pitying of him.*

Liz Is there anything I can get for you, Mr Clarke?

Stuart (*drains his glass*) Some more of this stuff, if you've got it.

She goes to the fridge and gets another bottle and starts to uncork it.

I hope it's bloody expensive.

Liz D'you like it?

Stuart Only if it costs. That's the point, isn't it?

Liz Is it?

Stuart That's what I thought. (*Beat.*) Unless I'm out of touch.

She brings the bottle down to him.

Liz Actually, it's £1.99 a bottle. Mr Cash gets a discount.

Stuart I'll bet he does. Tell you what, I'll have a brandy.

Liz Och . . .

Stuart A large one.

Beat. **Liz** *seems to want to say something.*

I've heard it all before, Liz, so don't waste your breath.

Liz I wouldn't bother. I've *seen* it all before.

She goes back to the kitchen and pours a brandy.

Stuart Thanks for the lunch, anyway.

Liz 'S OK.

Stuart It was very healthy.

She brings the brandy.

Liz Who is it you're punishing?

Stuart Oh no, please . . .

Liz It's somebody. I know in the long run it's you, but that's not where it started is it?

Stuart Look, I'll only say this once. Mind your own fucking business.

Liz Then get your own fucking brandy.

She takes it back.

Stuart (*laughing, trying to shrug it off*) OK, I'm sorry. Peace?

She puts the glass down in the kitchen and stands defiant.

It's not somebody. It's something.

He goes and gets the glass.

Liz Aye. That's what they always say. (*Beat.*) Why are drunks so predictable? Eh? I mean, you can take a hundred people, all completely different, and then you get them drunk, and they all turn into the same person. (*Beat.*) There was a documentary on the other night. Australian aborigines. They looked incredible, y'know? But they've given them drink, and Coca-Cola T-shirts and cut-off jeans, and now they look like every wino you ever saw in your life before. It was heartbreaking. (*Beat.*)

Stuart Isn't Cash responsible for some lager accounts?

Liz Aye. And vodka, and French liqueurs. (*Beat.*) But Mr Cash usually drinks mineral water.

Stuart Mais naturellement. (*He smiles.*)

Liz You know what happens to alcoholic men? Their breasts swell and their testicles shrink. (*Beat.*)

Stuart What about women?

Liz They've already had the experience.

He pours another drink.

Stuart Don't you have any vices then, Liz?

Liz Oh aye. Men.

Stuart Sorry, can't help you there. I'm a one-woman man.

She gives him a sorry look.

Liz I like Arab men, anyway.

Stuart Ah.

Liz My weakness. (*Beat.*)

Stuart You and . . . what's his name . . . ?

Liz Who? Robin? No way. He's more English than strawberries at Wimbledon. He's just a boy, in any case. I value finesse.

He raises his glass.

Stuart To quality.

Eric Bright *suddenly comes in, cheerful and lively.*

Eric Hullo, Liz. Little bit on the late side, I'm afraid. Couldn't be helped.

Liz Mr Cash is in Mr Gingham's office looking at some artwork. He won't be long.

Eric Smashing.

Liz I'll tell him you're here.

Eric That's smashing.

She goes out. **Stuart** *studies the label on the brandy bottle as* **Eric** *goes to the kitchen and opens the fridge. He opens a bottle of Guinness and pours, lovingly.*

Nectar of the gods. Dublin-brewed. Nothing like it. A glassful of history. Cheerio.

Eric *drinks and smacks his lips.* **Stuart** *studies his glass.*

Stuart French. Over-priced. Somebody else's. A goblet of bile. (*He knocks it back.*)

Eric (*busying himself with his case*) Waiting for Paul, are you?

Stuart Liz does the waiting. I'm a guest. (*Beat.*)

Eric *smiles.*

Eric Yes. But seriously.

Stuart Hmmm?

Eric Are we part of the same affair?

Stuart I sincerely hope not. We haven't been properly introduced.

Eric I sort of assumed you'd know who I was.

Stuart Yes, but I'm a stickler for protocol. (*Beat.*)

Eric Eric Bright.

Stuart We've met.

Eric Really? When?

Stuart Nineteen seventy . . . six. The terrace at the House of Commons. Photocall.

Eric Ah. Photographer, are you?

Stuart No. (*Beat.*) Arts for Labour. I was an artist. For Labour. You were an MP. For Labour.

Eric Don't remind me. (*Beat.*) I'm sorry . . . you're . . . ?

Stuart Stuart Clarke. (*Beat.*) Films. 'Red Sky over Clydeside'? 'The Poacher'?

Eric Of course, yes. I remember. Haven't done a lot this, er, decade, have you?

Stuart I was before my time. Tragic.

Eric Yes, yes. Arts for Labour. I was there, was I?

Stuart In body, at least.

Eric That's right. One of the problems with Labour, isn't it? We could always get Arts for the Party. Demonstrators for the Party, pop groups for the Party. It was *votes* for the Party where we came unstuck. (*Beat.*) Yes, I remember it now. Jim Callaghan was petrified somebody was going to smoke pot like the Beatles at Buck House. In fact, they were a very . . . respectable lot. Crusty even. Yourself excepted, of course. The electorate must have thought they were being asked to return the cast of 'Coronation Street' to Number Ten.

Stuart Instead, they opted for 'Miami Vice'.

Eric And who's to say they were wrong?

Stuart Not you, I'll bet.

Eric This is a democracy. The people made their choice. I merely observe.

Stuart Too modest. You're an example to us all.

Eric I like to think my mind was broad enough to change.

Stuart Don't we all. But, here I am, stuck in this straitjacket of ideals and ideology, of history and experience. I just can't seem to shake it off. If only I could be like you.

Eric Your cloth cap's showing, dear.

Stuart So's your fake suntan, but I'm too polite to mention that.

Pause.

Eric So what brings you to Paul Cash's office? Apart from the brandy?

Stuart Why, my undoubted talents as a film-maker, of course.

Eric Oh? Got the TUC account, has he?

Stuart You wouldn't be here if he had.

Eric That's true. I don't work for losers.

Stuart *pours another drink.*

I feel like I'm being judged here.

Stuart (*smirking*) Doesn't history judge us all?

Eric Oh God. One of the reasons I got out of the Labour Party was to escape from all that bloody council house, second-rate Leninist rhetoric. Or Dennis Skinner, as it's more commonly known.

Stuart *laughs.*

Ah. You were being ironic.

Stuart It's a possibility.

Cash and **Robin** *come in, mid-discussion.*

Robin . . . references, Paul. It's called visual wit. Remember?

Cash It's too prissy. Too bloody fey. Minimum impact. I want the truth about the product. Hello, Eric. (*He pats him on the shoulder.*) We're not pouring cream on, we're getting the cream out.

Robin But what's wrong with moving on to a larger canvas?

Cash Nothing, so long as it's not designed by another art school reject friend of yours.

Robin Get 1989 for Christ's sake, boss.

Cash Rob . . . try again. Dump the artwork. Keep the text if you must. But give me a wonderful experience. Please. And do it now. Sit this one out.

Robin *stares at him.*

We'll bring you in when we've got some basics worked out. OK?

Robin *stands a second then goes out.* **Cash** *presses the intercom buzzer.*

Liz, no calls. (*He pours coffee.*) Jesus, I want something bold and vivid to pass on to the agency, and he's giving me the history of art. OK. You two met?

Eric We're old friends.

Cash Yeah? Good. Sit down, Stuart. Come on, let's get formal. Right, Eric, did you tell Stuart where we are on this?

Eric I didn't really get a chance.

Stuart We were having such fun reliving old times.

Cash OK. Well, Eric and I have been working together since the last election, grooming Tory candidates. We show them the ropes as far as media techniques go, interviews and so on. Now, having got my foot in the door, I've been asked to put together some provisional ideas for party political broadcasts. To do that I need a team.

Stuart And we're it . . .

Cash For now yes. Quite simply Stuart I'm not alone in thinking Tory publicity has been handled very badly. I believe I can do better. I know I can do better. (*Beat.*)

Stuart So. We're all in love with the Tory Party.

Cash Yeah, that's right. For the purposes of this campaign, we are.

Stuart This is all a bit sudden.

Cash Last month I was heavily involved with British Airways. Next month I fully intend to be having a torrid affair with the South African Tourist Board.

Stuart You really put it about.

Cash That's the nature of the beast.

Stuart Mind you don't catch something.

Cash I've had the jabs. I'm germ free. (*Beat.*) Are you familiar with Eric's column Stuart?

Stuart Is that the one in Trafalgar Square . . . ?

Eric *chuckles.*

Cash Don't fuck about, man.

Stuart Well, if you ask me questions like that, it could very quickly be the end of a beautiful relationship.

Cash Come on. Have you read it?

Stuart Yes.

Cash And? (*Beat.*)

Stuart Forgive me, but, it's smug, self-satisfied, lowest common denominator crap.

Eric *chuckles.*

The guy's in love with the starch of Margaret Thatcher's skirts. (*Beat.*) He despises the working-class, because that's where he comes from. He's dangerously nostalgic, a cynic masquerading as a realist. In short, his bank roll's so far down his throat, it's coming out his arse. Oh, and he probably wants to travel and help children. (*Beat.*) Can I go now?

Eric *laughs.*

Eric You see! That's what they say. Grown men and women turn into little playground bullies. It's pathetic. We can nail this in the film, Paul. They don't want a Labour government, they want to take their bat and ball home so people like us won't be allowed to play any more. (*Beat. He's enjoying himself.*) Stuart, have you ever been to a Party conference?

Stuart Once.

Eric Let me tell you . . . the bit I hate most. It's those beady-eyed little fanatics with the badges and the look of the converted. Staring at each other in corners, repeating their mantra: 'Jobs and services, welfare state, jobs and services.' I used to stand there thinking: my dad was a metalworker, you pasty-faced little white-collar shits. He held my hand on the terraces at Old Trafford. He was a shop steward, a full-time union official when there was still something to fight for. And if one of you disordered little twerps had ever dared call him comrade, he'd have wrung your bloody neck.

Stuart So much for the brotherhood of man.

Eric Sexist.

Stuart The only time I went, I can't say as I was as revolted by the rank and file as you obviously were. No, it was the PLP who got up my nose. The sleek patricians of Westminster, with their directorships, their consultancies, their newspaper columns. You lot went into a room, and by the time you came out, something was decided. Because that's how it worked. The poor silly ordinary bastards worked like slaves to get you elected, and from then on you made the decisions. As if it was God's law. Well, I had a good chuckle watching those jaws drop when they realised they were going to have to stand for re-selection. Like someone had just told them the earth was flat.

Eric Re-selection, yes. The revenge of the pygmies. (*Pause.*)

Cash Well. Old wounds don't heal, do they?

Eric Not the oldest wound of all, the Labour Party. It still gushes blood, the poor old thing.

Cash The point is, Stuart, that your attitudes are no longer those of the ordinary Labour voter. You represent, shall I say, a hard rump.

Eric No, don't mention Eric Heffer.

Stuart Christ.

Cash Britain has changed, shifting class barriers, new technology, the environment . . .

Stuart Spare me the Murdoch memorial lecture.

Cash I know you don't want to hear it, but it's where we have to start from. Now somewhere out there is a mainstream critique of Tory policy. Which is beginning to give your ordinary Tory voter the jitters. I want us to identify it, agree on it and counter it.

Stuart Isn't that Bright's job?

Eric Don't look at me. I'm in love with the starch of Margaret Thatcher's skirts.

Cash Don't be shy, Stuart. Put the emotion on hold and let's have the intellect in functioning mode for a change. What are the Tories' main weaknesses?

Stuart How long have you got?

Cash As long as it takes?

Eric It *is* important to agree, *if* we're going to get into bed together on this one.

Stuart I'll keep my trousers on if it's all right with you.

Eric Oh dear. We shouldn't really be part of the same country, should we?

Stuart We're not.

Eric 'Twas ever thus. (*Beat.*)

Cash Finished?

Stuart Look, it's quite simple, Thatcher broke the unions to create a docile workforce, to get people back into a mobile labour market, a commodity, stripped of rights and representation. Also to push down real wages so the new industries could be manned at cheaper rates, making them economically viable for the immediate future. She financed unemployment with the money from North Sea oil, and floated a boom which let international capital alter the structure of British industry to such an extent that it would be impossible to reform it back again. How's that for an obituary?

Eric Right. Economic argument. Piece of cake.

Stuart The Welfare State has to be dismantled, sorry, rationalised, because it's an example of collective security, altruism if you like, which uses money, but, horror of horrors, doesn't make anybody a profit. Cannot make anybody a profit. So, smash it up. Private medicine makes a profit. Taxed benefits get something back at least. Stands to reason, push more and more people into private health care by making the NHS so piss-poor that only the dregs will still be able to *bear* to use it.

Eric (*writing*) Tory health cuts myth! (*Beat.*)

Stuart Down in Lambeth there's a derelict site, one of many, where young Londoners, dressed as New York hoodlums, chased Charles Bronson around for a couple of weeks while the cameras rolled. (*Beat.*) Where this recreation of Yankee social blight was being filmed, had once been a hospital. They knocked down a hospital and made 'Death Wish Three' on the ruins.

Eric Anti-Americanism. Good. (*Beat.*)

Stuart Is there anybody out there?

Cash You bet.

Eric That's really smashing, Stuart.

Stuart *goes to the kitchen and pours a brandy.*

We've got the right man here, all right, Paul.

Howard *and* **Gill** *have come into reception.*

Stuart Were you born a prat, Bright, or do you practise?

Cash Hey, this is work, Clarkie.

Eric Politics, not personalities. Right, Mr Clarke?

Liz *shows* **Howard** *and* **Gill** *into the office.*

Cash Howard

Howard Cash.

Eric *stands, rather sycophantically and holds out his hand.*

Howard Bright.

Eric Hullo.

Howard Still on our side, are you?

Eric Oh yes.

Howard *licks his finger and holds it up to test the wind direction.*

Howard Yes. Still blowing our way, I think. Cash, meet Gillian Huntley.

Cash Hello.

They shake hands.

Howard Gill's going to win the Lincoln by-election for us in a couple of weeks, we hope, so we need to teach her some of your television presentation tricks. Sprinkle some of your fairy dust, Cash.

Cash A pleasure.

Howard Friday week OK?

Cash Yes, fine.

Gill I've heard a lot about your expertise, Mr Cash.

Cash Good, I hope.

Gill Felicity Hammond sings your praises.

Cash Ah yes. We were very successful there.

Gill She won the seat.

Cash And so will you.

Howard Another one in the House. What's the world coming to eh?

Eric Well, you have an excellent example to follow, my dear.

Howard You surely don't mean me.

Eric I mean the PM.

Gill I think she's an example to us all. Including the men.

Howard Hmm. You're right of course. But I draw the line at twinset and pearls. (*Half-hearted laughter.*) Who's the wallah burglarising your best Napoleon, Cash?

Cash Stuart, come and meet Howard.

Stuart *ambles down.*

Howard Come on down, Stuart.

Stuart Why not? The price is right. (*He arrives.*)

Cash Howard, meet Stuart Clarke. Film director extraordinaire.

They shake.

Howard Stuart Clarke? Stuart Clarke?

Stuart Well, it was fun while it lasted.

Howard No, no, old man. Great fan of yours. And the good lady wife. Well, her especially.

Stuart Don't tell me you've seen my films.

Howard Of course.

Stuart And you like them?

Howard Like them? We had money in two of them. (*Beat.*) Bloody good stuff. Politics daft as a brush, but what the hell, it's a free country. Made us a few shillings if I remember. In fact, I think I'm right in saying, your film, what was it . . . something with 'Life' in the title . . .

Stuart 'A Backstreet Life'.

Howard That's right. Well, 'A Backstreet Life' bought us our villa in Greece.

Stuart (*not unfriendly*) So that's where the money went.

Howard 'Fraid so, yes. God, the wife will be so pleased. Listen, you must come to dinner. We'd be thrilled.

Stuart OK.

Eric I didn't know you were a patron of the arts, Howard.

Howard No? Well write it down for future reference. Look, can't really stop, Cash. Just wanted to meet the team. Talking of which, where's our dusky chum?

Cash Shall I get him?

Howard God, no. He makes me nervous. (*Beat.*)

Cash Can I get you anything? Coffee?

Howard Yes. Gill, you'll do that for me, won't you? It's up there in the little pot. Thanks.

She goes to pour the coffee.

OK. Those of you who haven't been down a dark hole for the last few years will be aware that the Conservative Party consists, crudely but accurately, of two factions. Known as the Wets and the Dries. Or Gentlemen and Players as I prefer it.

Gill Milk?

Howard What? Yes. You will also be aware –

Gill Sugar?

Howard No thank you. Also be aware that I'm not especially aligned with either party. Which is to say that I once served Heath loyally and prayed to Keynes every night, and I now serve Thatcher loyally. No prayers, you will observe, in conviction politics.

Gill gives him his coffee.

Thank you. Now, there has emerged, recently, a grouping which wishes to steer a middle course between these two opposites, wet and dry. We, they, see it as vital that we present a package to the electorate which stresses the strengths of the Party as a whole. In short, a balanced ticket. The Prime Minister obviously has great appeal for many people, but it is important that we don't allow our ability in depth to be swamped by just the one personality. So, some of us on the presentational side of things are keen to come up with a few examples of balanced, but effective, publicity. Not, I might say, without some opposition from both sides. I fear without it, we may lose the next general election. And HMS Britannia will be steering a course for the nearest bloody great iceberg. (*Beat.*)

Stuart Sort of a 'Did Six Million Really Die' exercise.

Howard In a way.

Stuart Were Four Million Really Unemployed?

Howard Not on our bloody figures they weren't! (*He laughs.*)
Cash, you know the form. Get me something good.

Cash Commitment to excellence. That's our promise, Howard.

Howard Good. (*Beat.*) Well, we must be off. I've promised this
young lady lunch somewhere she can throw bread rolls at Roy
Hattersley. Adios.

Gill Goodbye.

They all say goodbye etc. **Howard** *and* **Gill** *go.*

Stuart So. It's not even the Tory Party we're working for here. It's
the Eton and Harrow Tendency. (*He laughs.*)

Eric In my experience, you throw a bread roll at Hattersley, he
just eats it. (*Beat.*)

Cash I know Howard's a bit of a smoothie, but believe me, he
delivers. He got me the candidate training account against some
of the big boys, and that pays a lot of bills. (*Beat.*) If we get this
right, it could do us a lot of favours.

Eric I'm with you all the way.

Stuart Is that an election pledge? Because your track record's not
overly impressive on that score.

Eric This is the *real* world, Mr Clarke. (*Beat.*)

Cash Last time of asking, Stuart. No going back. Are you in?

Stuart In? I wouldn't miss it for the world. (*Beat.*)

Cash I'll have Liz draw up a contract.

Amanda *comes into reception.*

Eric Time I was off. Mr Murdoch wants three thousand words on
popular capitalism by Thursday. Can't disappoint him. When
shall we three meet again?

Cash I'll call you. See if you can draft out a few ideas for next
time.

Eric No problem. Oh, don't forget I've got a week's freebie in
Montserrat coming up.

Cash It's in the diary.

Amanda *comes in.* **Liz** *is behind her, but she gives up and goes back to her desk.* **Amanda** *sees* **Stuart** *and is taken aback.*

Eric Goodbye then. (*He goes.*)

Stuart What are you doing here?

Amanda Come to take my husband to lunch, what else? Assuming there's maybe something to celebrate.

Cash I'm just waiting on his references. Amanda, how are you? Long time no see.

They kiss formally.

Amanda You haven't changed much since I last saw you.

Cash Some things never change.

Stuart I've *had* lunch.

Amanda Liquid, by the look of it.

Stuart Salad. We can go to a boozer. I'll just take a leak. (*He goes.*)

Cash I thought you were busy today.

Amanda I've got an editorial board meeting at three. It could be very long and very bloody. I'm sorry. I thought Stuart'd be gone by now.

Cash You mean you came to see me?

Amanda Of course. I'm not the Sally Army. I don't follow him around like a soup kitchen. I gave that up years ago.

Cash It's a bit risky. I'm going to be seeing rather a lot of your husband.

Amanda Good. That means you can see more of me. (*Pause.*) Sod this. I want to kiss you. On the mouth. I want to lick your tongue.

Cash I'd like that.

Amanda You like everything. You're undiscriminating.

Cash It's this lust for life. I can't help it. (*Beat.*)

Amanda What about this evening?

Cash What about it?

Amanda Are you free?

Cash I could be.

Amanda Don't fuck me about Paul. You're not so hard to get.

Cash Ring me after lunch. (*Beat.*) I may be busy.

Amanda I could come late. Do it on your desk. Mess up your papers.

Cash How come we never do it on your desk?

Amanda Open plan office, darling. I may be many things, but an exhibitionist isn't one of them. Some things I keep to myself.

Stuart *comes back in.*

Stuart Right.

Amanda Did you wash your hands?

Stuart Shove it.

Amanda Anybody'd think you just *lost* a job.

Stuart I just lost *some*thing. Fuck knows what. (*Beat.*) Come on. (*They turn to go.*) Propaganda, Cash. That's what you said.

Cash That's right.

Stuart Pretty pictures. You're on.

Stuart *and* **Amanda** *go.* **Cash** *sits at his desk.* **Liz** *comes in.*

Liz D' you want some lunch?

Cash No thanks. (*Beat.*)

Liz I like him.

Cash Stuart?

Liz Aye.

Cash He's an easy guy to like. Or he used to be. (*Beat.*) He was nearly killed, you know. In Ulster.

Liz I didn't know.

Cash Yeah. (*He starts to smile.*) He was going to make a film. Pro IRA. Silly sod got caught in one of their city centre bombings. Complete accident. (*Laughs.*) Sorry. But you've got to laugh.

She stands for a second then picks up some papers from his desk.

Liz Are these signed?

Cash Yeah.

She goes. **Cash** *smiles to himself.*

Blackout.

Scene Four

About ten o'clock that night. The office is quite dark. **Cash** *is stretched out on the sofa. After a moment's pause, a young man,* **Dooley,** *comes in. He's drying his hands on a paper towel. He crosses the room and throws the towel into the waste bin.*

Dooley So. Paul. Are you often to be found in the Moulin Cinema Complex, Great Windmill Street? (*Beat.*) Are you?

Cash Occasionally. (*Beat.*)

Dooley Tell me, was it 'Ranch of the Nymphomaniac' or possibly 'Erotic Exploits of a Sexy Seducer' which drew you to this place? Or were you merely in out of the cold?

Cash It's a warm night. (*Beat.*) 'Prisoner of Paradise' was the film that particularly caught my eye.

Dooley The overtones of confinement, was it? You were expecting perhaps, bondage or some such? (*Beat.*) You should see the one with the Queen in it. 'Detained at Her Majesty's Pleasure.' (*Beat.*) I'll have that drink now.

Cash Help yourself. It's in the fridge.

Dooley One for yourself?

Cash I'll have a Scotch.

Dooley I hate the stuff. (*He takes a beer out of the fridge and pours a Scotch.*) Y'know, people say it's Scotch that makes the Scots the way they are. Well, I'm the way I am and I hate the stuff. (*Beat.*) Personally, I find the deletion of the erect male organ a great disappointment, don't you? (*He hands* **Cash** *his drink.*) In the films. I mean, we get to see every nook and cranny of the girls. The camera would appear to be fearless in its probing of the female extremities. But where are the throbbing willies? I sometimes feel like shouting out: 'Where are the cocks?' Y'know?

Cash You'd get thrown out.

Dooley What, by those wee Pakistani fellers?

Cash They carry knives. (*Beat.*)

Dooley Maybe that's where all the cocks have gone, eh? The Pakistani fellers slice them off and put them into samosas.

Cash Maybe.

Dooley Nah. It's a wee little Englishman somewhere who decreed that we were not to be allowed sight of the aroused male member. Has to be. It's so typically fucking English, that. (*Pause.*) I like cocks.

Cash You've told me.

Dooley Did you decorate this place yourself? Nah, course you didn't. I expect you had a firm of interior designers do it all for you.

Cash That's right.

Dooley I knew it. And d'you know how I knew it? It's like a public lavvy in here. That's how I knew it. (*Beat.*) A very nice public lavvy, but all the same . . . Do you ever go home?

Cash Not very often. I don't like going outside very much.

Dooley That's why you favour the erotic cinema, I suppose.

Cash No. (*Beat.*)

Dooley It's weird, is it not? That you never go home, though you have one, and I'm sure it's very nice, not like a public lavvy at all, and I don't have a home but would very much like to go there. If I had one. Is that not weird? That definitely says something to me.

Cash What?

Dooley Hey, I'm no philosopher. Which is just as well. Can you see one of them bastards sleeping in a cardboard box under the arches? No, you cannot.

Cash Why not? George Orwell did it.

Dooley Who?

Cash Orwell. Wrote '1984'.

Dooley Aye? Shite film. Fucking depressing. The music was OK. I like the Eurythmics. That Annie Lennox, she's worth a poke, eh? (*Beat.*) You've not got a clue who I'm talking about, have you?

Cash I have the Eurythmics on compact disc, as a matter of fact.

Dooley What, in your cheesy home you never go to?

Cash That's right.

Dooley Maybe I should burgle you. Steal Annie Lennox off you.

Cash Be my guest. I'm insured. (*Beat.*) Crap in the bed. Whatever it is you do. (*Beat.*)

Dooley You really wouldn't mind?

Cash Not in the slightest.

Dooley Don't you want all the things you own?

Cash I don't know what I want. All I know is, what I get isn't enough. (*Beat.*) What do *you* want?

Dooley Me? Fucking everything. I want a house, a couple of cars, flash, with stereo speakers and tinted windows. I want an American Express card. A video. Loads of coke. An Armani suit. And I wanna be on Wogan.

Cash (*genuine*) So? Do it.

Dooley Oh aye . . .

Cash Why not? It's there. You can have it.

Dooley Gonna give it to me, are you?

Cash No, it's easier than that. You just walk in and take it. (*Beat.*) If you weren't so bloody terrified of success, you could have it.

Dooley I'm not terrified of nothing.

Cash Wise up. You're all the same. You hang around Piccadilly Circus all day because you want to. You enjoy sleeping in a box. It's easy. You know that to go out and get what you want means standing on your own two feet. And that's something you never learned. Well I'll tell you, it's easier than spending your life whining on about how you're never going to get it.

Dooley If I get it, I'm depriving somebody else of it, am I not?

Cash So?

Dooley And you, at this very moment, are in fact depriving me of what is rightfully mine.

Cash But I'm sharing it with you.

Dooley Not sharing. Bartering. I'm allowed to dip my wee toe into your pool on the understanding that at some point I may agree to play with your erect member. Or allow you to play with mine. Or put it in my mouth. Or worse. (*Beat.*) You've bought me. Is that not right?

Cash In a sense. But in a sense, we're all bought and sold.

Dooley Aye. Except how come when *I*'m bought and sold I feel like a Filipino or a twelve-year-old Bangkok virgin?

Cash That's your speciality. That's your area. (*Beat.*) Anyway, who said anything about sex? (*Pause.*)

Dooley I'll help myself. (*He goes to the kitchen and gets another beer.*) Like I said, I like cocks. (*He smiles, thinking he may have gone too far.*)

Cash Do you have many friends?

Dooley No. Do you?

Cash (*Beat*) No. I don't.

Dooley Is that why you're talking to me?

Cash No. (*Beat.*)

Dooley What's your speciality, Paul? What's your area?

Cash I tell lies for a living.

Dooley Are you good at it?

Cash One of the best. It's a very crowded market these days, but I like to think I've carved out my own little niche.

Dooley Who do you tell these lies for?

Cash Whoever pays me.

Dooley And who do you tell them *to*?

Cash Everybody. You. All the people who can't afford to pay me.

Dooley Have you been telling me lies tonight?

Cash Who knows? (*Beat.*) Why have you been following me? Why did you leave threatening phone calls on my answering machine? (*Beat.*)

Dooley You must have somebody else in mind. I never met you before tonight. Halfway through 'Warm Nights, Hot Pleasures' at the Moulin Cinema. The bit where the young girl found herself alone in the kitchen with the chauffeur and the gardener. (*Beat.*) And then the governess came in.

Cash Why?

Dooley I believe she was interested in some form of perverted sex. I missed the crucial next section as you engaged me in conversation. Something to do with how much of the film had you already missed. Lucky, really, that you didn't turn up ten minutes earlier. Ten minutes earlier I had my hand in the pocket of a middle-aged gentleman, performing executive relief for the price of the cinema ticket. If you were after more of the same, I was going to have to ask you to change sides as my left wrist was flagging just a wee bit. The right's much stronger. Practice, y'see.

The doorbell in reception suddenly rings. They freeze. It rings again, more insistent. **Cash** *gets up and goes to the window. He looks down.*

Cash Shit. You have to go.

Dooley Now?

Cash Yes. (*He ushers him to the door.*) Go into the office on the right, and as soon as it's clear, get down the stairs and let yourself out. I'll meet you tomorrow. Same place. OK? (*Beat.*)

Dooley OK.

The doorbell rings again. **Dooley** *goes out.* **Cash** *goes to the intercom and speaks into it.*

Cash Hello . . .

Amanda Paul? It's me, Amanda.

Cash Oh, hello darling. Hang on. I'll let you in.

He presses the buzzer and goes to the office and arranges his desk to make it look as if he's been working. Then he sits and picks up a pen. He notices an empty beer can, gets up and puts it in the bin. He sits again. After a moment, **Amanda** *comes in with a bottle of wine.*

Amanda Help me drink this. Please.

He gets up and kisses her and takes the bottle and goes to uncork it.

Guess why Maxwell's back in town early. (*Beat.*)

Cash You're sacked?

Amanda No. Re-organisation.

Cash Sacked sideways.

Amanda Not even that. Sacked upwards. (*Beat.*) My salary's been raised by four thousand, my department's been enlarged, and I feel like I've been sacked. (*Beat.*) Of course, I've got a couple of placements in the department that weren't exactly my idea. Daughters of friends, that sort of thing. But, what the hell? I can cope. Nevertheless, there's a nasty smell of nepotism in the air. Also, a smell of impending reshuffle. (*Beat.*) Paris was mentioned. And New York.

Cash I see.

Amanda It's been mentioned before. Nothing ever came of it.

Cash Sounds like you're being given a trial.

Amanda It does, doesn't it?

Cash Is it what you want?

Amanda Yes. I suppose. (*Beat.*) At this rate, I'm never going to have kids.

Cash I didn't think you wanted any.

Amanda I don't.

Cash Well then.

Amanda (*she runs her fingers through his hair and kisses his face*) Mess up the papers?

Cash Darling . . . I've got to work. I'm behind on McLeish and Harper. And Robin's been playing silly buggers with the artwork. If I don't get it sorted a.s.a.p. we'll lose it.

Amanda Uh huh.

Cash I know it's a bastard, but what can I do?

Amanda I don't know. (*Beat.*) Shit, I'm miserable. (*Beat.*) Post-anxiety depression, most probably. What I need is to get zonked and roll in the hay.

Cash I am sorry.

She sits. He is not happy.

Amanda I think I'd prefer Paris to New York. The language is easier. (*He smiles.*) How was Stuart?

Cash Oh, you know . . .

Amanda No . . .

Cash He was a bit . . .

Amanda Prickly?

Cash That I can handle. It's just a very funny situation. Me employing *him*.

Amanda Somebody's got to.

Cash But he hates my guts. Always has done. (*Beat.*) Still, playtime's over. After all these years, Stuart's had to grow up.

Amanda You're enjoying it. (*Beat.*)

Cash Yeah. I'm helping the guy out, but . . . I guess revenge is sweet.

Amanda Very in tune with the times.

Cash What is?

Amanda Oh, revenge. (*Beat.*) Anyway, I'm glad it worked out. I've been on at him for months. In fact, I think *he* sees it as getting revenge. He likes to think you can't live without him. We both know you can, but you boys, you have to have your illusions.

Cash Why so keen to get us together?

Amanda Christ, Paul, haven't you ever heard of symmetry? (*Beat.*)

Cash You don't, by any chance, want to have your cake and eat it?

Amanda Don't be silly.

Cash Or maybe it's a way of softening the blow.

Amanda What blow?

Cash Letting one of us down easily. (*Beat.*)

Amanda I love you, Paul.

Cash And you love Stuart.

Amanda Not in the same way.

Cash How many different ways are there?

Amanda Hundreds. Look, don't get jealous, for Christ's sake. (*Beat.*) What am I saying? I'm telling my lover not to be jealous of my husband. Something's wrong here. (*Beat.*) Stuart and I have been together for a long time. We gave up bothering to love each other properly years ago. But I love you. (*Beat.*) We'll never have the same sort of relationship as I had with Stuart. I mean, I think once in a lifetime is enough for all that stuff. In fact, I don't think

I'm capable of it any more. I'm too proud now to become a couple again.

Cash So, basically, I'm your little bit on the side.

Amanda I like the sound of that. (*Beat.*) It's all there is. Take it or leave it.

Cash I'll leave it for tonight, if that's OK with you.

Amanda Sure. (*Beat.*) Paul, when I say I love you, that's what I mean. I don't mean I want to marry you and have your children and go all starry-eyed when you walk in the room and sing your praises to your boss and . . . look after you. I want someone to do that for me. And if they can't, then the occasional bout of lovemaking will do just as nicely thank you. I've got a job and a life to look out for. And it's a dirty job, but somebody's got to do it, and if it isn't me, then it's not going to be any other bugger.

Cash Yeah. (*Beat.*) I should have made my pitch for you nearly twenty years ago.

Amanda No way. You were foul. Then.

The phone rings.

Cash It's OK. It's on the answering machine.

Cash *and* **Amanda** *start to kiss.*

The machine clicks on. **Liz**'*s voice speaks.*

Liz Hello, Cash Creative Consultancy. There's nobody in the office at the moment, but if you'd like to leave your name and number, we'll get back to you as soon as possible. Thank you for calling.

The tone sounds. It is **Stuart***.*

Stuart Hi, Cash, uh, Paul . . . yeah, it's Stuart.

Cash *and* **Amanda** *look at each other, then kiss again and start to undress each other.*

Look, I just wanted to say . . . thanks. I hope I wasn't too much of an arsehole today . . . I'm a bit out of practice, that's all. (*Beat.*) I've started doing some research. Got some good ideas. If you want to give me a ring, I'll go over them with you. (*Beat.*) Hey, don't worry about Bright. He's a spiv. I know all about them. (*Beat.*) It'll be great to get behind a camera again. There's a lot of things I'm learning to do again. (*Beat.*) Listen mate, strictly between us . . . I made love to Amanda for the first time in months this morning. After you called. You're obviously a bigger turn-on than we ever thought, Cash.

Amanda *closes her eyes.*

Anyway . . . it's, uh, good to be on board. Yours for a great Conservative campaign and a Labour victory. Bye.

The line goes off. Pause. **Cash** *stands.*

Amanda Don't you dare give me a hard time for sleeping with my husband. (*Beat.*)

Cash I really have to get on with this. (*Beat.*)

Amanda Yeah. (*She stands and stares at him.*) Yeah.

She picks up her bag and goes. **Cash** *stands, hands in pockets, for a second, then finishes undressing. Finally, naked, he sits at his desk and finishes his Scotch.* **Dooley** *comes back in.*

Dooley But, as I soon became aware

Cash *starts.*

. . . you weren't in the market for executive relief of the kind only I can give in the stalls of the Moulin cinema. So you engaged me in idle chat and I thought to myself, this wee man's just a wee bit lonely. Company. That's all he's after. Am I right? (*Beat.*) I didnae leave, as you can see. I'll go if you want.

Cash No. That's all right.

Dooley I was browsing through your man's desk in there . . . (*He paces around, taking off his clothes as he goes.*) . . . and I was taking a look at some of the crap he had in there. Heavy. Intellectual stuff, no doubt. But surely you don't have to have a degree to lie to people. Maybe it helps. I dunno. But low, animal cunning must play a large part in this charade. And I am blessed with that particular commodity by the bucketful. I have a very resourceful nature. So.

He stands, naked, by **Cash***. After a pause,* **Cash** *stands.*

Dooley I want to be employed. (*Beat.*)

Cash I want to be loved.

Beat, then **Cash***'s hand goes out to* **Dooley***.*

Blackout.

Act Two

Scene One

Mid-morning a week later. **Cash** *is in the kitchen, leaning against the table drinking a cup of coffee.* **Robin** *is in the office setting up the video camera tripod.* **Liz** *enters with some papers and goes to the desk.*

Cash Is that the Benson stuff?

Liz And the Windfall contracts.

Cash Good. Liz, see if you can raise Billy at Machin and Drew for me, will you? If he's in court, leave a message. Say it's the Benson file.

Liz Uh huh. (*She goes.*)

Robin Windfall's definitely going through then, is it?

Cash You bet. They're convinced they can get a bigger share of mind now we've shown them how to unlock the strengths of the product.

Robin A two-year-old could have done that.

Cash But a two-year-old didn't. We did. Actually, I hate to say it, but your idea of putting them with Ronnie at the Tate agency was brilliant. Sticking with Todd's was flogging a dead horse. I'm eternally grateful.

Robin So give me a rise.

Cash See my lawyer.

Dooley *comes in with a portable video camera. He now wears a smart suit, shirt, and has a trendy haircut. He takes the camera to the tripod.*

Dooley This is a real beauty. Light as a feather. Feel that. Weighs nothing at all.

Robin I know.

They start setting it up.

Dooley I wouldn't mind one of these for Christmas. Hire myself out for weddings and that. Bar mitzvahs. Orgies. Make a fortune. That's how Spielberg started, y'know. Aye. I was talking to a guy in a pub, from one of the film companies in Wardour Street, and he said that Steven Spielberg started with home movies.

Robin Fascinating.

Dooley That's what I thought.

Cash *has come down and is looking through the papers on his desk.*

Cash You can set this up, can't you?

Robin Yeah.

Cash *goes out to talk to* **Liz.**

Dooley What's all this in aid of, then?

Robin If you were meant to know, somebody would have told you.

Dooley Well, I'm asking you. (*Beat.*) Is it your toy? Is that it? (*Beat.*) Well, the whole fucking place can't be your toy, now can it? (*Beat.*) Say something, even if it's only fuck off.

Robin Fuck off.

Dooley *laughs.*

Dooley You're fulla crap, you know that?

Robin Oh, just get out of my face.

Dooley *lights a cigarette.*

Dooley Pardon me for breathing, pal. Excuse me for polluting your air space. But I work here, much as you dislike it, I know. I am on the payroll. On the books. Official. So don't give me a hard time.

Robin Look, I know why you're here. I don't like it, but there you are.

Dooley You're breaking my heart.

Robin I know you're just a ponce. You'll be gone soon. To ponce off someone else. So it's no skin off my nose. Just don't get in my way, that's all.

Beat, then **Dooley** *grabs him by the collar.*

Dooley You smooth little bastard. Does it get that far up your nose, eh? Seeing someone like me in your place? (*He lets go.*)

Robin Just move on somewhere else.

Dooley I'm staying, pal. It's you who'll have to do the moving.

Robin I know it may be quite an effort, but think for a minute.

I've been here nearly two years. I know this business. I'm qualified. I'm fucking good. You've been here a week. You're a gofer. A nobody. You don't know the business. You don't know shit. (*Beat.*) Now, the first sign of unpleasantness, who do you think abandons ship? Got it? You. You're trash. The suit doesn't hide that. Pal.

Stuart *comes in to look through the videos.*

Stuart Ay ay. What's all this in aid of, then?

Robin Interview drill. Cash teaches the candidates not to pick their noses on 'Panorama'.

Stuart Really?

Stuart *has the video he was looking for.*

Cash *comes back in.*

Cash Cut the chat, boys. Let's see some work around here.

Dooley Sorry, Mr Cash.

He goes out to reception where **Liz** *gives him an envelope which he goes out with.*

Stuart Hey, Cash, I think I've come up with a slogan.

Cash Hit me.

Stuart 'Nobody with a conscience ever votes Conservative.'

Cash Snappy. But stick to the pictures.

Stuart Whatever you say. (*He goes out.*)

Cash Rob?

Robin What?

Cash Come on. Meditate on your own time. Is that thing ready to go?

Robin Yeah. (*Beat.*) I think we should talk.

Cash About what?

Robin About the company. About Young Lochinvar.

Cash Ho ho. How long did it take you to think that one up?

Robin Get smart, boss. He's a user.

Cash So am I. So, for that matter, are you. It's good for business.

Robin He could be very bad for business. Unless you want to be known as Rent Boy Limited.

Cash OK, shut up.

Robin No. And what's more, when do we get round to discussing making me a partner? It *was* part of the deal. (*Beat.*)

Cash First, I didn't notice anybody making any derogatory comments when I took you on –

Robin Well, Christ, at least I've had some formal education –

Cash Oh pardon me. Private school and Polytechnic of North London. I forgot you were so well connected.

Robin I mean, at least I have some qualification for the work.

Cash He's got the best qualification you can get. He wants it. I can turn him into anything. You'll always be an arty bastard, good for some things, but dodgy on the big stuff. You'll make a great living, no doubt about that, but you'll never take the world by the throat.

Robin And he will?

Cash No, I will. But he'll be there. (*Beat.*) And I'll think about making you a partner when you straighten out McLeish and Harper.

Robin What's wrong with it now, for Christ's sake?

Cash Nothing much. It could be better, that's all. Show it to Dooley. See what he thinks.

Robin You are joking, of course.

Cash No. (*Pause.*)

Robin OK, Paul, you've made your point. I'm sorry. Ideas above my station, etcetera. But please . . . ditch the rough trade. It's you I'm thinking of.

Cash I'm touched. (*Beat.*) If you weren't so precious, you'd understand. He's useful. To that boy, nothing is sacred. That's what I want. So for now, I'll let him run errands, hang around, upset you, I'll pay him, because one day, I'll open the box and there he'll be, fully formed. Ready to be unleashed on an unsuspecting world. And let's face it, the world saw *you* coming a mile off. We can't afford to stagnate, Robin, my old mate.

Howard *comes into reception.*

Robin You're going to fall flat on your face, you know.

Cash I got here by taking risks, not by worrying about my image.

Howard *comes in.*

Howard. Hello.

Howard Morning. No sign of Miss Huntley?

Cash Not yet.

Howard (*looking at his watch*) Good God. A fault. At last. I was beginning to think she could walk on water.

Cash Think about what I said, Rob. OK?

Robin Oh, yeah. Say goodbye, Rob. Goodbye Rob.

He goes.

Howard Is Bright in on this one?

Cash Yes.

Howard He's terribly good, isn't he? Terribly clever.

Cash Yes.

Howard I loathe him, though. Can't help it. Him and his kind, they're all the same. Stab their own in the back, then come over to us and start preaching the gospel. The fanaticism of the convert. (*Beat.*) Still, they're as nothing compared to this new breed of woman we keep getting. Clones of 'Herself'. Heads on one side, the voice of sweet reason, they're like a lot of little girls at a talent competition. All impersonating the same woman. One day, they'll be standing there in front of the voters, and suddenly the penny will drop. And the people will laugh. With every copied bloody mannerism the laughter will grow and grow until they all run from the podium screaming and crying, never to be seen again. (*Beat.*) I've been shafting her, you know.

Cash The Prime Minister?

Howard No, bloody fool. The Huntley woman.

Cash Oh.

Howard Back to her hotel after lunch, you know . . .

Cash Is this wise?

Howard No, it bloody well isn't. Don't know what came over me. Just have to hope she was too pissed to remember. Hasn't mentioned it since. But she's been behaving . . . as if she had something on me.

Cash Well she does. Not exactly in the job description, is it? I mean, candidate training doesn't usually involve sleeping with Party whips.

Howard No, not since matron took over. (*Beat.*) God, why are we always sexually attracted to danger areas?

Eric *has come into reception.*

Cash I'll take a raincheck on that one, Howard.

Eric *comes in.*

Eric Good morning.

Cash Morning.

Eric Where's the suspect?

Cash Not here yet.

Eric Black mark. Note that down, Howard.

Cash Sorry, let me get you something to drink. (*He speaks into the intercom.*) Liz. Coffee, please.

Eric Had dinner with Paul Johnson last night. We're going to be working together on the box.

Howard Crackerjack?

Eric (*chuckling*) No, Howard. New discussion programme on Channel Four. Politics and morality. (*Beat.*)

Howard Well. They certainly picked the right two there.

Eric Thank you.

Liz *comes in and goes to get the coffee.*

Cash It's good to see someone other than redbrick Marxists talking politics on the box. It's about time the Left orthodoxy was booted off our screens.

Eric Slow process, Paul. Slow process. But yes, it's happening.

Howard I won't believe it until the BBC's cleaned up.

Eric Privatisation. It's got to come. Then they won't have a rock to hide under. Daft middle-class Oxbridge Trots. Let them try and make a living in the real world.

Liz *puts a tray of coffee down and goes. They help themselves.*

Howard Tell me, Bright –

Eric Call me Eric, Howard, everybody does.

Howard Yes, Eric. How does it come about that someone with such an implacable hatred of all things middle-class finds himself on our side?

Eric Oh, Howard, didn't they tell you?

Howard What?

Eric The Tory Party's gone populist. Surely you'd noticed.

Howard But we haven't gone anti-middle-class.

Eric No, we're on the offensive against the trendy middle-class. The Left middle-class. The ones who consider themselves the natural allies of the proletariat. Islington. Lambeth. The ones who want to nanny the working-class. Who want them under-privileged. (*Beat.*) Unfortunately for them, whole swathes of working people vote Tory. You see them, horny-handed sons of toil with the *Sun* in their back pocket. Superhod. The brickie with the Roller. Holidays in Spain. Youth mobilised not against Fascism. Youth mobilised for Sangria and a suntan. And patriotism, that good old working-class virtue, is back in fashion. Pride, self-reliance. Working-class values, Howard. Many years ago, I joined the Labour Party because I thought it was a radical party. But it's a sheep in wolf's clothing. Margaret Thatcher's Tory Party is the true radical force in this country today. That's why I support you. This government has delivered what Labour promised. A genuine revolution. (*Beat.*)

Howard This is all most disorientating.

Eric You don't have to apologise for being rich any more, Howard. It's a bright new day. (*Beat.*)

Stuart *enters.*

Stuart Excuse me, is this the right room for the two-girl assisted sauna?

Cash Come in, Stuart. I've asked Stuart to sit in, Howard.

Howad Fine. Should raise the tone somewhat.

Stuart We aim to please.

Cash How d'you want to run things, Howard?

Howard Same as usual. We'll do the interview, you come up with any presentation stuff, Paul.

Eric Smashing.

Howard Just one thing . . . she's up against a pretty tough opponent in the election, majority's only a couple of thou, and the media are having a mid-term field day. So, let's not make it easy for her. OK?

Gill *comes in to reception.*

The rougher the ride, the more she'll benefit. Try to pierce the exterior. I want to see if she'll crack.

Liz *shows* **Gill** *in.*

Gill I'm most terribly sorry, My taxi was late, and then we got caught up in a demonstration. Honestly, the sooner we clear the streets, the better, in my view.

Cash Liz, another coffee.

Liz *goes and gets a cup.*

Gill It's monstrous that in a city as busy as London these people are allowed to march wherever the fancy takes them.

Stuart Have you ever tried to circumnavigate Buckingham Palace when there's a garden party on?

Howard Not to worry, Gill. Have a coffee and relax for a minute. Do you know everyone?

Gill Yes, Mr Cash, hello. Mr Clarke. And Mr Bright, of course, I know from his excellent television programme.

Eric You're too kind.

Gill I always make sure the whole family are watching. We gather round the television set every Sunday, all together.

Eric You make me sound like the abdication speech.

Gill (*laughing humourlessly*) Really, Mr Bright, nothing so dreary. (**Liz** *has poured her coffee.*) Thank you. That's very kind.

Cash Would you like to sit down?

Gill Thank you

They sit. **Liz** *goes.*

Cash Howard's explained all this set up to you, has he?

Gill Thoroughly.

Cash Good. Have you ever performed in front of cameras before?

Gill I was interviewed once. On a council matter.

Cash So it's not a completely new experience?

Gill Not completely.

Cash Fine. Eric will be conducting the interview with, I'm sure, some valuable guidance from Howard.

Howard *smiles at him.*

Stuart and I'll be watching the screen. Afterwards we can watch the video and take you through the interview again. Possibly suggest one or two ways you can present yourself more positively. If that's the case.

Gill I'm sure I'll be very rough.

Cash It's much easier than you think. Right. Let's get started.

They all stand and **Cash** *sits* **Gill** *on an uncomfortable chair in front of the camera.* **Eric** *and* **Howard** *sit just out of shot.* **Gill**'*s face is up on the screen.*

Gill Will questions be specific? Or. . . ?

Eric I expect we'll roam around all over the place.

Gill Jolly good.

Howard For the purposes of the test, assume us to be hostile.

Gill I'm sorry?

Howard 'Newsnight'.

Gill Got you.

Cash All right, then. In your own time.

Long pause while **Eric** *and* **Howard** *rake out sheets of prepared questions and flick through the pages.* **Cash** *settles down on the sofa with a pad and pencil, kicking off his shoes and watching the screen.* **Gill** *becomes uncomfortable.* **Eric** *suddenly breaks the silence in best interviewer style.*

Eric Gillian Huntley. Hello.

Gill Hello.

Eric May I first broach the thorny subject of the economy?

Gill Please.

Eric Very well. It is generally accepted that the economy is in trouble. The question is, just how bad is that trouble? On the definition that two straight quarters of declining national output constitute a recession, some economists would indeed claim that we are already in recession. Business confidence is slumping; many forecasters are anticipating falls in investment next year; the housing market is very clearly in recession. (*Beat.*) Of course, the Chancellor will say this is all fine, no need to panic, because it means domestic demand is slowing down, and this is good for our disastrous balance of payments figures. However, it also means, unfortunately for the Chancellor, that *supply* is also slowing. That is: output which can be sold abroad is slowing. And that is very bad news indeed. (*Beat.*) Now, here we all are, strapped into our seats, going through a little turbulence, and oh dear, one of the engines appears to be on fire. Pilot Lawson has availed himself of the ejector seat. Where will Pilot Major take us? Will it be a soft landing? Or will it be a crash landing? (*Beat.*) Miss Huntley?

Gill I have to say, uh, that your original statement was, uh, incorrect . . .

Eric Which statement? That the economy is in trouble?

Gill No, well . . .

Eric Because I want to be very clear on this.

Gill No, the bit about . . . recession. I mean . . . that's incorrect.

Eric I see.

Gill It is quite incorrect to say that we –

Howard No no no. Sorry to interrupt, Paul, Eric. Miss Huntley, when a questioner says something you know to be an untruth, you tell him so. What he said was not incorrect, it was wrong! Wrong! Plain and simple. Clear as a bell. Murder is wrong. Terrorism is wrong. Labour is wrong. Got me?

Gill Yes. Yes.

Howard All right. Do go on. (*Beat.*)

Gill Well, er . . . I'm not too sure about the . . . details. What I do know is: as a nation, we had been paying ourselves far too much for far too long.

Slightly stunned silence.

Eric Yes. If I may move on? Perhaps we'll come back to that one. Now then. The welfare state. Mrs Thatcher told us the health service was safe in her hands. The health service tells us it's dying the death of a thousand cuts. That august body, the British Medical Association, has been forced to set up a publicity campaign against Kenneth Clarke's NHS reforms. Reforms which he intends to foist on the nation in the face of near-unanimous criticism.

Gill Well . . .

Eric Please . . .

Gill Thank you. The Health Secretary's ambition is a very simple one. He wants to make the National Health service serve its customers better. We can't afford to cut and run now in the face of the BMA or the rest of the chorus of institutional wailers opposed to change, especially when the plain fact is that this government is spending more money, in real terms, on the health service today than at any time since its inception.

Eric All right, you've made yourself admirably clear on that one. What about education? The teachers tell us that they are at their most demoralised. Lack of basic facilities, books for heaven's sake, run-down classrooms, low wages, the list goes on. Here we see another of the traditionally moderate professions alienated, it would seem, by the government's antagonistic social policies.

Gill Well, you know, all we ask of the teachers is that they accept that they have responsibilities to the service in which they work. A service which will seek out those who are inefficient, those who abuse their position for political ends, those who are responsible for the breakdown of discipline in our schools.

Eric But the teachers say that this is all a smokescreen, a decoy behind which you keep their salaries down.

Gill I think anybody who has ever agonised over the plight of the young in our society will feel, as I do, that you cannot measure dedication in terms of financial reward. Goodness knows, we all want to respect and look up to our teachers, but, I ask you, how can we when they refuse to supervise dinner breaks, extra-curricular activities and so on, when they introduce the tactics of industrial anarchy into our classrooms?

Eric What about the principle involved? The Opposition have criticised you on just those grounds, that you have created two nations, with one set of workers being asked to accept a fall in their living standards while others are allowed pay rises way above the level of inflation.

Gill I don't think there's very much the Opposition can teach us about principle, do you? After all, they left us with rising inflation, debts, an economy in which we paid ourselves too much while not producing enough. Do you remember the winter of discontent? I do. And I never want to see another winter like it. And we have not. Since this Government came to power, the realism of our objectives has ensured stability and growth.

Stuart Unless you happen to be unemployed.

Gill We care passionately about the unemployed. We want to see Britain back at work. But we want to see real jobs, not feather-bedding and over-manning, practices which lead to disaster. Take the miners: they have realised now that the future of their industry lies in work, not in strikes, in hard work. There will have to be closures, naturally, because as pits become exhausted, so they have to close. That has always been accepted. We are simply applying the harsh remedies demanded by a competitive world market. (*Beat.*)

Eric Thank you. You've made yourself very clear. Now. The years of this Conservative Government have seen, have they not, a general rise in the level of lawlessness, real and perceived, as well as a sense of disillusion and cynicism about society as a whole. There is a feeling, correct me if I'm wrong, that we are on the whole a less happy nation. Litter on the streets, sewage on the beaches, dirt and infestation in the water, potholes in the road, schools without teachers, hospitals without nurses, an epidemic of crime and lawlessness, and a government that doesn't care.

Gill But, Eric, disorder, lack of discipline, lack of respect for authority are all things engendered in the young by that generation which grew up without benefit of guiding moral principles. The youth of the 1960s were encouraged to rebel, to profane, for no other reason than to annoy. At the same time, they were indoctrinated with decadent and anti-establishment ideas. These people now produce our television programmes, our films, our plays. They teach in our schools, they run many of our councils. They write for Left-wing magazines. They are people who try to use freedom to destroy freedom. They have encouraged the young, already under pressure from social circumstances bequeathed to us by successive Labour governments, under pressure from waves of immigration, to adopt the nihilistic pose so fashionable in the sorry sixties. Children are *encouraged* to worry about nuclear arms which have kept the peace in Europe for over forty years. They are positively encouraged to fear and worry about their future. And in so doing, they are made unreachable by reason and good common sense. They are no longer taught respect for private property. They are taught envy and greed. They are no longer taught to have pride in their country. Instead, they are given politically biased so-called accounts of our imperial past as if it were something to be ashamed of. They are taught 'peace studies'. Policemen are no longer allowed into our schools. But any crackpot black is invited, yes invited, to stir up racial hatred and hatred of authority. Is it any wonder, then, that these children steal, rape, riot, even murder, since without the restraint of civilisation and authority, that is human nature? (*Pause.*)

Eric Thank you. Most comprehensive.

Gill *relaxes as if the interview were over.*

Howard Miss Huntley. Just a couple of points.

Gill *tenses again.* **Howard** *is furious but in control.*

You're a librarian, I believe.

Gill That's right.

Howard And you live with your parents.

Gill Yes.

Howard You're engaged to be married.

Gill I am.

Howard What does your fiancé do for a living?

Gill He's a farmer.

Howard I see. (*Beat.*) And you were educated locally at a private school.

Gill Yes.

Howard And you studied English and Philosophy at St Andrew's University. (*Beat.*) You don't come from a very heavily industrialised area, I think I'm right in saying.

Gill No, it's very peaceful.

Howard I'm sure. And you've never worked in industry, or business.

Gill Neither has Neil Kinnock.

Howard Quite. (*Beat.*) You see, I'm just a little puzzled as to where you get your certainty from. I mean, it all sounds very familiar, it has the ring of truth about it, but . . . how do you know? (*Beat.*)

Gill I talk to people. I read. Books. Newspapers.

Howard Yes, of course, but forgive me, I detect a sense of something rather unpleasant in what you say.

Gill The truth often hurts.

Howard God yes, but I detect something other than the truth. I detect, pardon me for saying it, a fear, an underlying prejudice against your fellow Britons.

Gill If you mean I don't like socialists, you're quite right.

Howard No, I don't mean that. After all, not all teachers can be socialists, or all doctors, or nurses, or hospital administrators . . .

Stuart . . . or even miners for that matter . . .

Howard I mean, speaking as a fellow Briton, I get the impression that you feel we're just not good enough. We fail to measure up to some abstract standard you have for . . . attitude, behaviour. We're just not good enough, and you're jolly well going to do something about it! (*He smiles.*)

Gill I believe that is what politicians are for. (*Beat.*)

Howard Forgive me, but that is the most preposterous, dangerous nonsense it has ever been my misfortune to hear.

Eric *finds something fascinating to do in his case.* **Cash** *reclines with his eyes closed.*

I have been in politics all my adult life. I have known people who came into politics to further their business careers, to boost their egos, to fill an otherwise dull life, to fulfil the family tradition. I have even known people come into politics because they believe they have something useful to offer the nation. But I have never known anybody come into politics because they despise their country and wish to exorcise their fear and loathing with a good dose of corrective medicine. That is not political drive. That is psychological disorder. (*Beat.*) Please don't make the mistake of thinking that we want an army of steel-jawed, flaxen-haired warriors against all things decadent. Our leader is a one-off. She can't go on forever. She is useful in the short term for enabling us to do what we do best: running the capitalist economy. But in the long term, she is just another servant of the Party. (*Beat.*) I just don't think we need any more like you. (*Beat.*) I'm sorry, Miss Huntley, if one day you put your little foot outside Mother and Father's ivy-covered cottage and saw lots of frightening things. I'm sorry if you didn't understand what all those horrible big grown-ups were doing, in their factories, their offices, their pubs, their bedrooms. I'm sorry they called you nasty names, and swore and didn't go to church very often; they did things Mummy and Daddy said weren't very nice. (*Beat.*) But I've got news for you. They've been doing it since the dawn of creation, and they're going to go on doing it whether you stamp your little foot and tell them to stop it or not. (*Beat.*) It's not society that has the problem, Miss Huntley. It's not society that's deviant. It's you. (*Beat.*) My advice would be to marry your farmer, produce your incredibly heavily EEC subsidised crops, have a couple of children, go to church regularly and quietly shrivel up in the peaceful English countryside. That, after all, is what it's there for.

Gill *stands with a look of distress and betrayal and goes out. They watch her go.*

Cash Well, Howard. (*Beat.*) You shouldn't have messed around like that. You should have really let her have it.

Howard Cash, I've seen the future. And it freezes my water.

Eric *chuckles.*

What?

Eric I was just thinking. You're in the wrong party, old fruit.

Howard No. I'm not. She is.

Eric *laughs.* **Howard** *joins in.*

Cash Anybody need a drink?

Howard Please.

Cash *goes to the kitchen.*

I'll tell you what.

Cash What?

Howard I don't know why I'm laughing.

Cash No?

Howard No. Because if Miss Huntley opens her mouth, I'm going to be up to my eyeballs in shit.

He roars with laughter. **Eric** *laughs.* **Cash** *looks seriously at* **Howard**. **Liz** *enters.*

Liz I'm sorry, there's a phone-call from Central Office for Mr Lipton.

Howard Ah. I'd better take it outside.

He goes outside with **Liz** *and uses her phone.*

Stuart Anybody get the feeling there's something we're missing?

Cash Such as?

Stuart Such as: your man there may just not be a true believer.

Eric I would say that is a very definite possibility. (*Beat.*)

Cash So what the hell's he up to?

Eric And where do *we* fit in?

Stuart 'I think we should be told.' (*Beat.*)

Cash I need to talk to some people. Pronto.

Howard *comes back in.*

Howard Right. Now, where's that drink?

Blackout.

Scene Two

Later that day. Mid-afternoon. **Stuart** *is alone in the office, watching a video of Grosvenor Square or demonstrations, making notes.* **Liz** *comes in.*

Liz I'm sorry. Still no sign.

Stuart 'S OK, Liz.

Liz It's not like him. I mean, he doesn't even usually go out for lunch. A quick sandwich at his desk and that's it. I practically have to force-feed him.

Stuart You look after him, don't you?

Liz That's my job.

Stuart Being mother?

Liz Comes naturally. (*Beat.*)

Stuart Is he a good boss?

Liz Well, he expects a lot, but then he pays above the average. And he's very considerate sometimes. Let me go for a fortnight when my dad died. Even sent some flowers to the funeral.

Stuart That's nice.

Liz Yes, it was. Can I get you anything?

Stuart A Perrier. I'll get it. (*He goes to the kitchen.*) Does Cash have many women friends?

Liz I wouldn't know.

Stuart Oh, come on. You keep his diary. (*Beat.*) Between you and me, we used to think he might be gay. Not because of anything . . . specific. I suppose he was just a bit of a loner.

Liz He still is, then.

Stuart Fancy him yourself, do you?

Liz No! (*Beat.*)

Stuart I guess all his drive goes into this.

Liz Yeah. I guess so.

Stuart What a waste.

Liz I think he's very proud of the company.

Stuart He'd have to be.

Dooley *comes in, a bit drunk.*

Liz And where the hell d'you think you've been?

Dooley Fret not, hen. I've been engaged on important business. Company business.

Liz In the pub.

Dooley Christ, that's where deals get made.

Liz You're lucky Mr Cash is not back yet. Otherwise you'd be making a deal down at the broo.

Dooley Och, well, if he's no back yet . . .

He goes to the kitchen and gets a beer from the fridge.

Liz You put that back, Dooley.

Dooley Go fuck yourself.

Stuart Dooley . . . (*Beat.*)

Dooley Yes? (*Beat.*)

Stuart Don't talk to Liz like that. She's only doing her job.

Dooley Her job is to type out wee letters and post them. Her job is to make the tea and wipe the boss's bum for him when he has a shite.

Stuart And don't get smart with me, lad.

Dooley *snorts.*

Dooley What are you going to do about it? Going to teach me a lesson are you? Old man?

Stuart No.

Dooley That's right. No. (*Beat.*)

Stuart Look, lad, you'll be out on your arse if Cash comes back.

Dooley I won't be out on nothing.

Stuart Don't screw up. (*Beat.*)

Liz Come on, Dooley.

Robin *comes in.*

Dooley Oh fuck. It's the Bisto Kid.

He laughs and goes out with **Liz**.

Robin You've met the office yob?

Stuart Yeah.

Robin Everyone has to have one. Keeps the unemployment figures healthy.

Stuart What, is he on a scheme?

Robin No. Cash has taken him under his wing, so to speak.

Stuart Oh aye?

Robin Oh aye. (*Beat.*) So, how's it going with you, then?

Stuart Pretty good. You?

Robin Could be better. (*Beat.*) Look, I'm sorry we got off on the wrong foot.

Stuart Forget it. I have.

Robin Yeah. Uh . . . would you do me a favour?

Stuart If I can.

Robin Well, see, I've written this . . . film script. It's not finished or anything, not properly. I wondered if you'd have a look at it for me. Tell me if I'm doing it right.

Stuart What's it about?

Robin Uh . . . basically, it's about two guys who open an off-licence, then a cocktail bar, then a club. One guy's black, one's white. It's sort of a love story. (*Beat.*)

Stuart Yeah, I'll read it.

Robin Great I'll go and get a copy . . . if that's OK.

Stuart Sure.

Robin *goes out.* **Stuart** *looks amused and takes the video out of the machine.* **Liz** *comes in.*

Liz I'm sorry, Mr Clarke. Dooley's quite new.

Stuart You can say that again.

Liz Gives us Scots a bad name, him and his kind.

Stuart I've known enough Scots to be able to tell the difference.

Robin *comes in with the script and gives it to* **Stuart**.

Robin Here. No hurry. Just . . . I dunno. Let me know what you think.

Stuart This is the first script anybody's given me to read for over four years. I'll be very careful with it.

Cash *comes in looking harrassed.*

Cash Hi everyone. Stuart, I'm sorry, we said two-thirty, didn't we?

Stuart Not to worry.

Cash Liz, coffee, please. I'm drowning in bloody brandy. Why is it that some people only seem to think you're serious if you can down half a vat of brandy after lunch? Rob? Do something for you?

Robin No.

Cash OK, then. Off you go.

Robin Maybe if I wore a kilt, I might get a please.

Cash I don't have time, Robin. Just get out and come when I buzz you. Understood?

Robin Crystal. (*He goes.*)

Cash Jesus. Why is everybody a prima donna today? Liz, where's Dooley?

Liz I sent him out.

Cash Shit, why didn't you wait till I got back? (*She brings coffee.*) I want to send him over to Tate's for some artwork.

Liz He won't be long. I'll tell him as soon as he gets back.

Cash He should be here now. Wait until I'm back next time.

Liz I will. (*She goes.*)

Cash What a sodding day.

Stuart Actually Cash, the reason she sent him out was that he'd obviously had one too many for lunch and was being an obnoxious little git.

Cash Why didn't she tell me that?

Stuart Because she's a pro. (*Beat.*)

Cash Oh, fuck . . . (*He presses the intercom.*) Liz. Sorry. (*He releases without waiting for a reply.*) OK, Stuart.

Stuart Shall I tell you what I've got?

Cash First the bad news. I've just had lunch with . . . an old friend in the know vis-a-vis the to-ings and fro-ings of the Conservative and Unionist Party hierarchy. You were right. Howard has been a little naughty with us. This cosy little deal we're part of is news to everyone at Smith Square. I come out looking very bad. Not to mention more than a little silly.

Stuart That's how they are. You stab my back, I'll stab yours.

Cash It's worse than that. We, apparently, are part of a long-term campaign by Howard and friends to discredit the leadership in favour of their chosen successor.

Stuart Oh dear . . .

Cash Right. It's a full-blown bloody conspiracy. And it's all going to come out.

Stuart I'll clear my desk then, shall I?

Cash Not yet. We carry on. Only this time, we're bidding for the official campaign. (*Beat.*) I gave it my very best shot. We're in with a chance.

Stuart Nice one. And Howard?

Cash Backbench obscurity with any luck. Fuck him. Let him die. (*Beat.*) This is my life we're talking about. So I'm not playing softball.

Stuart Well. We're in with the big boys now.

Cash Too right. (*He indicates* **Stuart**'s *glass.*) Perrier?

Stuart You need a clear head when you're working for Fascists.

They smile.

Cash I'm glad you're with me. And Bright. He'll be setting the record straight this Sunday, in Fleet Street code.

Stuart Even rats have their uses.

Cash Not nice.

Stuart I know he's not.

Cash You could get to like him.

Stuart I could get to like ulcerative colitis. But I won't. (*Beat.*)

Cash OK. What have you got? Talk to me, baby.

Dooley *comes in.*

Dooley, run that over to Tate's.

He gives him an envelope.

Dooley What, the noo?

Cash Yes, 'the noo'.

Dooley *sways.*

And then go home. Take the afternoon off.

Dooley *stands there.*

What?

Dooley I'll need a key.

Stuart *pretends not to hear.* **Cash** *gives a key to* **Dooley** *who goes.*

Stuart Right, the idea I have here, very much planning stage at the moment, is that we concentrate on the opposition. Because I'll be perfectly frank, Cash, I hate the bloody sight of Thatcher. And I reckon so does a goodly portion of the nation at large. Her material's thin. She needs to be used sparingly.

Cash Yes, but we *do* need to use her. Particularly now. Forget the balanced ticket. Think you can handle it?

Stuart Oh yes. I can handle it.

Cash Good. (*Beat.*)

Stuart Anyway, I've had a whale of a time, going through archive stuff, and I've come up with a potted history of the Labour movement in revolt since about 1965. Now, to me, this stuff is beautiful. There's the miner's strike. The three day week. Arthur looking great. Heath looking like a twat, not difficult to find, that one. All the Vietnam stuff. Lots of coppers getting booted. Winter of discontent. Strikes, marches, punch-ups. And d'you know what's most beautiful about it? It's in black and white. It's the fucking ark! What is black and white? Black and white is Old, it's depressing, it's the Past. Now, you intercut pictures of today's opposition leaders, also in black and white, with appropriate quotes, but, every time you mention this fucking awful Government's record, you switch to colour, fists, blood, blah-blah, black and white. New technology, sunrise industry: glorious colour. Trade unions, strikes, power failures: black and white. Home ownership, the Falklands: living bloody sensurround. (*Beat.*) I hate it. But I love it.

Cash Sounds good. Sounds very good.

Stuart You ever been on a picket line Cash?

Cash Stuart, please.

Stuart OK, so imagine it. Get the image. What d'you see? (*Beat.*)

Cash Strikers, banners . . .

Stuart Yeah . . .

Cash Police . . .

Stuart Where?

Cash Hmmm?

Stuart Where are the police?

Cash Oh. In front of me.

Stuart Between you and the pickets.

Cash Yeah.

Stuart Protecting you, right?

Cash If you like.

Stuart It's a simple point. Can you ever remember the camera making you feel a part of the picket line? That those people around you were protecting you, your job?

Cash No. But then, that wouldn't be objective, impartial reporting, would it? (*He smiles.*)

Stuart I'm a film-maker. I know the camera's never neutral. The public's so-called objective position is with the police, the bosses, the government, capital. The camera has given the silent majority its politics. The Politics of the State. (*Beat.*) That is what I want to exploit in this broadcast. It'll be very good. You can trust me, I'm a doctor.

Cash So the whole thing'll have a newsy, documentary feel to it.

Stuart Totally. Make it like a news broadcast. Use news pictures. Tap that deep-rooted response. Labour is violence, chaos, fear.

Cash We're not talking major subtlety here, I take it.

Stuart No.

Cash What about sound? Voice over?

Stuart Authoritative. Doom-laden. Get the bloke who does the nuclear warning. And music. Grand and heavy. Scare the public shitless. (*Beat.*) You said think Goebbels.

Cash I didn't know you had it in you. You're not just selling out. You're having a grand closing-down sale.

Stuart Yeah. Everything must go. (*He's down for a moment.*) What d'you reckon?

Cash I like it. A lot. I think you've cracked it. Well done. We'll run it by Eric, then I think we might go with it.

Stuart I've still got loads of archive stuff to go through. Between you and me, I'm trying to turn up a shot of Bright at a miners' gala.

Cash You'll be lucky. When d'you think you can have a mock-up for me?

Stuart Couple of days, tops.

Cash That's great. (*He pours a coffee.*) Coffee?

Stuart No thanks.

Cash How are things at home? How's Amanda?

Stuart OK. (*Beat.*) OK? It's a fucking shambles. (*Beat.*) Cash . . .

Cash I'm not being funny, mate, but . . . not in office hours, eh?

Stuart (*beat*) I reckon . . . I'm pretty certain . . . she's been having an affair. (*Beat.*) I know she's not happy. With her job, with me. (*Beat.*) Every now and again I try to make contact again. Go on the wagon. Be nice. Be whoever it is she wants me to be. It never lasts. I get the feeling sometimes that she doesn't actually like me. Me. Who I am deep down. I mean, I don't always like myself. I let me down a lot. But I always find I have a sneaking residual regard for myself. (*Beat.*) I'm not a bad man.

Cash Maybe just not good enough.

Stuart Yeah. I want to make it work. I don't know how.

Cash You're asking the wrong man. I'm not exactly a paragon of family virtue. (*Beat.*)

Stuart What's it like, being on your own?

Cash It has its moments. Its compensations.

Stuart I don't think I could face it. (*Beat.*) That's why I'm doing this, y'know. For Amanda. That's why I want it to be good.

Cash It's a good enough reason.

Stuart It's the best.

The intercom buzzes.

Liz Mr Cash. Miss Huntley's here to see you.

Cash Oh right. Ask her to come in. (*Beat.*) I hope it works out.

Stuart So do I, mate. Because if it doesn't . . .

Gill *enters.*

Cash Gillian, hello.

Gill Hello.

Cash Just keep at it then, Stuart.

Stuart Yeah. (*Beat. He smiles.*) Right-wing thinking. It ought to carry a government health warning. (*He goes.*)

Cash Hard to believe, but he's the nearest thing to a genius I've ever met.

Gill He doesn't seem very happy.

Cash They never are. That's left to us ordinary mortals. Can I get you anything? Drink?

Gill No, I like to . . . keep a clear head. Nothing, thanks.

Cash OK.

Gill I hope you don't mind me just turning up like this.

Cash Not at all. As a matter of fact I left a message at your hotel. Didn't you get it?

Gill No, I, er, haven't been back there yet.

Cash Ah. (*He offers her a seat.*) I'm sorry we never got a chance to go through your interview.

Gill So am I.

Cash Howard's behaviour was unforgivable. I'm sorry.

Gill That's all right. He'll pay. (*Beat.*)

Cash Yes. (*Beat.*)

Gill One hears whispers.

Cash Oh?

Gill All very malicious, probably. (*Beat.*)

Cash Right. The interview. I just want to give you some presentation points. Nothing to do with substance, that's not my area.

Gill Don't you have any political beliefs, Mr Cash? (*Beat.*)

Cash Oh yes.

Gill What are they?

Cash Not far removed from yours. More . . .

Gill What?

Cash I was going to say: more ruthless, perhaps.

Gill Oh, don't let my sex fool you. I'm as ruthless as any man.

Cash You'll go far. (*He smiles.*)

Gill Let's hope so. (*She smiles.*) Have you ever thought of standing for office?

Cash Often.

Gill Then why not? Not lack of ambition, surely.

Cash Far from it. My problem is I don't think I could keep up the public face. I think I might look like I was enjoying myself too much. I might look a little . . . smug. Cruel, even. Something a politician can't afford.

Gill I understand.

Cash That's something you have to look out for.

Gill It's difficult, though, when you know you're right, don't you find?

Cash I do. But I'm not after people's votes. And that's the name of the game. Making yourself attractive and credible to the voters.

Gill Mr Cash, you're a cynic.

Cash Probably. But I'm right.

Gill I must think about it. (*Beat.*) I suppose it would be asking too much for you to come to Lincoln next week.

Cash Well . . . I am very busy.

Gill I know . . . I just hoped . . .

Cash But it might be possible. (*Beat.*)

Gill I'd be very grateful. I'm just not sure who I can trust.

Cash I want to see you win. You can depend on that.

Liz *appears at the door.*

Liz Sorry. I've got Mr Benson on the line.

Cash Damn. Uh, look . . . get his number, tell him I'll get straight back to him.

Liz OK. (*She goes.*)

Cash Damn.

Gill I'm sorry, if I'm . . .

Cash No, it's just somebody I've been trying to track down.

Gill Look . . . why don't we meet up again? Somewhere more relaxed. (*Beat.*)

Cash Lunch? Dinner?

Gill Dinner would be nice. (*Beat.*) Why don't you call me at the hotel?

Cash Yes. I will. (*Beat.*)

Gill I think we'll find lots to talk about. There's a lot I want to learn.

Cash I'll do my best. (*He stands.*)

Gill I'm a very determined woman, Mr Cash.

Cash I admire that.

Gill Good. I'll be off, then.

Cash Right.

Gill Goodbye.

She goes. **Liz** *comes in. She gives him a piece of paper. She stands and gives him a look.*

Cash What?

Liz I don't like her.

Cash (*smiles*) I know. Isn't she absolutely bloody awful?

He laughs. **Liz** *goes.* **Stuart** *enters.*

Stuart Sorry, forgot the video.

Cash Help yourself.

Stuart Last time I saw that look on your face Harold Wilson had just resigned. (*He goes to the door. Stops. Turns.*) What did Shirley Temple want?

Pause.

Cash The lot, matey. (*He smiles.*) She wants the lot.

Blackout.

Scene Three

Evening, a week later. The kitchen table is spread with buffet food. There are bottles of wine and champagne. In the lobby are **Cash, Liz, Robin, Gill, Eric** *and* **Amanda**, *drinks in hand, looking at the pictures on the wall and talking.* **Stuart**, *in the office, pops a bottle of champagne. He's a bit drunk.* **Amanda** *comes in. She too is slightly drunk.*

Amanda (*seeing* **Stuart**) Oh God. (*Beat.*)

Stuart What? (*Beat.*) I don't know why he doesn't just write a cheque for ten grand, frame it and stick it up on the wall. There's no need to bother with all that paint and canvas. Messy bloody stuff. A good crisp Barclay's cheque. That's all he needs.

Amanda *pours a drink.*

After all, he has the artistic appreciation of a brain-damaged two-toed sloth.

Amanda How do you know?

Stuart We go back a long way. We're old muckers.

Amanda You didn't know Cash twenty years ago and you don't now. You never bothered.

Stuart D'you blame me? (*Beat.*) Have you ever looked into his eyes? Which are the windows of the soul? Have you? I have, I peered in and saw all these pricey pictures and nobody home.

Amanda I thought you weren't going to drink.

Stuart Celebration, isn't it? Thanks to me, Cash got the account. And thanks to Cash, there's another bloody Tory woman in Parliament. Anyway, you're pushing it back.

Amanda I'm allowed. I'm not an alcoholic. (*Beat.*)

Stuart D'you know what he was telling me about the other day? Banking. Advertising jargon and banking. D'you know what a high net-worth individual is? I didn't. Well. A high net-worth individual is a rich bastard. Yeah. And, d'you know what they call banking for people who aren't high net-worth individuals? People who are, in fact, poor? D'you know? It's called cloth-cap banking. (*Beat.*) Don't you just love it? (*Beat.*)

Amanda Stuart. Behave. Please.

Stuart Why?

Amanda I don't know. When in Rome?

Stuart Bollocks. When in Rome, act like a cunt.

Eric *comes in.*

Talking of which . . .

Eric Letting it all hang out, Clarkie?

Stuart In short, yes. Brightie.

Eric Well you deserve it. You did a very professional job of work. (*Dialling the phone, to* **Amanda**.) I love this man. A joy to work with. Never a dull moment.

Stuart That's what you think. I had a few, I can tell you. The dullest has got to be Brightie giving me the gen on popular capitalism. How it's the saviour of Great Britain and all who sail in her. That was dull. Very, very dull.

Amanda You, of course, are never less than riveting.

Eric *is speaking on the phone.*

Stuart Hey, less of the smut if you don't mind. (*Beat.*) Who you calling, Brightie? Eh? Heavy breathing to the blessed Margaret? A bit of insider trading?

Eric *puts the phone down.*

Eric Minicab, actually.

Stuart Minicab? I had you down as a Roller man. Merc at the very least.

Eric Can't leave the Rolls in the car-park at Heathrow, can I? It would only get vandalised by a disaffected member of the progressive class.

Stuart With any luck.

Amanda Where are you flying?

Eric Montserrat. Fact-finding freebie for the Colour Supp.

Stuart He likes to keep his ear close to the ground. Find out what the chap in Club Class is thinking.

Amanda It's supposed to be beautiful there.

Eric I hope so.

Stuart I don't. I can't imagine you with a real tan.

Amanda We've never been anywhere like that, have we?

Stuart (*thinking hard*) I don't know. Is it anything like Barnsley?

Eric Not especially.

Stuart Well then, I don't think we've been anywhere like that.

Amanda No.

Stuart I took you to Derry. Ungrateful bag.

Amanda (*looks upset*) Yes. I forgot. Thanks.

Stuart *raises his hand in a gesture of apology but says nothing.* **Liz** *comes in.*

Liz Everyone OK?

Amanda Fine, thanks.

Eric I'd love a Guinness.

Stuart Me too. Sabrina. That's the one I'd like.

Amanda Oh God . . .

Liz I thought you were reformed, Mr Clarke.

Stuart This isn't really happening. It's a nightmare. Nothing is real.

Liz That's all right then. (*She gives* **Eric** *his drink and goes.*)

Eric Nectar of the gods. Dublin-

Stuart -brewed. Nothing like it. (*Beat.*) You got shares in Guinness or something?

Eric Yes. (*Beat. They both laugh.*) See. We *can* get on.

Stuart I haven't got the energy to hate you, Brightie.

Eric That's good.

Stuart Is it?

Amanda You're all the same. Get a couple of drinks inside you and it's all chaps together. The saloon bar brotherhood. Bloody men.

Stuart My wife's hatred, on the other hand, knows no bounds. She can hate. My God, how she can hate. Bring down a man at a hundred paces with her hatred, she can.

Amanda Most men seem perfectly capable of bringing themselves down, thank you very much.

Stuart (*bitter*) But you just love to give us a little nudge.

Eric Do I detect a whiff of cordite in the air?

Stuart No. Just the embers of a fire that went out.

Again, **Amanda** *is visibly upset. She goes out and joins the others in the lobby.*

Eric Tell me, Clarkie, pre-brewer's droop, were you a whips and chains man?

Stuart Do what?

Eric The black leather hood. Manacles in the cellar. Fag butts on the chest.

Stuart You feeling all right?

Eric Mas-o-chism. (*Beat.*) You do seem to enjoy a good frolic in the broken glass.

Stuart Oh. I dunno. (*Beat.*) Fuck it.

He goes and opens another bottle of champagne. **Robin** *comes in.*

Robin Art fatigue already?

Stuart What Cash knows about art could be written on the back of a cheque stub. In fact, probably is.

Robin But he knows what he likes.

Stuart I wonder.

Eric Why is it that people like Cash and myself attract such venom from the left-wing, artist class? Is it because we achieve? Grammar-school boys in a comprehensive world? Because we make money? Fine for the print worker, not for the journalist? Because we don't swallow the old orthodoxies? What? What is this heinous crime we've committed?

Stuart You're a couple of mercenary shitbags.

Eric God, is that all?!

Stuart Yes. That's all.

Robin Whoah, time out. Left-wing, artist class, moi? Nyet, comrades. What you see before you is the new man. No-wing, hedonist, post-industrial, post-modern –

Stuart Post-early-for-Christmas.

Robin (*mocking*) Style. Dancing on the ruins. It's a hit and run culture. Bizarre connections. Stop making sense. Death to syntax. Long live the slogan. I'm talkin' 'bout my generation, daddio.

Stuart *guffaws and comes down to* **Robin**.

Stuart (*putting his arm round* **Robin**'s *shoulder*) Oh, I love this boy. He means it, he really means it. He reckons his jacket is a political statement. And d'you know what, Brightie? He's not afraid to put his money where his designer boxer shorts are. This boy has given me a film script. This cultural buzz-saw has written a piece for the modern cinema. Post-modern cinema, sorry. A love story! About two blokes, agreed, but that's not exactly risque in these days of Sodom and Gomorrah, is it? I was expecting Fellini, Bukowski, Burroughs, Buñuel at the very least. And what did I get? A polyunsaturated Colin Welland. An absolute beginner! (*Beat.*) And we're going to make the film, aren't we?

Robin (*smiling*) That's right.

Stuart I love him!

Stuart *plants a smacker on Robin's forehead as* **Amanda** *comes in.*

Amanda Now that is grounds for divorce.

Stuart You don't want to divorce me. It's too much fun watching me twitch around with my wings pulled off.

Amanda Fun? Now there's a novel concept. (*Beat.*) C'mon, Paul wants your opinion on something.

Stuart *Paul* wants *my* opinion?

Amanda All right then, *I* want your opinion. Your company. Your presence.

Stuart My balls.

Amanda I've got 'em.

Stuart Yeah.

Amanda C'mon.

Stuart *goes off with* **Amanda**, *taking a champagne bottle.*

Eric You say you're making a film. Is that for real?

Robin Yuh.

Eric You've got finance?

Robin Yuh. TV tie-in.

Eric Well, good luck with it. (*Beat.*) And it's about two blokes, is it?

Robin Yuh.

Eric Interesting. (*Beat.*) You don't get a lot of films like that.

Robin Oh, I don't know.

Eric Well I don't see many like that.

Robin Obviously you don't go to the right places.

Eric Obviously. (*Beat.*) It's a shame you aren't in on the campaign with us. It would have been nice to work together.

Robin Politics isn't exactly my strong suit. I'm easily bored.

Eric Oh, absolutely. That's why I gave up Parliament. I mean, everybody seems to think I did it for money, but it's not true. Not entirely. I did it because it was so boring. The shiny trouser seats. The dandruff on the collars. The shabby, boring ritual of democracy: a lot of middle-aged men reeking of mothballs and stale whisky; a total sham. So I made my excuses and left. (*Beat.*) All the interesting folk have gone. There's only the bores and the lonely left. (*Beat.*) I find the real world so much more stimulating.

Robin Yuh. Me too. (*Beat.*)

Eric Listen, Robin. When I get back from Montserrat, what do you say we meet up. Dinner maybe. I know some very interesting people from your point of view.

Robin Uh . . .

Eric TV, films. All very necessary if you want to go big time.

Robin Sure. Look, Mr Bright . . .

Eric Eric . . .

Robin Eric . . . about the film. The two blokes thing.

Eric (*laughing*) Robin, Robin, don't say what I think you're going to say.

Robin I just don't want any misunderstanding.

Eric What's to misunderstand?

Robin Well, if you write about a gay theme, people sort of assume . . .

Eric I never assume. Assumptions are the death of spontaneity. (*Beat.*) So. Don't worry. I'm not assuming you're gay.

Robin Oh no, it's not that. It's just . . .

Eric What?

Robin Well . . . I don't fancy you. (*Beat.*)

There is a noise from the lobby. **Dooley** *lurches into the room, followed by* **Cash** *and* **Liz**. *He goes straight for the champagne.*

Dooley You cannae have a party without Dooley. I am vital to the smooth running of any social function. Am I no right, boss?

He swigs from the bottle. **Cash** *smiles, trying to placate him.*

Cash Yes, but you have to keep it nice.

Dooley Nice? Fucking nice? Get to fuck . . .

Cash Because if you don't, you get your bottom smacked.

Dooley Ooh, I am all aquiver.

Eric (*amiable*) Trouble with the staff?

Cash Over-exuberance.

Dooley Bollocks to that. I'm on drugs, you bampot.

Liz Dooley . . .

Dooley What is it, hen? You want a good shagging?

Cash OK, that's it.

Dooley Don't you come anywhere fucking near me. I am not your property.

Cash You're fired.

Dooley You did that already.

Cash I'm just reminding you.

Stuart, Amanda *and* **Gill** *come in.*

Stuart Cash, who sold you that bullshit?

Cash It was a commission.

Stuart You actually paid someone to paint it? Jesus. I didn't know you were involved in charity for the blind.

Cash It's an investment.

Stuart Then put it in the bloody bank. Get it out of sight.

Gill I think it's rather good.

Stuart Are we speaking artistically or financially here?

Gill I would say it conforms to certain traditional rules, and as such, is pleasing to the eye.

There is a general frisson at this. **Stuart** *giggles.*

Gill Yes, I know you'll mock, but that's what I feel.

Stuart And you obviously feel things very deeply.

Gill Some things, yes.

Eric Surely it's all in the eye of the beholder.

Stuart Christ, Brightie, with a penetrating and original mind like yours, how come when you ratted on Labour, you never joined the SDP?

Eric I'm not principled enough.

Stuart You said it.

Liz *is bringing round a tray of food.*

Stuart God, Liz, don't wait on me. I hate it.

Liz It's what I do. It's what I'm paid for.

Stuart Well don't do it at me.

Cash Don't you find your social conscience a bit of a millstone, Stuart?

Stuart It's nothing to do with conscience. It's demeaning.

Gill But everybody has to work. Somebody has to do the waiting.

Stuart You do it, then. Or let's see Nigel Lawson's daughter cleaning toilets. Mark Thatcher washing cars for a quid an hour.

Eric Oh Clarkie, you're so tribal. So socialist.

Amanda Huh.

Stuart What's wrong with that? It's not illegal, yet.

Eric Everything's wrong with it. It's what's wrong with the whole bloody country.

Gill Hear hear.

Eric I mean, you're an intelligent man, Stuart. A talented man.
Yet you waste your talent desperately trying to dupe the people
into swallowing your idiotic vision of a New Jerusalem. I've seen
your vision. It's grotesque. It's sentimental. It's a bloody lie.
(*Beat.*) Christ, how can a country ever progress if a whole group of
people like yourself explode with apoplexy at the injustice of the
class system every time they're offered a canape? It's not rational.

Stuart Neither is exploitation.

Eric *laughs.*

Eric Leaving aside the fact that I disagree, look at Liz, Stuart.
Does she look exploited?

Liz *gives him a fierce look.*

No, she doesn't. She's simply doing a job of work.

Amanda She's not a specimen, Eric.

Liz I can speak for myself.

Amanda Well, excuse me.

Eric She sells her labour. We all do. It's nothing to be ashamed of.
She's hard-working and loyal. Those are virtues. Not things to be
sneered at.

Stuart I'm sure you've never noticed, but that's what socialism's
all about.

Eric Oh God. Not socialism. *Again.* If only we could wave a wand,
make it disappear. Chant a spell, or something. Socialism's
irrelevant.

Cash It's also destructive.

Eric Absolutely. It *is* an alien ideology. The majority of people
neither understand nor want it. It hangs over us all like a black
cloud, desperately kept aloft by the huffing and puffing of the
activists. Oh, the activists. The great fat cuckoos in the Labour
nest. A nice left-of-centre party, with sensible managerial policies,
totally hijacked by a combination of the sentimentally gullible,
yourself, and the beady-eyed fanatics, the revolutionaries. Let's
face it, socialism's not on the agenda, old fruit. It's history. The
people are scared to death of it.

Amanda You, of course, would know all about the people and
what they want. With your intimate knowledge of them. From

your Channel Island tax haven and your pied-à-terre in
Bloomsbury. I think, if you were to be completely honest, you'd
have to say that you're making educated guesses based on
self-interest and innate prejudice. Oh, I know those are the perfect
qualifications for membership of your little club, the Sunday
pontificators, but they're sod all to do with the real world. God,
we used to go to church to be preached at and told what was
wrong and what was right. Now we just open the paper and up
pops the pulpit and there's little Eric Bright telling it how it really
is. You and your little chums, all barking away together. D'you
know what you make me think of when you're on your soap box?
D'you know what I see? I see good lunches. Fine wine. And great
fat cigars. (*Beat.*) You're the self-appointed loudhailers for a
government that's turned this country into a land fit for Rupert
Murdoch.

Gill What an utterly absurd statement.

Amanda Oh . . . naff off. It amazes me that you'll all give
credence to this dim-witted country cow, who, by some freak of
nature, is now a Member of Parliament for Christ's sake, and yet
you pour all the shit you can on the idea, just the idea, of
socialism. Well, it's not the people who are scared of socialism, it's
you. Because it would drop your lovely lunch in your lap, and
stick your great fat cigar up your arse.

Gill Is this what passes for politics where you come from?
Foul-mouthed abuse?

Amanda You want politics, sister? I'll give you politics. Not my
husband's soggy labourist crap. That's just Tory paternalism
with a collectivist face. Thanks to their silly soft-centre deference
we still live in one of the most class-ridden, tradition-bound
societies in the modern world.

Eric Don't tell me your wife's a Trot, Clarkie.

Stuart I don't know.

Amanda No, you bloody don't. (*Beat.*) Socialism hasn't failed
Britain. It's never been tried.

Eric Someone's been reading her *New Left Review*.

Amanda I used to write for it, you condescending shithead.

Cash Amanda . . .

Amanda I'm sick of it. Your little parliamentary game. Your boys' club with its crappy rules and its honorary men. Pretending to be alternatives to each other. Well, you're all petrified. Every last one of you. Petrified of anything that'd shake you out of your cosy embrace.

Dooley *swings round with the video camera in his hand.*

Dooley I cannae understand a word you people say. You make a lot of noise, but I don't get any meaning from it.

Robin For once, we agree.

Cash It's called conversation.

Eric Cut and thrust.

Dooley Oh aye? Well the only cut and thrust I know is with a broken bottle.

Gill Really . . .

Dooley *goes over to her.*

Dooley Really . . . Who are you? *What* are you?

Dooley *points the camera at* **Gill**. *Her face comes up on the screen.*

Are you a very important person? A VIP?

Beat. He points it at **Amanda**.

And you? What are you?

Amanda Oh go away.

Dooley Ooh, I like you.

Beat. He points the camera at **Cash** *and then at* **Robin**.

Well, I think we know all about you two.

Beat. He points it at **Eric**.

You. I've seen *you* on the box. Yap yap yap. I've seen you. But . . . I don't know what you *do*. I mean, Leslie Crowther, I know what he does. He gives people suites of furniture and mopeds. Les Dawson, he gives them a Blankety Blank cheque book. But *you*. What do you give away?

Eric Nothing.

Dooley Then what the fuck are you doing on my television set?! (*Beat.*) When I lived at home with my family, I used to watch the TV all day. And I can tell you what good television is. It's where they give you something. You wave your arms about and act like a prat and you win a prize. Fucking great, eh? Well, where's my prize? I've come all the way to London to win something and all I've got is a cardboard box to sleep in and a lot of men playing with my willy. Somebody tell Bob Monkhouse. Tell him what it's really like. (*He turns the camera on himself.*) Look, I'm on TV. Look, there I am. Ask me a question. Ask me where I'm from. What do I do for a living? Actually I'm unemployed at the moment. Aaah. No, I'm not married, Cilla, but I wouldn't mind poking you, eh? I like windsurfing and I fuck dogs. Now, gimme a prize. I'm on. I want something. *You owe me* something! (*Beat.*) I'm on . . . you bastards.

Cash *takes the camera from him and hands it to* **Robin**.

Dooley You've got everything, you, and you won't give me a prize.

Cash *turns round suddenly, giving* **Dooley** *a backhanded belt across the face.* **Dooley** *goes flying. The others gasp etc.* **Cash** *picks* **Dooley** *up, blood round his mouth.*

Mind the fucking suit . . .

Cash It's mine. I paid.

He throws **Dooley** *onto the sofa. People are shocked. Nobody does anything.*

Liz Mr Cash . . .

Cash Job training, Liz.

He picks **Dooley** *up and thumps him in the stomach.*

Stuart Stop it, Cash . . .

Dooley (*hardly able to speak*) It's not even my own clothes I'm bleeding on.

He laughs. **Cash** *hits him in the face again.*

Amanda Make him stop.

Cash *lifts him up.*

Cash I owe you nothing! Nobody owes anybody else a thing. Got me?

Dooley (*laughing*) Lend us a fiver . . .

Cash *is about to hit him again.* **Liz** *suddenly steps in and grabs* **Dooley** *away.* **Robin** *rushes out.* **Stuart** *helps* **Liz** *lift* **Dooley**. **Cash** *goes to the* *kitchen and pops a bottle of champagne.* **Eric** *has looked at his watch and out of the window.*

Eric Is it written on tablets of stone somewhere that minicabs will always be late?

Beat. **Gill** *goes to* **Cash** *and fills her glass.*

Stuart You really believe it, don't you, Cash? Nobody owes anybody else a thing!

Cash Having studied all the available evidence, yes.

Stuart You've studied nothing. You're working from instinct. Lust. That's why you're such a vicious bastard.

Cash I operate, Stuart, that's all. Nothing new, nothing special in that. But it means I don't have time for the emotional garbage people like you carry round. I won't be trapped like you. I won't let you trap me. I'll just operate. And screw the cost.

Stuart It'll come back to you. It always does.

Cash Not if you keep moving.

Stuart It'll get you. Even if it's just one night where you wake up, and the dark frightens you.

Cash I'll sleep with the light on.

Stuart Very smart.

Cash I like to think so. (*Beat.*)

Stuart You'll never understand, will you? You haven't got the humanity to understand.

Gill (*pointing at* **Dooley**) Are we supposed to understand that?

Stuart Yes!

Amanda Patronising bastard.

Stuart Not now. Please. (*Beat.*)

Liz *stands* **Dooley** *up. He's in a bad way.*

Liz Come on . . .

Stuart Need a hand?

Amanda Don't you run out now.

Stuart He's in pain, for Christ's sake.

Amanda Well, you're not going to stop that. You'll only be making yourself feel good.

Liz Fuck you . . .

She walks **Dooley** *out.*

Stuart Doesn't hide it, does it? All the high-tech. It's still a fucking jungle.

Cash What did you expect?

Stuart Oh, God, I dunno. What did I expect? Nothing, I suppose. (*Beat.*) What did I want? (*Beat.*) Love. (*Beat.*) This . . . ruthlessness. It's not human, that's all.

Cash You see, that's your mistake. It is human. Quintessentially bloody human. You're a freak of nature. You've forgotten you're an animal.

Stuart Yeah. It's what's known as civilisation.

Amanda *sits by him.* **Howard** *suddenly appears, very upset.*

Howard Ah. (*Beat.*)

Cash Howard.

Eric *looks out of the window.*

Eric At last. (*He gets his bag.*) Can't stop, Howard, my cab's here. I'll call you next week, Paul.

Cash OK.

Eric *'s almost gone*

Howard You're a treacherous bastard, Bright.

Eric *stops, half-turns and looks as if he's going to reply, then he smiles.*

Eric Yes, see you then. (*He goes.*)

Howard And as for you two . . .

Cash What can I do for you, Howard?

Howard Take the knife out from between my shoulder-blades.

Cash Oh, come on . . .

Howard *takes out a photo wallet.*

Howard Look. My wife. My children. Do you know what you've done to them?

Cash Frankly, no.

Howard Joint effort, was it? The two of you cook it up together?

Cash Who?

Howard You and the wicked witch here.

Cash Gill? What's she got to do with it?

Howard Oh Jesus, spare me that one, please. OK, Cash, you get a better offer, fair enough, do some politicking of your own. That I can take. That, I possibly even expect. But why, dear God, why drag me all the way down?

Cash I changed clients, that's all. You hadn't been exactly honest with me, Howard. In fact you could have ruined me.

Howard So you ruined me.

Cash I changed clients. And Eric wrote a small piece. Hardly treacherous.

Howard And what about the fact that I am now officially branded a criminal? (*Beat.*)

Cash Sorry, Howard, not with you.

Howard I'll draw you a bloody map, shall I? I have just been forced to offer my resignation. Due to ill health. Didn't know I was ill? No, it came as a surprise to me as well. I was accused of an abuse of my position. I was accused of a criminal offence. To stop it going public, I had to resign. That was the price. I am no longer a Member of Parliament. I'm now an irrelevance. Finished.

Cash But why?

Howard God, because this woman accused me of raping her. (*Beat.*)

 Cash Ah.

Howard Is that all you can say?

Cash Well . . . (*Beat.*)

Howard And so, they're rid of me. Opposition y'see. They know it's a lie.

Gill I beg your pardon, but they do not know that it's a lie. Because it isn't a lie. You're a filthy animal who takes advantage of his power to compromise women Party members in order to secure sexual favours. I risked great harm to my personal and

professional reputation to expose you. However, I felt it was
something I had to do, if only to protect other women like myself.

Howard For Christ's sake, somebody switch her off! (*Beat.*)
Listen to me you tart, you disgusting automaton, I'm going to do
everything I can to ruin you. My life is shattered, all for the sake of
an afternoon in the sack with a whore on the make. For that, I've
lost everything. (*Beat.*) I've got a wife at home who hasn't stopped
crying for two days. Three children who are going to have to live
the rest of their lives with whispers and innuendoes about their
father. You don't do that to somebody and expect to get away
scot-free. I'll drag you down. I have friends. People with
influence. I'll see to it that nobody in the party will ever trust you.

Gill You're a bad loser. That's a flaw in a politician.

Howard I think I have a right to be a bad loser, considering I've
lost everything.

Cash Come on, Howard, that's not strictly true. At last count you
had, what, four company directorships, a thriving family
business, and homes on three continents. Hardly destitute.

Howard And the disgrace?

Cash What about it? Probably do your reputation good in some
quarters. (*Beat.*) You thought you were invincible. You
underestimated the stakes. Fatal. Old boy. (*Pause.*)

Amanda I'm sure it won't hurt for very long. Have some
champers.

She holds the bottle up. **Howard** *starts to cry.*

Oh God . . .

Howard My whole life . . . gone . . .

Stuart You're only out of a job.

Amanda Now you know how it feels.

Beat. **Howard** *looks at them and goes out.*

Gill What a pathetic individual.

Amanda You should know.

Cash Did you shop him?

Gill Yes, of course.

Cash Harsh.

Gill You think so? (*Beat.*)

Cash No.

Gill Good. (*Beat.*) I have to go. My fiancé's picking me up at the hotel. We're driving back to Suffolk.

Cash Give him my regards.

Gill I will, thanks. (*She kisses* **Cash** *on the cheek. To* **Amanda** *and* **Stuart**.) I hope you can come to terms with what we're doing.

Stuart Or else?

Amanda Up against the wall.

Gill I don't think so. Well. Wouldn't be very English, would it? Goodbye. (*She goes.*)

Amanda Stuart . . . oh God . . . I want to confess something. (*Beat.*) I've had an affair. (*Beat.*) I'm sorry.

Cash *stares straight ahead.*

Stuart Had. Is it finished? (*Beat.*)

Amanda Oh yes.

Cash *stands and goes out.*

Stuart It hurts.

Amanda I know. (*Beat.*)

Stuart What do we do now?

Amanda Christ, I don't know.

Stuart Do we have another go?

Amanda I don't really know what I want any more. I just feel drained, and angry.

Stuart What can you do about it?

Amanda I don't know. (*Beat.*)

Stuart Between the two of us, we don't know very much at all, do we?

Amanda Nothing that's of any use. (*Beat.*) Let's . . . 'have another go'.

Stuart OK.

Cash *comes back in with some papers.*

Cash Might as well get on with some work.

Robin *comes in and gives* **Cash** *an envelope.*

What is it?

Robin Resignation.

Cash Why?

Robin *shrugs.*

Another job?

Robin Sort of.

Stuart It's my fault, Cash. He gave me a script. I showed it to David at Channel Four. We go into production in March.

Cash You finished it.

Robin It was finished all the time. (*Beat.*) I've got a couple of commissions as well.

Cash Well done. (*Beat.*) Well. (*He extends his hand.*) Good luck.

They shake.

Robin See you in the movies.

He goes. **Stuart** *stands.*

Stuart Sorry I won't get to do the broadcast.

Cash You've done all the work. I can get a hack in.

Stuart Well. It's been really real.

Cash You don't have to go.

Stuart (*looking round the room*) Oh . . . I think I do. (*To* **Amanda**.) Fancy a meal?

Amanda Japanese?

Stuart You're paying.

Amanda OK. (*She stands.*)

Cash Take some champagne.

Stuart No. You keep it. For a celebration.

Cash There's still work for you, if you want it.

Stuart I'm gonna be a bit busy, as a matter of fact.

Cash Sure.

Stuart Thanks.

Cash Nice to see you again, Amanda.

Amanda Same here.

Cash Keep the faith.

Amanda What else is there to do? (*Beat.*) C'mon.

They go. **Cash** *surveys the room.* **Liz** *comes in and starts clearing up.* **Dooley** *comes in holding his stomach.*

Cash Did I hurt you?

Dooley (*trying to smile*) Get tae fuck.

Cash You can take it.

Dooley Aye. (*He takes a bottle of champagne and curls up on the sofa.*)

Cash Leave it, Liz.

Liz It's got to be done.

She starts washing up. **Cash** *sits at his desk.*

Cash First thing tomorrow, I want to chase Benson. (*The phone rings.*) And don't forget I'm at Smith Square in the afternoon. (*The answering machine goes on.*) So, anything urgent, you can get me there.

Cash *switches the answering machine speaker on.* **Liz**'s *message is just finishing.* **Cash** *gets up and pours himself a glass of champagne.*

Liz . . . as soon as possible. Thank you for calling. (*The machine beeps.*)

Berkowitz Cash, hi. Berkowitz, New York. Things are really starting to happen, pal. I lunched Forbert like you said, and the guy is jumping without a parachute. His tongue is so far up my ass he's licking my lips. I don't know what you did over there, Cash, but you've got Buckley and the whole crew creaming themselves. You better think about opening up over here. Better still, get yourself down to Heathrow and come see us. I mean it. So. Call me. And let's bust this thing wide open, OK? They need you. They love you. So come and explore, you hear?

Beat. The machine goes off. **Cash** *raises his glass.*

Cash You got it.

Blackout.

Grace

Characters

Ruth Hartstone, *in her fifties, an artistic English gentlewoman*
Freddy, *in his late thirties, of mixed race, he tends the grounds of Hartstone*
Rev Neal Hoffman, *in his fifties, American evangelist, founder of Enterprise Faith, a multi-media Christian Church*
Amy Hoffman, *in her late thirties, Neal's wife, a Christian screenwriter*
Gavin Driver, *in his forties, an American-trained English evangelist-businessman*
Lance, *in his late twenties, Driver's assistant, a zealot of the new right*
Felicia, *in her early twenties, an American actress/singer*
Joanna Hope-Collier, *in her early twenties, an English actress, straight out of drama school*

The play takes place over a June/July weekend in the drawing room and garden at Hartstone, a house deep in the country.

Grace was first staged at Hampstead Theatre, London on 3 December 1992.

Ruth Hartstone	Anna Massey
Freddy	Ben Thomas
Rev. Neal Hoffman	James Laurenson
Amy Hoffman	Kate Fahy
Gavin Driver	Peter Wight
Lance	Kevin Dignam
Felicia	Kristin Marks
Joanna Hope-Collier	Emma Lewis

Directed by Mike Bradwell
Designed by Sue Plummer
Songs by Doug Lucie, *arranged by* Kevin Curry

Scene One

The drawing room at Hartstone. Summer, early evening. **Ruth** *is sitting at the table reading from a book into a portable tape cassette machine. She is reading from* The Water Babies.

Ruth 'In fact, the fairies had turned him into a water baby. A water baby? You never heard of a water baby? Perhaps not. That is the very reason why this story was written. "But there are no such things as water babies." How do you know that? Have you been there to see? And if you had been there to see, and had seen none, that would not prove that there were none. No one has a right to say that no water babies exist till they have seen no water babies existing; which is quite a different thing, mind, from not seeing water babies; and a thing which nobody ever did or perhaps ever will do.

Freddy *enters through the french windows. He is mixed African / English. He wears a green shirt, fishing waistcoat, cord trousers and waders. He holds a fly fishing rod in one hand and seven or eight fresh-caught trout in the other.* **Ruth** *holds her hand up to stop him speaking and carries on reading.*

Wise men know that their business is to examine what is, and not to settle what is not.' *(She turns off the tape.* **Freddy** *holds up the fish.)*

Freddy Is that enough?

Ruth I've no idea.

Freddy Well how many are coming? *(Beat.)*

Ruth Four, five, six, I don't know. Just gut them and wrap them in foil. I'll chuck them in the oven when they arrive. *(Beat.)*

Freddy *(nodding to the book)* The Water Babies?

Ruth I'm recording it for old Annie Bradley. She's blind as a bat now, poor old thing.

Freddy Very uplifting.

Ruth   You used to love it when you were small.

Freddy   Yes. Except I never understood why little Tom was so ecstatic when the black washed off. (*Beat.*)

Ruth   Proper little Malcolm X, aren't we? (*Beat.*)

Freddy (*starting to move off*)   Anyway, it's definitely more than four.

Ruth   What is?

Freddy   For dinner. The buyers.

Ruth   How do you know?

Freddy   They were swarming all over the gatehouse as I came in. Acting like they own the place already.

Ruth   They're almost an hour early.

Freddy (*going*)   Definitely more than four, anyhow.

Ruth   You utter . . .

He's gone. She gets up and goes to the window and looks out. She looks alarmed, comes back to the table and picks up the book and some papers as we hear a car draw up on the gravel outside. **Ruth** *goes off into the house.*

Sound of car doors opening and shutting. We hear talking from offstage. **Gavin Driver** *and* **Neal Hoffman** *appear, each with a shoulder bag,* **Gavin** *with a set of plans in his hand.* **Gavin** *walks straight in,* **Neal** *stands in the entrance out into the grounds. He turns and comes into the room, smiling hugely.*

Gavin   Did I lie?

Neal   No, you did not. Praise the Lord. This ground is holy. I feel it.

Amy Hoffman *comes in. She is pale and drawn. She goes straight to the table and sits, taking out a small bottle of mineral water and some pills. She swallows one.*

Neal   How you feeling, honey? (*She pulls a face.*) Maybe take a nap later . . .

Gavin (*goes to the door and shouts*)   Hello?! Miss Hartstone?

Neal   Gavin, Amy has a headache . . .

Gavin   Sorry, Neal . . .

Amy   I have an inner-ear imbalance . . .

Neal   Whatever . . .

Amy   It's a whole different thing . . .

Neal   You had a headache in the car . . .

Amy   I felt *dizzy* in the car . . .

Freddy *comes in.*

Gavin   Ah, Freddy, hello, is Ruth about?

Freddy   She's in the kitchen. She'll be up in a minute. D'you need a hand with the bags?

Gavin   That's very kind.

Freddy   No problem. (*He goes out to the car.*)

Neal   Who in the heck is that?

Gavin   That's Freddy. He looks after the place.

Felicia, Joanna *and* **Lance** *appear.* **Lance** *carries cases.*

Felicia   Some place . . .

Joanna   I bet it's a fridge in winter.

Felicia   So, this is where it happened, huh?

Gavin   Right here.

Felicia   Neat.

Neal *is holding his arms out.*

Gavin   Just leave them there for now, Lance.

Lance *puts the cases down.*

Neal   Brothers and sisters . . . (*They all assume a solemn, prayerful attitude.*) . . . Let us pray. Lord, we thank you for your guidance and protection in bringing us safely to our destination. We thank you for shining your light in the darkness to lead us to this holy place. This place from which we will expand our mission of spiritual enlightenment. This place of miracles.

Freddy *comes in with some cases.*

Neal   Thank you Lord. Amen.

All   Amen.

Freddy   That's all the bags.

Gavin   Thanks, Freddy. Oh, everyone, this is Freddy. And Freddy, this is the Reverend Neal Hoffman.

Neal   God bless you brother.

Gavin   . . . His wife Amy, Felicia, Joanna and Lance. (*They say hello, wave, etc.*)

Freddy   So. Good journey?

Gavin   Yes, we made very good time.

Neal   The Lord cleared a path to expedite our arrival.

Freddy's *not sure how to take this.*

Freddy   Good. (*Beat.*) Uh, shall I show you the rooms?

Gavin   Yes, would you? I think the ladies might want to freshen up a little.

Freddy   OK. It's this way. (*The women follow him off.*)

Gavin   You might like to take the cases up, Lance . . .

Lance   Oh, sure. (*He picks up some cases and goes, leaving* **Neal** *and* **Gavin** *alone.*)

Gavin   Well.

Neal   Well yourself. (*They smile.*) And *is* it a fridge in winter?

Gavin   It won't be. Not with central heating. Don't worry, it's all in the conversion budget.

Neal   Uh huh. So what do these people do for heat?

Gavin   Don't laugh, but they wear lots of woollens. They put on three jumpers, throw plenty of logs on the fire and huddle together in one room.

Neal   Real pioneer spirit. I think our pilgrims will be expecting hot and cold running, however.

Gavin   And they shall have it.

Neal   Praise the Lord.

Gavin   Amen.

Neal   OK, that land on the right, as we drove up to the house . . . that part of the estate?

Gavin   All of it. Everything you can see, and then some. (*He spreads out the plans on the table and points to various parts.*) This is the section you saw. That'll be the campsite. And down this way . . . (*He points out into the grounds.*) . . . that's where we'll put up the church marquee. I'll take you down there later. And that whole front area where we drove in, there we have space for a thousand cars, with optional space on the upper pasture for another five hundred.

Lance *comes back in and picks up more cases.*

Neal   Everything OK?

Lance   Mrs Hoffman changed your room, the first one was South . . .

Neal   South facing, yeah.

Lance   Apart from that, everything's fine. And I think this place is absolutely brilliant.

They smile. He goes.

Neal   Fine boy.

Gavin   Yes, absolutely first class. Very committed.

Neal   Now, how about these outhouses and stuff we're going to convert?

Gavin   Ah, they're out this way, down towards the river. It's a beautiful spot.

Neal   Can't wait to see it.

Gavin   I can show you round the estate before dinner, if you're not too tired.

Neal   Never too tired to do God's work, Gavin.

Gavin   Amen.

Neal *breaks away, smiling, and inspects the room.*

Neal   I feel a permanence here. It's real.

Ruth *appears at the french windows and stares off in the direction of the limousine.*

Gavin   Ah, Ruth.

Ruth   What a most extraordinary motor car.

Neal (*chuckles*)   It's a Mercedes stretch limousine.

Ruth   Good grief. Is it yours? It must have cost a fortune.

Neal   The Lord has been very generous to my automotive needs.

Ruth   How awfully good of him. (*Beat.*) You must be Gavin's partner.

Neal   Correction, his boss. Reverend Neal Hoffman. Honoured to meet you, Miss Hartstone. (*He shakes her hand.*)

Ruth   Yes . . .

Neal   The house is more beautiful than I ever imagined.

Ruth   Yes, lovely, isn't it? The old place is falling to bits, mind . . .

Neal   That's history, Miss Hartstone.

Ruth   Do please call me Ruth.

Neal   Things decay only for the Lord to build them up again, Ruth.

Ruth   He deals in motor cars *and* does building repairs. Gosh. Or am I being too literal? (**Neal** *smiles.*)

Neal   When you've been slain in the spirit, anything is possible with the Lord.

Ruth   Really?

Neal   John, three, three. 'Except a man be born again, he cannot see the kingdom of God.'

Ruth   Oh, I see. He's a sort of spiritual freemason.

Neal   Except everybody can join.

Ruth   It would appear they're obliged to, if they want to get anywhere.

Gavin   You're wasting your time Neal. I'm afraid Ruth's just an old fashioned sceptic.

Neal   You're not like your sister, then?

Ruth   Not at all like my sister, no.

Neal   That's a real shame.

Ruth   Is it? She died aged fifteen. I'm still here. I think I can confidently say I got the better deal.

Neal   She didn't die, Ruth, she didn't die.

Ruth   Sorry to contradict you, but I saw them carry her body away. I kissed her in the coffin. She was cold. (*Beat.*) But I understand what you mean.

Neal   I still can't quite believe I'm standing where it happened.

Ruth   What did?

Neal   Grace. Your sister. Where she passed over.

Ruth   Oh. Well, if you want to be strictly accurate she actually popped her clogs in her room upstairs.

Gavin   Yes, we were hoping to conduct a service up there, as a matter of fact.

Neal   A thanksgiving. For a short but miraculous life.
(*Beat.*)

Ruth   Be my guest. It's a bit of a broom cupboard,
though. I doubt you'll all fit in.

Gavin   We'll manage. (*Beat.*)

Ruth   Well, let me offer you a sherry.

Gavin   Lovely, thank you. (*She goes to the drinks and pours
three sherries.*)

Neal   So, Ruth, is Freddy all the workforce you employ
now?

Ruth   Freddy doesn't work for me, he *lives* here. I don't
have anybody working for me any more.

Neal   I guess not. My motto, Ruth: let the businessman
get on with business. We know how to look after people.
And I reckon the people round here deserve a few breaks
after the mess you got them in to.

Ruth   We ... did our best.

Neal   Well I've been in business twenty five years, and
good intentions are fine things to have, but they don't
guarantee a profit and a paycheck.

Ruth   Our failure was hardly unique.

Neal   But you made elementary mistakes, if you don't
mind me saying so. I mean, you went into production with
an untested product; you borrowed way past your ability to
pay back; you didn't lay people off when you should have.
And worst, you didn't research your market. If you had,
you'd have discovered there wasn't a demand for your jam.

Ruth   High-class organic preserves, actually.

Neal   Whatever. (*Beat.*) The fact is, Ruth, you tried to sell
a product nobody needed.

Ruth   But I thought that was the basis of the entire
system.

Neal   And as a consequence, the good people around here who'd put their faith in you were dragged down along with you.

Ruth   They knew there were risks. Nobody was coerced.

Neal   And you owe the banks an awful lot of money.

Ruth   But you're here to put that right.

Neal   Correct. (*Beat.*)

Ruth   You've certainly been doing your homework on us.

Neal   You can bet we have. (*Beat.*) And tell me, did Gavin show you the 'Grace' screenplay?

Ruth   He did, yes.

Neal   And how did you find it? (*Beat.*)

Ruth   Fascinating.

Gavin   We've obviously taken a few liberties, you know . . .

Ruth   Feel free. Artistic licence, and all that.

Neal   But I think you'll have to agree, it's jam packed with spirituality.

Ruth   Oh, jam packed. Absolutely.

Neal   Amy, that's my wife, she wrote the script.

Ruth   Yes, I'm very much looking forward to meeting her. I've just been reading some of her short stories. (*Beat.*)

Neal   She, uh, won't thank you for bringing that up.

Ruth   Why ever not?

Gavin   They were written before she was born again.

Ruth   So? (*Beat.*)

Neal   They were the work of the Devil, Ruth. (*Beat.*) And the Devil wants your soul. He wants my soul, too, but you better believe it, he's gonna have a war on his hands if he tries to get it.

Ruth   I see.

Neal   Because I'm with the Lord.

Gavin   Amen.

Ruth   Another sherry, anyone?

Neal   No, thank you. (*Beat.*) I need to freshen up a little before dinner.

Ruth   Of course. We eat at eight. Informal. No need to dress.

Neal   Thank you, ma'am. (*He looks at his watch.*) Gavin, what do you say we take that walk at seven thirty?

Gavin   Seven thirty it is. I'll come and get you.

Neal   Fine. Ruth.

Ruth   Reverend.

He goes. **Ruth** *pours a sherry.*

Tell me, Gavin . . . would I be right in thinking that the Reverend Hoffman is just ever so slightly bonkers?

Gavin (*laughs*)   Ever so slightly American would probably be nearer the mark.

Ruth   I've known plenty of Americans. But never one quite like the Reverend.

Gavin   That's because he's a true Christian, Ruth. (*Beat.*) Us Brits, you see, we're brought up to see some virtue in quiet, reserve, the stiff upper lip. Even when we discover Jesus we've been loath to shout out the good news. Whereas our American cousins have no such inhibitions. They believe that good news is worth spreading. If you don't holler it out at the top of your lungs, you're letting the Lord down.

Ruth   Doesn't that presuppose that the rest of us are all deaf?

Gavin Can you be so sure that you're not?

Ruth Excuse me, Gavin, my family were missionaries. I was clubbed senseless with the word of God from the tender age of two. I am not deaf. I stopped listening. (*Beat.*)

Gavin Sorry.

Ruth Don't be. Just don't try to convert me. I've been there and back again and the trip was most definitely not worth it.

Gavin You know . . . something I realised very early in life: that scepticism is a darn sight easier than belief.

Ruth Gavin, please understand . . . God, Jesus, the Devil, all that . . . I find it very painful, that's all. (*Beat.*) Well, if you'll excuse me, I believe I've got a lot of trout to gut, otherwise we shall all go hungry.

Gavin Well, we can't have that.

Joanna *comes in.*

Gavin Ah, Ruth, before you go, let me introduce you. This is Joanna Hope-Collier. Joanna, this is Miss Hartstone.

Joanna Crumbs, hello . . .

Ruth Hello . . .

Joanna I'm playing you. You know, as a young girl. In the film.

Ruth Well. I hope you have more luck with it than I did.

She goes.

Joanna Did I say something stupid?

Gavin No.

Joanna Shit, I bet I did. (*Beat.*) Oops, sorry.

Gavin Profanity is totally unnecessary at any time.

Joanna   Sorry. (*Beat.*) Incredible place, isn't it?

Gavin   Yes.

Joanna   I mean . . . so historic. (*Beat.*) That black bloke showed us the room where Grace died, where Jesus appeared. Just a little bed and a table.

Gavin   I cried. When I first stepped into that room I felt the physical presence of the Lord and I wept for joy.

Joanna   Amazing.

Gavin   Yes. (*Beat.*) Where's Felicia?

Joanna   Taking a nap. She's still jet-lagged.

Gavin   Make sure she's up in time for dinner.

Joanna   Yuh. (*Beat.*) Any news on your wife?

Gavin   No. We just have to pray that the baby can wait until after this weekend.

Joanna   What if it doesn't? Will you have to go back to London?

Gavin   I can't possibly. Not until those contracts have Ruth's signature on them. (*Beat.*) I was there for the births of the other four. I can hardly be called uncaring.

Joanna   Hardly that.

Lance *comes in.*

Lance   Joanna, there you are.

Joanna   Oh, hello, Lance.

Lance   Been looking all over for you. A guy could get well and truly lost in this place, I tell you. They've stuck me out in the West wing or whatever you call it. The bathroom's route march distance.

Joanna   I'm much closer.

Lance   Yeah, lucky beggar. Still, quite a thrill to be here at all, eh, Gavin?

Gavin   Yes, quite a thrill.

Lance   The old order. They had it easy all right. Still, que sera? Our turn now. (*He and* **Gavin** *smile.*) And all done without a single shot being fired.

Gavin   Amen. (*Beat.*)

Lance   Jo, fancy a poke about? Explore the place?

Joanna   OK. Oh, I just have to ask Gavin something. You go on, I'll catch up with you.

Lance   Righto.

He goes out.

Gavin   I think Lance has taken rather a shine to you.

Joanna   I think so too. (*Beat.*)

Gavin   What did you want to ask me? (*Beat.*)

Joanna   Oh . . . should I come to your room tonight? Later? (*Beat.*)

Gavin   Sometimes when I look at you, I shake. I try not to, but something takes me over. Forgive me. (*Beat.*)

Joanna   Shall I? (*Beat.*)

Gavin   Please.

Joanna   Thanks.

She goes out.

Gavin   Thanks.

Blackout. On speakers **Felicia**'s *recording of 'He is the Cord' is heard:*

'There's someone up there caring, watching from above.
You may not have met him, but you know his name is love.
He watches daily over us, he keeps us all from fear
For he is all around us now, he is everywhere.'

Scene Two

After dinner, about 10.00 p.m. **Felicia** *is in the centre of the room playing an acoustic guitar and singing 'He is the Cord'. Watching are* **Amy, Joanna, Lance** *and* **Freddy**.

Felicia (*singing*)

> He is the light, he is the might.
> He is the man, his is the hand.
> He is the Lord, he is the cord,
> That binds us to eternal life.

She exhorts the others to join in the reprise of this final chorus. All but **Freddy** *join in.* **Felicia** *finishes on a big flourish. The others clap,* **Lance** *whoops American style.* **Felicia** *claps and whoops.*

Felicia (*cries out with joy*)   OK! Right! OK!

Amy   Praise the Lord.

Felicia   Amen. (*To* **Freddy**.) Well? How'd you like it?

Freddy   Great. Thanks.

Felicia   You're welcome. That song's what we call 'easy listening inspirational', but on the album I really get to rock out. That's why it's called 'Rowdy Worship'.

Freddy   I'd like to hear it some time.

Felicia *takes a cassette tape from her bag and hands it to him.*

Felicia   OK, you got it. Here you go. Don't worry, I have plenty of copies.

Freddy   Thanks a lot.

Felicia   You're welcome.

Freddy (*looking at the tape*)   Have you sold many?

Felicia   That album you have in your hand there has sold 250 thousand units and still climbing. Watch out, people, the electronic Gospel is coming to save the world, hallelujah.

Freddy I never knew it was such big business.

Lance Mega. Absolutely ginormous.

Felicia You talk the rock'n'roll faith thing, you're talking growth. See, people want the music to plug into their belief systems.

Freddy Is that right?

Lance And do you know what the catalyst was? What started it all off?

Freddy Let me see . . . Gospel music?

Felicia No, that was just, you know, for black folks.

Lance What started it off was Jesus Christ Superstar. (*Beat.*) No kid. Another Brit triumph.

Felicia The Reverend started up Enterprise Faith Records after he saw the show. Isn't that right, Amy?

Amy That's correct.

Felicia Christian ethics in today's musical idiom is how he describes it.

Freddy You mean you appropriated modern secular musical forms to propagate your specifically religious message.

Felicia I guess . . .

Amy You got it.

Freddy Very clever.

Amy We discovered a product gap and filled it, to the glory of the Lord. That's all.

Freddy Well, nice one, as they say. (*Beat.*)

Joanna I am totally cream crackered. Anybody mind if I hit the sack?

Amy Not at all, honey.

Lance (*standing*) Find your way OK?

Joanna   I should think so. Goodnight. (*They all 'goodnight'. She goes.*)

Felicia   Uh, excuse me, what is cream crackered?

Lance   Cream crackered, knackered. Er, bushed, beat.

Felicia   Oh . . .

Amy   Cockney rhyming slang, that right?

Lance   That's right.

Felicia   Joanna's a cockney?

Lance   No. People of her class sometimes use the slang. They find the incongruity what they call 'a bit of a wheeze', apparently.

Felicia   Cute.

Lance   Yeah. (*Beat.*)

Freddy   So . . . let me get this right . . . Joanna's playing Ruth, in the film . . .

Felicia   Right.

Freddy   And you're playing Grace . . .

Felicia   Right. Hey, don't worry, I have a voice coach.

Freddy   I'm sure you'll be wonderful.

Neal, **Ruth** *and* **Gavin** *appear from the grounds, mid-conversation.*

Felicia   Thank you.

Neal   . . . and of course, something many people don't know is that the word 'evangelical' comes from the Greek, meaning good news. Did you know that Ruth?

Ruth   Yes I did as a matter of fact.

Gavin   Can you excuse me for a minute, Neal? I have to call the clinic, check on Sophie.

Neal   Take your time. And hey, be sure to tell that little lady we all love her and we're all praying for her.

Gavin   I'll do that.

He goes outside and talks into his mobile phone. **Neal** *flops down into a chair and undoes his tie.*

Neal   Lance, you have those visitor projections ready for me?

Lance   Uh, yeah, I think so. You want them now?

Neal   First thing tomorrow.

Lance   I'd better go over them now, then.

Neal   That would be much appreciated.

Lance   OK. (*He gets up.*)

Neal (*to* **Felicia**)   And you, little lady, you get your beauty sleep. I don't want any wrinkles showing up on that film. OK?

Felicia   Yes sir. Goodnight.

Neal   And God bless.

She and **Lance** *go.*

And you honey? Tired?

Amy   I guess so.

Neal   OK then. (*They kiss.*) Sleep tight.

Amy   Goodnight everybody. (*She goes.*)

Ruth   Just how many people are we expecting for this filming on Sunday?

Neal   Only two or three, it's not a full shoot. We're making a trailer for transmission on our TV station back home, then our viewers send in their donations, and we've raised the cost of our movie.

Ruth   I see.

Neal   I hope you'll come along and watch. We'd be joyed to have you.

Ruth I may do that. (*Beat.*) I must say, I'm amazed at
the way the youngsters do exactly as you tell them. That's
very rare these days.

Neal Self-discipline. One of the first things you learn
when you're with The Lord. Without it, you're nothing,
nobody. Take me, Ruth, I didn't always walk in God's
light. You may not know, but I was brought up in poverty.
I never knew my father. He left before I was born. And
my mother was an alcoholic, so I was raised mostly in
institutions and foster homes. (*Beat.*) I may look to you now
like a respectable old clergyman, but I was a real wild
young man for a time. Oh yes. You know how it was.
Change the world, equality, peace, drugs, free living, I
bought the whole store.

Ruth Well, we all did some very strange things in those
days. Take me, I married a plumber. Name of Brian.

Neal Really?

Ruth Yes. He fixed all my taps then disappeared to
Amsterdam with a Moroccan stilt-walker.

Neal Well. (*Beat.*) I didn't realise at the time, but what I
had was a hunger. I swallowed everything . . . booze, grass,
acid, and still I was starving. I had no father to respect; I
had no respect for anything or anybody, myself included. I
ran around spitting hatred everywhere, round and round,
confused, angry and deeply, deeply unhappy.

Ruth And then, don't tell me, you found God.

Neal No, Ruth, no. What I'd found was the Devil. (*Beat.*)
He spoke to me. I went around in a dream for I don't
know how long, with the Devil speaking to me, on and on
and on. And do you know what he was saying? (*Beat.*) He
was telling me to kill. Yes, to kill. So I went out and I
bought a gun. I didn't know who I was going to kill, it
could have been the President, it could have been the
check-out girl at the K-mart. (*Beat.*) But I found myself in a

huge stadium. I didn't know why I was there, what was
going on, I only knew I had to kill. Surrounded by
thousands of people, but who? And then I knew. There he
was, framed in lights. There was the man I was going to
kill. (*Beat.*) Dr Billy Graham. (*Beat.*) I had my hand on the
gun in my jacket pocket as I pressed forward to get close
enough. And the Devil was screaming at me, and Billy was
preaching, and I had these voices, yelling and hollering,
fighting for my soul. And Billy was telling us to come
forward to Jesus, and I was going forward, and I had the
gun in my hand. And at last I stood before him. And I
was shaking, Lord I was shaking. And then I looked up.
(*Beat.*) And the Devil was gone. No more yelling in my
head. For the very first time in my life, I felt peace.
Complete, silent, loving peace. So I tore off my jacket and
threw it way behind me. I fell to my knees. And I said,
'Dr Graham, forgive me, but I came here to kill you.' And
he smiled, and fell to his knees and we prayed together.
(*Beat.*) A miracle. (*Beat.*) And that was when I understood. It
was me that had to change first. Only then could I change
the world.

Ruth   Rather like St Paul.

Neal   Yes! Precisely. Just as it happened in the Bible, so,
two thousand years later, it happened to me. Isn't that just
incredible?

Ruth   Oh, incredible.

Neal   You see, God's purpose never ever changes. From
the time of the Scriptures to now, the message is the same:
reject the Devil and come to the Lord. (*Beat.*)

Ruth   The problem I have, Reverend, is that in my entire
life, I have never had any inkling of the existence of God.
Or the Devil. I can accept, for the sake of argument, that
they exist, but then that acceptance brings with it a
question: if they are constantly struggling for possession of
the soul of humankind, then why have so very many
people, myself included, never had any sign of this titanic
struggle raging all around us?

Neal   I expect they were trying to get through, but I'll bet
your line was always busy.

Ruth   No. It's not deliberate on my part. If God were to
manifest Himself to me I shouldn't complain. In fact, I
would be grateful for some answers. (*Beat.*) It's just that it
will never happen, that's all. (*Beat.*)

Neal   God's love is there, Ruth. You've chosen to ignore
it.

Ruth   So it's my fault.

Neal   Of course. That's why you're so unhappy. That's
why you're having to sell this place. Without the Lord,
there is no happiness or success. There is only the saddest
state in the world: Godlessness. The endless black eternity
of living without his love.

Freddy   And why, specifically, should eternity be black?

Neal (*he laughs*)   A figure of speech, brother, a figure of
speech.

Freddy   Yes, it always is.

Neal   Black like the night is black.

Freddy   And where does, say, poverty rate on this sliding
scale of sadness?

Neal   Very high indeed. You should read your Bible,
brother. The poor man who accepts Jesus Christ into his
heart possesses all the riches of the kingdom of God.

Freddy (*exploding with laughter*)   Oh, man, you are priceless!
It's just words, for Christ's sake. (*He stalks out.*)

Ruth   Freddy . . . (*Pause.*) Sorry.

Neal   That's OK, Ruth. A lot of people get sentimental
about poverty. (*Beat.*) If he cares so darn much, why isn't
he out there doing something about it like I am?

Ruth   I wasn't aware you were a philanthropist. I was
under the impression that you were a businessman,

somebody who looks to make a profit.

Neal I'm a Christian businessman. Every cent I earn goes to the glory of God. And that employs people, that puts bread on the table, that gives people hope.

Ruth It's also given you that enormous limousine outside and that lovely Rolex on your wrist.

Neal The Lord has blessed me in kind. He has chosen to reward me financially because I've put to use my God-given business talent. (*Beat.*)

Ruth So there really *is* an answer for everything.

Neal Yes. God is the answer.

Ruth I'm sorry, but I believe that anybody who thinks God is the answer has seriously misunderstood the question.

Gavin *comes back in.*

Gavin Well. Sophie sends you her love, Neal.

Neal God bless her. How is she?

Gavin Bearing up. But nothing's happening as yet, so we can get right on with business.

Ruth Yes. You were going to show me your brochure. All the exciting things you intend doing with my home. (*Beat.*) Ex-home.

Gavin It's still yours for at least a couple of months.

Ruth I shall be glad to be rid of it.

Gavin No, I can't believe that.

Ruth Oh, believe it. And the two million pounds you're paying me for it has seen off any lingering doubts I may have had.

Gavin (*having taken a large brochure out of his case*) Here we are.

Ruth It's very professional looking.

Neal   What did you expect?

Ruth (*reading the cover*)   'Hartstone. Christian leisure and
satellite broadcasting complex. Hartstone: Retreat. Church.
Shrine. Hartstone: The truly Christian experience.' Hmm. I
suppose in a year or two I won't recognise the place.

Gavin   Apart from the obvious building and alteration
work we'll have to undertake, we've gone to great lengths
to retain the essential character of the place.

Ruth   Don't worry. The essential character went long ago.
It's all yours.

Neal   Ruth . . . I love this place.

Ruth (*holding up the brochure*)   No. You love *this* place.

Neal   Same thing. (*Beat.*)

Ruth   No. (*Pause. She looks through the brochure.*) I must say,
I'm intrigued to know how you got planning permission for
some of this. I mean, aren't we an area of special scientific
interest, or some such? I should have thought the DOE
would have tied you up in red tape. (**Gavin** *smiles.*) Or am
I mistaken?

Gavin   We have satisfied every aspect of government
concern, I think you could say.

Ruth   Oh. You went to school with the minister.

Gavin   Not quite. But I have done a little consultancy
work for the government in the past. I have very good
contacts.

Neal   But don't think this is achieved by graft, Ruth. The
government wants the same thing we want for this area:
jobs and prosperity.

Gavin   And we really have bent over backwards to
accommodate the Green lobby and the inevitable local
nimbies.

Neal   So, everybody's happy. (*Beat.*) Uh, let me see if I
can't offer a little something that might make *you* even

happier Ruth. How would you like to stay on here? (*Beat.*)
I happen to believe there is a role here for you at
Hartstone after we take over.

Ruth   Doing what?

Neal   Bearing witness. Telling our visitors the fantastic
story of your family and Grace in particular. Showing them
round the place, giving them the true picture of life as it
was for you here back then. (*Beat.*)

Ruth   There are a few things I feel I may have been cut
out for in life, Reverend, but I'm afraid Redcoat isn't one
of them.

Neal   Excuse me?

Ruth   I'd make a lousy spiritual tour guide.

Neal   What the heck has that got to do with the
Redcoats?

Gavin   I'll explain another time, Neal.

Neal   You people have got to stop talking in riddles.
(*Looks at his watch.*) Well, my lovely Rolex tells me it's time
I got some sleep. What time's our first meeting tomorrow?

Gavin   The contractors will be here at ten, then it's pretty
solid through the day.

Neal   That's how I like it.

Freddy *comes back in.*

Freddy   Sorry. I shouldn't have blown up like that.

Neal   Thank you, brother. Apology accepted. (*Beat.*) OK.
Sleep. God bless you all. (*He goes.*)

Gavin   Looks like I missed something.

Ruth   The merest altercation.

Gavin   Ah. (*Beat.*) By the way, Ruth, Neal just threw *me* a
curve there as well.

Ruth   I'm sorry?

Gavin   Staying on. I know it wouldn't appeal to you.

Ruth   No.

Gavin   He can be rather impulsive at times, but, you know, next to Billy Graham, Neal is the most ... inspirational man I ever met. Do you know about his conversion? How it came about?

Ruth   Yes, it was in the literature you sent me. And, oddly enough, we were just treated to a word for word rendition of it while you were out. Luckily, I got in with St Paul before he could reach the finale. (*Beat.*)

Gavin   Well. We all love him very dearly, despite his little foibles.

Ruth   Unfortunately, he reminds me of my father.

Gavin   Is that unfortunate?

Ruth   In as much as I hated my father, yes.

Gavin   That is very sad.

Ruth   Why?

Gavin   Well ... we believe that manliness is Christliness; that much sorrow and pain has been caused by women refusing to accept the authority of their fathers and husbands. (*Beat.*)

Ruth   Which century precisely is it, Gavin, to which you would drag us back?

Gavin   We simply go back to the Bible.

Ruth   Very convenient.

Gavin   There's nothing convenient about it at all. It's the word of God and must be obeyed, that's all.

Ruth   I wonder how enthusiastically you'd obey if it turned out not to suit you so very well. (*Beat.*)

Gavin   I forget, your mind's made up about us already.

Ruth   Long, long ago.

Gavin   Well, I'll pray for God to open your mind and enter your heart.

Ruth   Please, don't bother.

Gavin   It's no bother. (*He smiles.*) Right, well, I'll get off to bed, too. Big day tomorrow. Goodnight, and God bless. (*He goes.*)

Pause. **Ruth** *gets her copy of* The Water Babies *and sets up the cassette machine.*

Ruth   You shouldn't get so worked up.

Freddy   Me? (*Beat.*) It's just that they're such . . . bastards. Sorry.

Ruth   Feel free. Very soon, they'll own the world. (*Beat.*) Those poor innocent souls in Gdansk, Bucharest, Vladivostock . . . they won't know what's hit them. The joys of the free market, and in less than one year, the Reverend Hoffman beamed into their homes via satellite, twenty four hours a day. Makes you shudder, doesn't it? (*Beat.*) Forget the rubbish about the meek inheriting the earth. This bunch are buying it up in one job lot.

Freddy (*beat*)   And you're not going to tell them the truth. You know . . .

Ruth   No. Why should I?

Freddy   Because it's dishonest.

Ruth   This is England. Nobody is honest any more. There's no return on honesty. (*Pause.*) Have you seen what they're going to do to your river?

Freddy   He told me.

Ruth   No, look, there's an artist's impression of it here. (*She hands him the brochure.*) Hideous, isn't it?

Freddy   Don't.

Ruth   A marina, boating, water skiing.

Freddy   Yes . . .

Ruth 'A total riverside leisure environment.' It says here.

Freddy (*beat*) It's obscene. They're going to kill that river. For money.

Ruth Welcome to the real world. (*Beat.*)

Freddy I won't forgive you, you know.

Ruth Look ... They've made a film about the Apostles. Available only on video, it says. A film about the Apostles entitled 'The Magnificent Twelve'. (*Beat.*) No sensible God would allow his followers to be so idiotic, surely.

Freddy It's not a joke.

Ruth I'm afraid the jury's still out on that one.

Freddy Oh, I know, disguise it with irony, as per usual. But the pain in this house is real. *My* pain is real.

Ruth (*reading from the brochure*) 'Enterprise Faith is at the forefront of the major revival of the Church in Europe – East and West. We are putting the Church into the marketplace. We are changing the hearts and minds of *people*. That's where the revival begins. That is the Gospel of Faith. Enterprise Faith.' (*Pause.* **Freddy** *stands to go.*) Freddy I have no desire to be forgiven anything.

Freddy I'm going to the river.

Ruth (*throws the brochure and opens the book and switches on the tape recorder. She reads out loud*) '"And now, my pretty little man," said Mother Carey, "you are sure you know the way to the Other-end-of-Nowhere?" Tom thought; and behold, he had forgotten it utterly. "That is because you took your eyes off me." "But what am I to do, ma'am? For I can't keep looking at you when I am somewhere else." "You must do without me, as most people have to do, and of course, you must go the whole way backward." "Backward!" cried Tom, "Then I shall not be able to see my way." "On the contrary, if you look forward, you will not see a step before you, and be certain to go wrong; but, if you look behind you, and watch carefully whatever you have passed, then you will know what is coming next as plainly as if you saw it in a looking glass."'

Scene Three

Saturday morning 11.00 a.m. **Felicia** *and* **Joanna** *are rehearsing a scene from the film. This is not immediately obvious, although* **Felicia** *is trying to speak with an English accent, because their scripts are on the table.*

Felicia   Do you ever wonder what Heaven must be like?

Joanna   Sometimes.

Felicia   And what do you think?

Joanna   Oh, I expect it's very light and warm . . . with nice trees for shade and cool streams, and everybody happy. Yes, lots of singing and laughing . . . (*Pause. She's forgotten the line.* **Felicia** *prompts.*)

Felicia   How about you?

Joanna   Shit, sorry. (*Beat.*) How about you?

Felicia   Oh . . . I think of Heaven as being cradled in God's bosom . . . a deep warm feeling, with His strong arms around me. And Jesus there, smiling. A smile like all the nicest things in the world. A smile like healing medicine. (*She coughs badly.* **Joanna** *goes to her.*)

Joanna   You're going to be all right. I've been praying for you. You're going to be well again, soon.

Felicia   I don't mind, you know. I'm not afraid to die, if it's the Lord's will.

Joanna   You're so brave. (*Beat.*) Uh . . . no, I've lost my objective, sorry. (*She goes and consults her script.*)

Felicia   That's OK. (*Beat.*) You think I need to work on the cough?

Joanna   No, it sounds really . . . death rattle, you know?

Felicia   Thank you. Hey, I can't wait till we get our costumes. We can just hang out, and, like, really become Grace and Ruth.

Joanna   Yeah, dead method. (*Beat.*) God, I hope they didn't wear corsets.

Felicia   Uh uh, too young.

Joanna   I wore one once in a telly I did. Nearly killed me. (*Beat.*) Maybe they wore suspenders.

Felicia   Suspenders?

Freddy *comes in from the grounds carrying a shotgun.*

Joanna   Oh, hello.

Freddy   Hello.

Felicia   Shoot anything?

Freddy   No.

Joanna   Good. Dead things, yuk.

Freddy (*he laughs*)   You eat meat?

Joanna   Yeah. But . . .

Freddy   Humanely slaughtered, right? My favourite contradiction. Dead is dead, whichever way you look at it.

Joanna   At least my dinner's been killed for a reason. It hasn't been killed for fun.

Freddy   I have never in my life killed anything for fun. (*Beat.*) Bye. (*He smiles and goes.*)

Joanna   Guns give me the creeps, that's all.

Felicia   Every man has the right to defend himself.

Joanna   Against what? Rabbits? (*Beat.*)

Felicia   I guess we're just a lot more comfortable around guns in the States.

Joanna   Well I hate them.

Felicia   I grew up with them. My daddy has a real big collection. And he always says it ain't the bullet that kills you, it's the hole.

Joanna   What a cop out.

Felicia   Why? Any how, I think Freddy looks kinda neat with a gun.

Joanna   Whoah, I get it.

Felicia   Get what?

Joanna   You know . . .

Felicia   What?

Joanna   You've got the hots for Freddy.

Felicia *looks angry.*

Felicia   No, I do not. That's not right.

Joanna   I'm sorry. Just a joke.

Felicia   Yeah. (*Beat.*)

Joanna   You're not . . . I mean . . . don't be offended . . . you're not prejudiced, are you? (**Felicia** *is furious.*)

Felicia   No. How dare you say that?

Joanna   Sorry.

Felicia   How dare you? (*Pause.*)

Joanna   Look, uh, I've got a big mouth, OK? I don't always check my brain's in gear when I open it. Sorry.

Felicia   I had a Negro boyfriend, as a matter of fact.

Joanna   Oh. (*Beat.*)

Felicia   He's a real great guy. A real strong Christian. He works at Faith records, we met when I was cutting the album. (*Beat.*) My mom thought Bob, that's his name, she thought Bob was a great guy, the best, she told me so. But when I told her I was in love she said she'd been praying that this wouldn't happen. She'd been praying. (*Beat.*) And we couldn't tell my Daddy. Daddy wouldn't have understood. (*Beat.*) And folks at Faith, well, they were kind of weird about it, too. Bad career choice was how Reverend Hoffman put it. (*Beat.*) We never fooled around, nothing like that. We were just a good Christian couple. But we had kind of an acceptance problem. (*Beat.*)

Joanna   Do you still see him?

Felicia   Not really. (*Upset, she goes to her bag and takes out her walkman.*)

Joanna   Funny place, your country.

Felicia   Yeah, real funny. (**Amy** *comes in.*)

Amy   Hi.

Felicia
Joanna } Hi.

Felicia   Sleep OK?

Amy   More or less . . .

Felicia   So how you feeling?

Amy   Better, you know . . . a little bit dizzy at times . . .

Felicia   Take it easy.

Amy   Yeah.

Felicia *is preparing to listen to her walkman.*

You kids been out yet? Round the property?

Joanna   I had a look round last night. It's fantastic.

Felicia   I just need a scripture moment. Excuse me.

Amy   Go right ahead.

Felicia *puts on her headphones and closes her eyes. As she listens, she sometimes sits swaying gently, sometimes paces around with her hands clasped.*

Joanna   What's she doing?

Amy   She's taking a spiritual supplement. (*Beat.*) It's a two minute reading from the scriptures. So, you're stuck in traffic, or doing the laundry, or waiting on line at the bank, and you feel what we call Bible hunger, you just put in the tape, close your eyes and get filled right up with the word of God.

Felicia *is nodding her head and occasionally saying amen.*

Joanna You're kidding.

Amy No.

Joanna *(laughing)* Like taking an aspirin.

Amy Except the word of God brings greater relief and comfort than aspirin ever could. *(Beat.)*

Joanna Felicia was telling me about Bob . . .

Amy Oh yeah?

Joanna Yeah. I think it got her a bit upset.

Amy Well, y'know, it can be pretty distressing when a guy, y'know, when a relationship breaks down one side. She got awful hurt.

Joanna What, you're saying he dumped her?

Amy Uh, well, I guess . . . well, yeah. *(Beat.)*

Joanna So it had nothing to do with his colour.

Amy Excuse me?

Joanna She seemed to think it might have had something to do with . . . well, y'know.

Amy No.

Joanna He's black.

Amy Yes.

Joanna Well . . . I don't know. *(Beat.)*

Felicia Amen.

Amy Hey, have you guys been rehearsing my script?

Joanna   Yeah.

Amy   A-plus. I'm flattered.

Joanna   We love it.

Amy   It's a great story. Wrote itself.

Joanna   And it's just so incredible actually being here.

Amy   Yeah, I've been trying to soak it all in. It's like every brick in this old house could tell a story. (*Beat.*) And that room . . . boy.

Joanna   Oh, yeah. (*Beat.*) When I went in there, you know . . . I cried.

Amy   Really?

Joanna   It was like I was overcome.

Amy *puts her hand on* **Joanna**'s *shoulder.*

Amy   That is *so* sensitive.

Joanna   Well . . .

Amy   No, honestly, that is beautiful. (*She strokes* **Joanna**'s *hair and smiles at her.*)

Felicia   Praise the Lord. (*She takes off the headphones, smiling.*)

Amy   Amen.

Felicia   Amen.

Neal, **Gavin** *and* **Lance** *appear from the grounds. They carry plans and papers.* **Neal** *is in a hurry as he walks though the room.*

Neal   OK. Give me two minutes while I go get those charts. (*He looks at his watch.*) Call me if the marquee guy arrives. (*He's gone.*)

Gavin   OK. (*Beat.*) Morning everyone. Beautiful day.

Amy   Did Neal eat breakfast?

Gavin   Hours ago.

Amy   Make sure he gets a sandwich by eleven thirty.

Gavin   I will.

Amy   And promise me you'll stop for lunch. You know his intestinal situation.

Gavin   We're having lunch in town, it's all arranged. Don't worry, I'll look after him.

Amy   Good.

Gavin   You've all got plenty to do? Not bored?

Joanna   We've been rehearsing.

Gavin   Smashing. Which reminds me, did you ring the camera crew?

Lance   Yes, they finish in London at midnight, so they're driving down overnight. They'll be here five a.m. at the latest.

Gavin   Good.

Lance   And they have to be back in town for three o'clock.

Gavin   We'll be wrapped by ten, so that's no problem.

Lance   They were a little bit stroppy about the early start.

Gavin   Typical. We're paying them three times the rate and still they manage a whinge. Welcome home Gavin. Honestly, you'd think people over here would have learned the lesson of the past thirteen years. In the States, I call someone up, I say: we've got a problem. They say: great, how do we solve it? Over here, they say: cor, blimey, guv, that's a tall order, it'll cost you.

Joanna   My father says it's got a lot better, though.

Gavin   Of course it has. But that was just the shake-out. Sadly, there's something soft in your average Brit that stops him going all the way.

Amy   Maybe the Lord can change that.

Gavin Amen to that. But he may need a helping hand, and that, God willing, is part of my mission.

Neal *hurries back in with some papers.* **Lance** *goes to the windows.*

Gavin All set?

Neal Can't wait.

Lance Looks like the marquee guys have finally arrived.

Neal Great, let's do some business. (*He,* **Gavin** *and* **Lance** *go out.*)

Felicia Where does he get his energy?

Amy From the Lord, where else? (*They smile.*)

Ruth *comes in in her dressing gown, holding a cup of tea.*

Ruth Oh, good morning. (*They all 'hello', 'hi' etc.*)

Amy Been catching up on some sleep?

Ruth No, I suffer from insomnia. I usually spend most of the night writing. In actual fact I've had approximately two and a half hours of something only vaguely like sleep.

Amy I know the feeling.

Ruth One gets used to it, I suppose. (*Beat.*)

Amy And what do you write? When you can't sleep?

Ruth Oh, this and that. Furious letters to the newspapers, that sort of thing.

Amy What, all night? (*Beat.*)

Ruth No. Bits of memoirs, short stories, sometimes, like you.

Amy No. I don't. Not any more.

Ruth Well, that's a terrible shame. I read two of your volumes and liked them very much. (*Beat.*)

Amy You have my stories here?

Ruth   Yes.

Amy   In this house?

Ruth   Upstairs.

Amy *is agitated.*

Ruth   Why?

Amy   What must you think?

Ruth   Of what?

Amy   Nothing. (*Beat.*) Of me.

Ruth   For a start, I think you're a very good writer. Why on earth you bother with all this evangelist claptrap is beyond me. It's a criminal waste of talent.

Amy   A talent put to God's purpose is not wasted.

Ruth   Ha. I'll bet you could write that on the gravestones of a few million poor buggers.

Amy *stands.*

Amy   Excuse me.

Ruth   Ah. Sudden pressing business.

Amy   I have some things to do.

Ruth   Of course you do.

Amy   No, I really do.

Ruth   Of course you really do. (*Beat.*)

Amy   What have I done to you? (*Beat.*)

Ruth (*indicating the scripts*)   Is that the script you wrote?

Amy   Yes.

Ruth   Your talent put to God's purpose?

Amy   I hope so. (*Beat.*)

Ruth *just smiles.* **Amy** *goes.*

Ruth   First one of the day.

Felicia   Miss Hartstone . . .

Ruth   Hmmm . . . ?

Felicia   Excuse me, but Mrs. Hoffman is a good Christian lady.

Ruth   I'm very happy for her.

Felicia   Has she offended you?

Ruth   I don't know. Possibly.

Felicia   Well, I believe you've offended her.

Ruth   That, my dear, is because I'm a crabby old cow. Especially before I've had my herbal tea. (*She sips.*)

Felicia   Politeness doesn't cost, you know. (*Frisson. Beat.*)

Ruth   Yes. That's true. (*Beat.*)

Joanna   Miss Hartstone, how old were you when you first wore suspenders? Oh God, that sounds stupid. I mean, when you were young, when Grace was here, you know, the film . . .

Ruth   My dear, you've totally lost me.

Joanna   Sorry. We were reading a scene, you see, and we wondered what sort of clothes you wore.

Ruth   I see. Well, most definitely not suspenders. I normally wore corduroy trousers. And a sensible sweater.

Felicia   And Grace? (*Beat.*)

Ruth   Any old thing, really. A simple dress. Sandals.

Felicia   Do you have any photographs?

Ruth   Only from years before, in Africa.

Felicia   That's a real shame. (*Beat.*)

Ruth   Actually, somewhere, I have the last dress she ever wore. Yes, I have it somewhere.

Felicia Wow, that is incredible.

Joanna Fantastic.

Felicia Do you suppose we could . . . ? No, I guess it's too personal.

Ruth What is? (*Beat.*)

Felicia Could I wear it in the movie? (**Ruth** *smiles.*)

Ruth Oh, no. No, I don't think so.

Felicia Sorry, I shouldn't have asked.

Ruth Why on earth not?

Felicia I realise it would probably be too painful for you.

Ruth Too painful?

Felicia Yes, I mean, your sister's dress, and her dying and everything . . .

Ruth Oh, I see. No, the reason you couldn't possibly wear the dress is that it would be far too big for you.

Felicia Excuse me?

Ruth *stands.*

Ruth Look like a tent on you. (*She goes.*)

Felicia Man, is she flaky, or what?

Joanna Grace must have been, you know, fat when she died. You're going to have put on a few pounds.

Felicia No way. I can't play large. That is not a possibility. I have an image.

Joanna Have to eat lots of cream cakes.

Felicia Absolutely no way. (*Beat.*)

Joanna If you don't let on about the corduroy trousers and the sensible sweaters, I won't tell anyone about Grace's weight problem.

Felicia   Deal.

Lance *comes in from the grounds.*

Lance   Anybody seen my damn case? (*He spots it.*) Ah, there it is. (*He opens it and searches through some papers.*)

Joanna   Busy busy busy.

Lance   You're telling me. Still, all right for some, eh?

Joanna   Do you mind? We've been working.

Lance   Yeah. (*He snaps his case shut.*) This is great, isn't it? I feel really ... (*He clenches his fist.*) ... y'know?

Freddy *comes in to go through the grounds.*

Joanna   Has someone been putting something in your tea, Lance?

Lance   No, listen, to be on the ground floor on an operation like this ... it's unreal. I mean, this place, it's a beacon for the future. Broadcasting to the whole of Europe, giving people what they want: God and freedom. I love it. What do you say, Freddy?

Freddy   What do I say?

Lance   Yeah. (*Beat.*)

Freddy   Nothing. (*Beat.*)

Lance   Well, there'll be stacks of work when we come on stream next year. Stick around.

Freddy   No thanks. I'd rather not see what you do. I'd rather not know.

Lance   Well, your loss.

Freddy   Yeah. My loss. (*Beat.*)

Joanna   Did *you* catch those trout we had yesterday, Freddy?

Freddy   Yes.

Joanna   How clever. Real countryman, aren't you?

Freddy   I suppose so.

Lance   Funnily enough I caught some massive salmon in the States last year.

Joanna   Do you look after everything all on your own?

Freddy   More or less.

Joanna   Sort of like a gamekeeper.

Freddy   That's right.

Joanna   Must be a heck of a job.

Freddy   It's my life.

Joanna   That's really romantic. Very D.H. Lawrence. You know. Lady Chatterly.

Freddy   Miss, I may be a little shy, but I'm not stupid.

Joanna   Didn't say you were. (*Beat.*) Any chance of showing us where the kitchen is? I feel a snack-attack coming on.

Freddy   Sure.

Joanna   Felicia?

Felicia   Yeah, OK I'll watch.

Lance   Meanwhile, some of us will get on with some work.

Freddy *gestures the way and they start to go.*

Joanna   Don't strain yourself, Lance.

The women go. **Freddy** *gives* **Lance** *a look and follows them.* **Lance** *stands, case in hand.*

Lance (*American accent*)   Goddam nigger. (*He smirks, turns and walks briskly off.*)

Scene Four

The drawing room, 2.30 a.m. In the semi-darkness we can just about make out a figure in a nightdress crouched beside the drinks cabinet. Pause. **Ruth** *comes in carrying two books, a notepad, pens and a cup of tea. She puts these on the table and brings a table lamp across and switches it on. As she does so, the figure,* **Amy,** *shifts and tries to become smaller.* **Ruth** *pulls up a chair and sits down.* **Amy** *shifts again.* **Ruth** *looks up, sees something and slowly looks round to check the windows. She looks back and very slowly and quietly opens a notebook and picks up a pen. She sits. Slight movement from* **Amy.** **Ruth** *puts the pen down.*

Ruth   You know, I really can't concentrate terribly well with you scuffling around down there. (*Pause.*) I say . . . ? (*Pause.*) Oh, well, suit yourself. (*She begins packing her things up.*)

Amy   Help me.

Ruth   What? (*Pause. Softly.*) What did you say? (*She stands and goes over to* **Amy.**) Mrs Hoffman? What are you doing? (*Beat.*) Are you all right?

Amy   No.

Ruth   Whatever is the matter?

Amy *looks up. Cradled in her arms is a two-thirds-empty vodka bottle. She's very drunk.*

Ruth   Oh my good Lord . . . (*She gently takes the bottle and puts it on the table.*) Right, let's have you up. (*She tries to help her up.* **Amy** *shakes her head and waves her arms.*)

Amy   No . . .

Ruth   All right. (*Beat.*) All right. Wherever you feel most comfortable. (**Ruth** *goes and sits again.*) What is it? Insomnia? Same as me? (*Beat.*) You know, if I ever for one moment allow the possibility that there might be a God, then it's always about now. The middle of the night. Not to be able to sleep is a kind of hell. A terrible punishment. (*Beat.*) That's why I'm not very keen on the idea of eternity.

When my time comes, I'm really rather looking forward to closing my eyes and knowing that for the first time in many, many years I shall sleep. Deep, long and quiet.

Pause. **Amy** *slowly crawls across the floor to the table. She puts her arm up and feels for the vodka bottle. She finds it and hauls herself up onto her knees. She takes the top off the bottle and takes an incredibly long swig. She puts the bottle back and curls up.*

Good grief. (*Beat.*) Not many people know this, but my father, my sainted, light-in-the-darkness-bringing father could polish off a bottle of port before lunch. Yes, port. Horrible sickly stuff if you ask me. But there you are. (*Beat.*)

Amy *takes another swig.*

This is very strange, you know. I mean, I was under the impression that you Americans always had your drinks on the rocks. (*Beat.*) No? I could get you some ice. (*She takes a sip of tea.*) Perhaps you'd like some herbal tea? (*Beat.*) I'm sorry, I'm sounding like a mother hen, aren't I? Anyway, it's your choice. If you want to crawl around on the floor at the dead of night, drunk as a lord, then that's up to you. Crawl away. (*Beat.*) It's just that I thought you asked me to help you. (*She stands and comes round to where* **Amy** *is crouching.*) This is quite a stroke of luck, really. I've got your books here. I was going to make some notes and ask you some questions tomorrow. I've always wanted to quiz a living writer.

Amy (*her speech is very slurred*)   'S all fucking true.

Ruth   What?

Amy   'S all true. It all happened.

Ruth   Ah. (*Beat.*) Yes, I was going to ask you about that. Don't misunderstand me, I wasn't shocked. (*Beat.*) Well, actually, yes I was. A bit. But it occurred to me that . . . well, that anybody who went through all, or most, or even some of what's in your books . . . then things must be very difficult for them. (*Beat.*)

Amy   Up the fucking ass. You ever been fucked up the ass? (*Beat.*)

Ruth   No. Thankfully. I've always maintained a discreet distance from men who discussed sodomy too enthusiastically. (*Beat.*) I take it you have. Been. You know. (*Beat.*) Ah yes . . . (*She picks up one of the books.*) Yes, I know the one you mean. (*Beat.*) God. That's real, is it? The video tapes and everything.

Amy   I was paid. (*Beat.*) Couldn't see my face, not at first. I knew it was me 'cause I had a fucking band aid on my big toe. Nearly tore the nail off that morning, caught it in the shower. Fucking band aid. Little smudge of blood, the top corner. My big toe. Those guys. Those fucking assholes. They were the big guys, y'know? Extra big guys. Cocks like fucking airplanes. (*Pause. She takes another swig.*) I saw the video. (*Beat.*)

Ruth   You survived, at least.

Amy   Yeah, look at me. A survivor.

Ruth   And your stories . . . some of them are beautiful.

Amy   Fuck beauty. (*Pause.*)

Ruth   Do I take it that your conversion is only temporary?

Amy   No. (*Beat.*) But it's all messed up. Sometimes, I can't help it, I just see these things. And I pray and I pray and they don't go away and it's my fault. I'm not good enough.

Ruth   That's silly. None of us is. (*Beat.*)

Amy   My sins should be forgiven. But they're not. God won't forgive me. (*She takes another huge swig and crumples up.*)

Neal *has come in, unseen, in his pyjamas and dressing gown.*

Ruth   Then He's not half the Deity He's cracked up to be. (*She sees* **Neal**.) Ah. It's your wife. I think she needs help.

Neil *walks across to* **Amy** *and takes the bottle from her. He puts* *the top on it and returns it to the drinks cabinet. He walks back to the table and picks up one of the books. He looks at* **Ruth** *and drops the book back on the table. He drops to his knees, elbows on the table, hands clasped together.*

Neal   Lord, give me strength in this hour of need. Give me strength to bring this beautiful woman back to your love and goodness, to save her from these torments, to help her live again in Jesus Christ. Thank you, Lord. Amen. (*He puts his head in his hands for a few seconds then slowly gets up.*) Ruth . . . Amy and I have a beautiful daughter, Kimmy. She'll be sixteen years old this fall. (*Beat.*) Since the day Kimmy was born, Satan has been trying to claim her. Not a day goes by without he throws us a new challenge. Satan has targeted our daughter, he's targeted us, because of the strength of my mission. The power of the message of God's love is so strong in me that the Devil keeps on coming back, trying to destroy me and my beautiful family. (*Beat.*) Before we left on this trip, he sent a boy from Kimmy's school to claim her. He gave her rock albums that said 'Satan will reign forever' when you played them backwards. He tried to seduce her, until I exorcised the Devil from his body. Then Satan gave Kimmy nightmares, physical ailments, nosebleeds, a skin condition. I've been fighting him through my daughter, and now he's trying to destroy me through Amy. And I have to fight him again.

Pause. **Ruth** *suddenly laughs.*

Ruth   Excuse me asking, but why would anybody want to play a record backwards? What on earth could possibly be the point? And I'm hardly surprised your daughter has nightmares after seeing her father do a spot exorcism on one of her schoolfriends. That's enough to make anybody a candidate for the funny farm. (*Beat.*) Really, Reverend, you do rather seem to come at everything the wrong way round. (*Beat.*)

Neal *picks up the books.*

Neal   You brought these into this house. Why?

Ruth   Obviously I wanted to see what kind of writer she was.

Neal   We sent you the script.

Ruth   Yes . . .

Neal   So who made you bring these books here?

Ruth   Who? It was intellectual curiosity, for heaven's sake. Or have you never heard of that? (*Pause.*) Oh, I see. Who. Yes, very good. (*Beat.*) Well, you tell me.

Neal   I already know. (*Beat.*)

Ruth (*she points to* **Amy**)   So your answer to this is that I am a stooge of Satan?!

Neal   Yes! Satan loves a failure. And that's what you are. He smells out people like you, failed, bitter people, to use in his battle with the success of God's love. (*Beat.*)

Ruth   Stop blaming it all on Satan. It's you, and you bloody well know it.

Neal *throws his arms in the air and stands in front of her.*

Neal   In the name of our Lord and Saviour . . .

Ruth   Oh no you don't . . .

Neal   Jesus Christ . . .

Ruth   Not to me you don't . . .

Neal   I bind you, Satan . . .

Ruth   That's enough . . .

Neal   And cast you out . . .

Ruth   ENOUGH! (*She slaps his face. Pause.*) Anyone can see Satan didn't do this.

She walks out. Pause.

Neal *kneels by the upright chair.* **Gavin** *enters wearing his dressing gown.*

Gavin   Neal? What's going on? What's wrong with Ruth? (*He sees* **Amy**.) Heavens, Amy . . . (*He goes to her.*) Are you all right? Amy? (*He's holding her.*) Neal, what's wrong with her? Neal?

Neal   Get her onto the chair please, Gavin. (*He's suddenly very businesslike.*)

They lift her up as **Lance** *comes in.*

Gavin   Lance, help us here.

Lance   What's happening?

Gavin   Just help.

Lance *takes over from* **Neal**, *who paces slowly around.* **Gavin** *and* **Lance** *get* **Amy** *onto the chair.*

Neal   Gavin, Lance. Brothers. (*Beat.*) Satan is among us.

Lance   Do what?

Gavin   Sshh.

Neal   Through his agent, he has entered my wife and dragged her from the path of righteousness. Her faith has been poisoned, infected with sinfulness. (*Beat.*) Satan has my wife. (*Beat.*) Pray. We need the Lord here now. We need him here in this room with us. Only the Lord can bring my wife back to me. (*He drops to his knees and prays.*)

Lord, I know you're there, looking out for the welfare of your daughter, Amy, in her hour of need. Lord, give her the strength to get through this and cast Satan out of her mind for good. Bring her back to your bountiful love to live in your light for evermore. Amen.

Gavin/Lance   Amen.

Neal *stands.*

Neal   Amy, Amy, remember what the scripture says: for God so loved the world, that he gave his only begotten son, that whosoever believeth in him should not perish, but have everlasting life. For God sent not his son into the world to condemn the world; but that the world through him might be saved.

Gavin Lord, I don't believe you want to take Amy away from us now. We trust you to see us through this time, and to bring our beloved sister back to us. Amen.

Neal/Lance Amen.

Amy *is stirring.*

Neal Lord, we believe in Jesus Christ. We believe that to deny him is to die in our sins. Only by believing in him can we come into your presence.

Amy's *eyes are open, she watches* **Neal.**

Lord, rekindle the fire of faith in Amy, because before Satan got a hold of her, she was burning for Jesus Christ. (*He picks up the books.*) Satan is strong, but we know the Lord is stronger. We know God loves us and forgives us our sins. Forgive these, Lord. (*He brandishes the books.*) Cast Satan out. In the name of our Saviour Jesus Christ, cast Satan out, cast him out, Lord, cast him out forever! (*He rips the books apart and throws them from him.* **Amy** *gasps.* **Neal** *goes to her.*) Amy, your sins are not a problem for God. He can handle your sins, no matter how bad, no matter how low, God does not have a problem with that. What he cannot tolerate is when you shut him out, when you deny him, when you don't accept that he is Lord in your life. That is when he gets mighty angry. And when the Lord is angry, the heavens shake and men go mad. Do you hear me? Am I getting through?! (**Amy** *nods.*) Disown the Lord and you wind up in Hell. Where every breath feels like fire, every thought burns your brain, until you can't breathe or think any more. Except you have to. You have to breathe. You have to think. And all the time, you're on fire, your lungs, your brain, burning, burning for all eternity. (*Beat.*) So come back to the Lord. Don't make him angry, make him joyous in his heart. Accept that he and only he is Lord. I tell you, I command you, in the name of Jesus Christ, come to the Lord. Right now!

Amy *leans back in the chair and begins a low moan that slowly turns into an incoherent babble, bizarre and chilling.* **Neal** *sinks to his knees, as do* **Gavin** *and* **Lance**.

Neal   Praise the Lord!

Gavin   Amen!

Neal   Speak, Lord, speak!

Amy *babbles on, slowly coming to a halt. When she's finally silent, she opens her eyes and half smiles.* **Neal** *throws his arms around her.*

Thank you, Lord, thank you Jesus. (*He repeats this.* **Amy** *joins in, then* **Gavin**. *They reach a crescendo.*) Thank you, thank you, thank you, thank you. (*They subside.* **Neal** *extends a hand to* **Gavin**.) Gavin, thank you. (**Gavin** *takes his hand and embraces both of them,* **Neal** *extends a hand to* **Lance**.) Lance.

Lance *takes it self-consciously then puts his arms around them. They stay like this for some time, then* **Neal** *and* **Amy** *gently pull away.*

OK, OK. Everything's fine now. Right honey? (*She nods.*)

Gavin   Do you need anything?

Neal   No, we're just fine.

Gavin   OK, God bless. Come on, Lance.

Lance   Goodnight.

They go. **Neal** *lets go of her.*

Neal   Amy … honey … you promised me … you promised me … (*Beat.*) Well. OK. We'll just have to keep a tighter grip, that's all. (*Beat.*) We are going to beat Satan here every day. We'll have thousands of people here coming to God. And we'll be sending his word out to this whole continent. There's a real craving, I can feel it. They've lost sight of their moral destiny. But we'll bring them back to the fundamentals of the Christian faith, and we'll create a true kingdom of God, right here. Right here. This is where it begins. (*Beat. He puts his arm around her.*)

Believe it. The word is love.

Fade

Scene Five

The terrace or lawn outside the drawing room, 12.00 midday, Sunday morning. **Joanna** *is sunbathing on a sun-lounger, wearing only bikini bottom and sunglasses. To one side is a set of garden furniture. The church bells fade. Pause.* **Joanna**'s *hand goes down to a glass of orange juice on the ground beside her. She picks it up and sips leisurely through the straw, then puts the glass back down. Pause.* **Freddy** *comes from round the front of the house to go out into the grounds. He sees* **Joanna** *and stops and stares.* **Joanna** *realises he's there and peers over her sunglasses at him.*

Joanna   Hello.

Freddy   Hello. (*Beat.*) You didn't make it to church, then?

Joanna   No fear. (*Beat.*)

Freddy   You want to be careful.

Joanna   Hmm?

Freddy   Too much sunlight, it's not good for you. Skin cancer.

Joanna   Oh yeah, right. Thanks.

Lance *appears from the house. He's wearing baggy shorts, a gruesome Contra shirt, baseball cap and shades. He carries a basketball, American football, baseball bat and ball and two catchers' mitts.* **Freddy** *starts off into the grounds.*

Freddy   Looks like you bought the whole toyshop.

Lance   What? (*He laughs mirthlessly.*) Oh, yeah. Sort of.

Freddy *goes.* **Lance** *walks down to* **Joanna**.

Hi, Jo.

Joanna   Hi.

Lance *sees she's topless and stops in his tracks.*

Lance   What are you up to?

Joanna   Silly question, Lance.

Lance   Yeah, trust me. (*Beat.*) Hey, great shoot this morning.

Joanna (*perking up*)   You think so?

Lance   You were ace. It was really moving.

Joanna   Thanks. 'Course, I'll give it a lot more when we make the actual movie. Turbo-charged, you watch me.

Lance   I will. (*Beat.*)

Joanna   Hey, Lance . . .

Lance   Yeah? (*He moves closer.*)

Joanna   Listen . . . what did you think of Felicia?

Lance   Uh, great.

Beat.

Joanna   You don't think she's . . . y'know . . . a bit wooden?

Lance   I don't know . . . I mean, what do I know about it?

Joanna   Listen, don't get me wrong, I'm not knocking her. It's just, I don't get a lot *from* her, y'know? There's no electricity.

Beat.

Lance   The thing *I* noticed . . .

Joanna   What's that?

Lance   She doesn't sound very English.

Joanna   Yeah, I asked Gavin about that. He said it doesn't matter, 'cause the Yanks won't notice anyway, and everywhere else it'll be dubbed.

Lance   What about over here?

Joanna   Gavin says people are used to it. Apparently most people think the American accent sounds quite normal. Anyway, only the God squad'll see it. It's not as if we're talking Barry Norman.

Lance   Right. (*Beat.*)

Joanna   So. You looking for someone to play with?

Lance   I just thought, maybe, a little one on one, hit a couple of flies or even whack a few homers. (*Beat.*)

Joanna   I'll ask that question again, shall I? And perhaps I can have the answer in English.

Lance   Got to learn the jockspeak, otherwise you look stupid.

Joanna   Yes . . .

Lance   It's true. You turn up at a game in the States and get it all wrong, they treat you like a total pinhead.

Joanna   That's very friendly of them.

Lance   It's their game, it's their privilege. Funnily enough I play every Sunday, y'know. In Regent's Park. Softball in Summer, touch-football in Winter. You should come along, a lot of girls do.

Joanna   Not really my scene.

Lance   And they're a great bunch of guys. Then afterwards there's this great bar in Camden where we all go to hang out and talk sports.

Joanna   I didn't have you down as the sporty type.

Lance   I wasn't till I moved to the States. Going to a game over there is a real experience. Comfortable seating, giant screen replays, food and drink franchises. It's a whole culture. Not like here. Here, the overpriced, soggy hot-dogs and the putrid toilets are legendary.

Joanna   I thought that was part of the charm.

Lance   Yeah. That's one of the problems with the Brits, isn't it? They feel shortchanged if they're not being shat on. (*Beat.*) 'Scuse my French. (*Beat.*) You ever been to the States.

Joanna   No. I'm going in the Autumn.

Lance   The Fall. You'll love it. The greatest country on earth. There's a brilliant story. Apparently, in some town down South, there's an old guy sitting on his porch, and he's got a can of beer in one hand and a rifle in the other and a Bible on his knee. And as people walk by, he's shouting: 'Where else in the world can a man do this?' (*He laughs.*) Brilliant. (*Beat.*)

Felicia *comes out of the house carrying her guitar.*

Felicia   Hi.

Lance   Hello there.

Felicia (*seeing that* **Joanna**'s *topless. Beat*)   Joanna . . .

Joanna   Hi.

Felicia   Jo-*anna* . . .

Joanna   Fel-*icia*. What? (**Felicia** *is looking away.*)

Felicia   What are you doing?

Joanna   Soaking up some rays, obviously.

Felicia   But . . . you're not wearing anything.

Joanna   Not a lot, no. I find that's the best way to get a tan.

Felicia   But it's obscene. (*Beat.*)

Joanna   What?

Felicia   It's not right. It's unchristian to flaunt your body.

Joanna   I'm not flaunting it.

Felicia   You're lying there . . . and, there's a man present.

Lance   I'm not looking . . .

Joanna   What am I supposed to do? If I was draped halfway up the side of the house whistling at passers-by, then perhaps I might be accused of flaunting myself. As it is, I'm simply lying here minding my own business. (*Beat.*) Which is something you might care to consider doing.

Felicia   I'm sorry, but public nudity is obscene.

Joanna   So don't look.

Felicia   Joanna, your body is a temple, given to you by God. Show disrespect for your body and you're showing disrespect for Him. Drink and drugs and promiscuity, all these things people do with their bodies, they hurt God. They hurt him bad. And I mean, do you want to cause the Lord pain? Do you? It's like someone who loves you gives you an incredible gift on your birthday, and you take the wrapping off and go 'Hey, wow, neat gift' and you throw it down in the dirt and trample on it. Is that what you do to someone who loves you so much he gave you the gift of life? (*Beat.*)

Joanna   Christ . . . beam me up, Scotty. (*Pause.*)

Felicia   You know, in the States people get arrested if they appear like that in public.

Joanna   'In the States . . .' I'm sick of the bloody States frankly. We're not in the States, in case you hadn't noticed. We're in stupid old England, where it's not considered a criminal or moral offence to want to get your tits brown. So lay off, for Christ's sake. Stop trying to make everybody conform to your Sunday school bloody morals.

Felicia   There's no need to be offensive.

Joanna   OK. Stop calling me obscene and I'll stop being offensive. Let me live my life my way and I promise I won't comment again on your tedious bloody sermonising.

Felicia *turns away and starts to strum the guitar. She begins humming a Christian song.*

Oh for crying out loud . . . (**Felicia** *sings.*) Shut that bloody racket up, *please.* (*Beat.*) This really is too much. (*Beat.*) All I want is a suntan! Is that too much to ask?

Felicia *sings.* **Joanna** *gets up, furious, and collects her things together. As she's about to go,* **Lance** *talks to her out of* **Felicia**'*s carshot.*

Lance   We could, er, maybe go skinny dipping. (*Smiling.*) Well? (*Beat.*)

Joanna   You complete and utter PRAT! (*She walks off into the house.*) JESUS FUCKING WEPT!

She's gone. **Felicia** *stops playing.* **Lance** *stands. Long pause.* **Felicia** *turns round.*

Felicia   What's gotten into her?

Lance   Search me. (*Pause.*) That's a nice song.

Felicia   Thanks. (*Beat.*) Joanna's not born again, is she?

Lance   I don't think so, no. (*Beat.*)

Felicia   I expected everyone who worked for Reverend Hoffman to be Christian.

Lance   You'd have thought so, wouldn't you?

Felicia   I mean, how are we supposed to reach the correct spiritual level if one of the cast behaves the way she just did? I'll be in the middle of a scene, a really crucial scene maybe, and I'll suddenly look at her and think: I've seen those breasts.

Lance   I know what you mean.

Felicia   And I can't be expected to act under those conditions.

Lance   It's not on. (*Beat.*) I thought you were great this morning, by the way.

Felicia   Why thank you. I was real nervous.

Lance   It didn't show.

Felicia   Really? That's nice of you.

Lance   I thought Joanna was possibly a bit . . .

Felicia   What?

Lance   I don't know the right word. (*Beat.*) Wooden? Is
that right?

Felicia   That is absolutely right. You know, I am so
pleased to hear somebody else say that.

Lance   Maybe you should say something to the Reverend.
I mean, he's the director.

Felicia   Maybe I should. (*She picks up the other mitt.*) C'mon,
pitch me one.

Lance   I'm not much good . . .

Felicia   Go for it. (*He throws.*)

Ruth *appears from the house and shouts.*

Ruth   Freddy! (*Beat.*) Freddy!

Lance   Lost him?

Ruth (*giving* **Lance** *a hostile look*)   I doubt it. Damn, I
want him to move some furniture.

Lance   Can I help?

Ruth   No thanks. In fact, I'd rather you didn't even come
into the house while you're wearing that obscenity. (*The T-
shirt.*)

Lance   It's a free country.

Ruth   Not when the United States disapproves of your
elected government, it's not.

Lance (*he smirks*)   Oh, that old line, really . . .

Ruth   I beg your pardon? (*Beat. He decides to go for it.*)

Lance   I don't suppose you've been? To Nicaragua?

Ruth   No, I haven't, so what?

Lance   So many people haven't been, but think they

know what went on there. So many people. Well I've been.
And I know what went on.

Ruth   And what would you have been doing there,
precisely?

Lance   I was there working for the Free World
Foundation.

Ruth   Oh my God, The Oliver North Fan Club.

Lance   Ma'am I'm just the simple follower of an
unemployed Jewish carpenter from Nazareth.

Ruth   Give me strength. (*Beat.*) Please remove that T-shirt
before you enter my house. And please refrain from
discussing politics while you're here. (*She goes.*)

Lance   Whatever happened to free speech?

Felicia *has picked up her guitar.*

Felicia   I guess Miss Hartstone's a radical or something.

Lance   About as radical as a boiled sweet. Champagne
socialist, that's what she is. She lives in this place, and she
wants everybody else to vote Labour. That really makes me
want to barf.

Freddy *appears from the grounds.*

Freddy   Did somebody call me?

Felicia   Ruth. She wanted you to help her with the
furniture.

Freddy   Oh, yeah.

Lance   She declined my offer of help.

Freddy   What a surprise.

Felicia   Would you like some juice?

Freddy   Yeah, why not?

Lance *is a bit put out.*

Felicia   OK. (*She pours him a glass and hands it to him.*)

Freddy   Thanks.

Felicia   You're welcome. (*Beat.*) I just wanted to say how beautiful I think Hartstone is. You must really love it here.

Freddy   Yeah.

Felicia   And I guess we're kind of taking it away from you.

Freddy   Yeah. (*Beat.*)

Felicia   Where will you go?

Freddy   I may go to Africa.

Felicia   Oh, wow, roots and stuff.

Freddy   I don't really know. I've never been. I was born here.

Felicia   Really?

Freddy   Yeah. (*Beat.*) Right. (*He drains his glass.*) I'd better find Ruth.

Felicia   Yeah.

He goes. She and **Lance** *look puzzled. We hear* **Neal**'s *voice from offstage.*

Neal   Where is everybody?

He appears from round the front of the house followed by **Gavin** *and* **Amy**. *They are dressed for church.* **Amy** *wears dark glasses.*

Felicia   Out here.

Neal   Well, this is very pretty.

Gavin   How agreeable. Drinks on the terrace. Lovely.

Amy *sits at the table.*

Felicia   So how was church?

Neal   Honey, one word: boring. Am I right or am I right?

Gavin *smiles.*

Felicia   Church was *boring?*

Neal   Like you would not believe.

Gavin   I'm afraid that's the good old Church of England.
All hush and carpet slippers.

Neal   You don't pussyfoot around the subject of sin. You
don't apologise to folks for even bringing it up. What we
just experienced, that is not a living Gospel, that is living
death. Heck, what in the world is wrong with these people?

Amy   I kind of liked it. It was . . . reflective.

Neal   Honey, shiny surfaces reflect, mirrors reflect. You
don't go to church to reflect. You go to praise the Lord
and hear his word. You go to hear that miracles can
happen. To *see* miracles happen. (*Beat.*) The only miracle
this morning was that I stayed awake.

Gavin   Neal, what you saw this morning was the past.
That's why I wanted you to go. Organised religion over
here has totally lost its way. It is presided over by a group
of men, some of whom proudly claim not even to believe
the truth of the Bible. And they don't even *know* their
Bible. 'Seek ye first the Kingdom of God and His
righteousness.' A pretty simple instruction, you'd think. But
if you only heard the naive political rubbish waffled out
today by people who pretend to be Christian leaders, you'd
despair. These people no longer meet the Biblical
qualifications for Christian leadership. Along with
Communism, on which so many of them were so very soft,
they are already in the dustbin of history.

Neal *beams.*

Neal   Amen. (*Beat.*) Felicia, honey, seeing as you have
your guitar there, what do you say we shake off some of
this Church of England dust and praise the Lord the way
we know how?

Felicia   Amen. You bet. (*She starts to play.*)

Neal   Let's hear it for the Lord!

When they sing, they sway and hold out their arms, occasionally raising them aloft. **Felicia** *starts the song then they all join in.*

Felicia (*singing*)   Lift up your hearts, lift up your hands, lift up your eyes to Jesus.

All   Trust in his word, trust in his love, trust in the hands of Jesus.

Joanna *appears U/S in the house, still topless. She sees them and quickly pulls on her shorts and top and runs out to join them. She stands next to* **Gavin**, *who smiles at her, and joins in the singing.* **Felicia** *looks at* **Lance**, *then at* **Joanna**, *then at* **Lance** *again. He smiles. They sing the chorus.*

Take him on board, for he is the Lord. The family of man is safe in his hands.

Scene Six

The garden, late afternoon. **Freddy** *is tying a fly at the table as* **Ruth** *comes out of the house, carrying a manuscript. He looks up at her then back to the fly.*

Ruth   You said you'd help me with that table earlier.

Freddy   I couldn't find you. Do it later.

Ruth   It's done now. (*Pause. She walks across and puts the manuscript on the table.*) There. I dug it out. (*Pause.*)

Freddy. And what are you going to do with it?

Ruth   What do you think? Send it to the publisher. The offer's still open.

Freddy   When are you going to send it?

Ruth   Tomorrow.

Freddy   And when are you going to tell them? (*Pause. He shakes his head.*) You really are something.

Ruth   Don't. I've had enough. I don't need any lectures.

Freddy   You know it's wrong.

Ruth (*angry*)   It is not wrong! What they're doing is wrong. What I'm trying to do is wring some benefit from a hopeless situation.

Freddy   Stand up to them, then.

Ruth   And starve.

Freddy   Don't make me laugh. (*Pause.*)

Ruth   Freddy, anything I can do to mess things up for Reverend Hoffman, I'll do it. The man is a virus. I've seen it before. God knows I've seen it.

Freddy   So you shaft Hoffman, and you posthumously get to shaft your father. Well, fine, Halleluiah. But what about me? Do I figure in *any* of this?

Ruth   Of course you do. (*She touches the MS.*) This is for you.

Freddy   What they do here will outlive your book. And I still won't exist. Ruth, I've lived my life as nobody. This is all I've known, this is my identity. Give them Hartstone and you give them me. (*Beat.*) Tell them now. Please.

Ruth   Freddy, virtually every penny we get from the sale will go to pay for our debts. And, it will also mean that all those people we ruined will be able to go on living in something like comfort. And we owe them that. (*Beat.*) If I tell Hoffman and Driver *now* . . . Well, the house was on the market for over a year. If I tell them now . . . Oh Christ. I'd be better off dead. (*Long pause.*)

Freddy   It's just like I remember when I was young. Half a world away, people were dying. And you organised a summer school to discuss the implications. A lot of talk about alternatives. Wigwams in the upper pasture. And half a world away, where *I* should have been, people were dying. (*Beat.*) And now you're irrelevant, living proof of the uselessness of free speech. You don't even know what hope is. And your country's been colonised while you talked.

Ruth   It's your country too.

Freddy   No.

Ruth   Freddy . . . (*Pause.*)

Freddy   I'm going to Africa. (*Pause.*) I told you I was thinking about it. I've got a job, if I want it. An irrigation project in Kenya. (*Pause.*)

Ruth   You're leaving me.

Freddy   I'm going home.

Ruth   This is home. (*Pause.*) Freddy, don't leave me, please.

Freddy   I've got to.

Ruth   Why?

Freddy   Because nobody who cares about anything can possibly live in this country any more. (*Pause.*)

Ruth   That's just . . . despair.

Freddy   No, I'm leaving, moving on. You're staying. That's despair. (*Pause. She looks at him.*)

Ruth   I wish I could believe in God.

Freddy *starts tying his fly again as* **Gavin** *appears from the house.*

Gavin   Ah, there you are. Isn't this just . . . idyllic? You must have been so happy here over the years. (*Beat.*) Thanks again for that splendid lunch, it really was delicious. Everything so fresh.

Ruth   Yes, we grow it all here.

Gavin   Of course.

Ruth   I believe you're going to asphalt over the vegetable garden, though.

Gavin   Are we?

Ruth   According to the groundplan you showed me. (*Beat.*)

Gavin We'll be buying in bulk, you see. What with thousands of visitors and everything, well, the vegetable garden would be a bit pointless.

Ruth Yes, pointless.

Gavin I mean, I don't always like it, but we have to think in terms of business. If something doesn't pay its way or could be put to better use, then it has to go. It's tough sometimes, but hey, that's why we're in this game, to turn a buck.

Freddy Then God help us.

Gavin (*chuckling*) Honestly, you two, let go. Some of us have.

Freddy Let go of what?

Gavin The old left/liberal tosh. Come on, forget it, we're all in this together. Let's make it a success. We're all Brits, after all.

Ruth I do wish you wouldn't use that word.

Gavin Which word?

Ruth Brit. It's ugly. It's a word with its head shaved and a tattoo on its forearm. I am British. Or English. I am not a stunted, monosyllabic spit of a word.

Gavin I'm sorry, Ruth, but Brit is what they call us in the States, so as far as I'm concerned, Brit it is. In fact, I feel quite proud to be called a Brit. You arrive at a foreign airport these days and you're greeted with respect. Not like the seventies when anybody with a British passport was a laughing stock.

Ruth So the last thirteen years . . . we went through all that so people like you could hold their heads up in VIP lounges around the globe.

Gavin Britain can hold its head up in the world again. That's the lesson. You see, in the States, the first thing you learn is that with belief and hard work, anything is possible. You also learn working nights to pay your way through Bible college as I did, that there is actually no such thing as class. You are what you are, and you either have character and ability or you don't. You are an individual, not a member of a class. Except in the UK. Here, if it's not some scruffy Trot telling people their place, it's the snobocracy, the Oxbridge elite. (*Beat.*) When I came back to this country, I saw something I'd never realised before. I saw that what we like to think of as respect for tradition was nothing more than a reverence of the decrepit. And the great thing about America is that it is constantly reinventing itself, it's always young and vibrant. We have to make this country more like America, so that *we* can be reinvented. (*Beat.*)

Ruth   The eternal present. Never look back. Forget the past. It sounds like hell. (*Beat.*) Anyway, Gavin, I'm glad your youthful passion wasn't for the Soviet Union. Because if it had been, and you were standing here now extolling the virtues of Mother Russia, I'd be tempted to regard you as the trained agent of a foreign power. Kim Philby in a Mickey Mouse hat. (*Beat.*)

Gavin   It's very easy to sneer when you see a bit of enthusiasm . . .

Ruth   I'm not sneering . . .

Gavin   Very easy for people like you. Sitting in your perfect garden on a perfect summer's day, your inherited wealth earning interest with every second that ticks off on the antique grandfather clock in the hallway.

Ruth   Now who's sneering?

Freddy   I want to know what you think gives you the right to do what you do. Who asked you to reinvent us? What right do you have?

Gavin   Given the last four election results, wouldn't you say the people have given us the right.

Freddy   A minority of people.

Gavin A parliamentary majority.

Freddy Semantics.

Gavin Democracy.

Freddy Bollocks. Your only mandate comes from American big business and American foreign policy ambitions.

Gavin Oh, really . . .

Ruth Tell me, why is it that with all your talk about change, about what this country needs, you never once express any sort of respect for this country or its people? You impose the American way of life on us as if we're just laboratory rats. And all for what? Because you're in this game to turn a buck. Not a pound, I notice. A buck. (*Beat.*) Nothing about this country has ever been good enough for you, has it? (*Beat.*) And you don't really give a damn, you don't care what awfulness you create, because you never gave a damn for us in the first place. (*Beat.*)

Freddy And I'm sure you know, Mr Driver, we're bankrupt. There's no inherited wealth earning any interest. What little extra Ruth ever had, she tended to give away to good causes. Libraries, mostly. And when the local school couldn't afford textbooks, she bought them some. (*He starts to go.*) And the grandfather clock hasn't worked since nineteen seventy two. (*He goes.*)

Ruth I'm sure you'll be glad to know that thanks to me your future workforce has at least *seen* a book.

Gavin Not especially, no.

Ruth I don't know why that surprises me.

Gavin The skills children need to learn today won't be found in books.

Ruth Skills?! Books are about more than skills.

Gavin Sentimental claptrap. Another liberal hobby horse rears its ugly head. Look, literacy is only a phase in human development. As soon as more efficient forms of information technology become established, books will die out. It's already started to happen. Look at the States, Japan. Children are visual-literate now. They read comics, they watch TV, they use computers. They don't read books! There's no need.

Ruth   No need? (*Beat.*) My God ... that is the saddest thing I have ever heard. That makes me despair. (*She is very upset. He laughs.*)

Gavin   Really, Ruth, the world moves on.

Lance *appears at the French windows.*

Lance   Gavin, the clinic is on the phone.

Gavin   Oh no, not now, please ... (*He goes to the house and turns back to* **Ruth**.) Of course, there's one book that will never go out of print. Praise the Lord.

He disappears indoors. **Lance** *hovers.*

Lance   Lovely day. (*Beat.*) God's in his heaven, all right. (*Beat.*)

Ruth   Just go away, please.

Lance   Sorry?

Ruth   Go away. (*Beat.*)

Lance   Yeah, sure ...

He hovers a moment then goes into the house. Pause. As she is about to go, **Amy** *appears from the grounds with some picked flowers. They look at each other.*

Amy   I picked these. I hope that's OK. (**Ruth** *nods.*) The lilies of the field. (*Beat.*) You OK?

Ruth   Mmmm. You?

Amy   I guess. (*Beat.*) I wanted to apologise ...

Ruth   No, don't.

Amy   I should ...

Ruth   People behaving badly has never bothered me. Anyway, I think you have cause. It's just . . . your husband . . .

Amy   Isn't he a wonderful man? (*Beat.*)

Ruth   Is that really what you think? (*Beat.*)

Amy   I have problems. My husband understands and helps me through them.

Ruth   You never stop to wonder whether he might not be your biggest problem?

Amy   My biggest problem is sin.

Ruth   According to your husband.

Amy   According to God.

Ruth   They are not one and the same thing.

Amy *looks puzzled.*

Have you ever tried counselling?

Amy   No.

Ruth   Why not?

Amy   Obviously, secular counselling would be no use. Those people don't have a message. Without Christianity as their base, they have no hope to offer.

Ruth   According to your husband, no doubt.

Amy   Until . . . until I met Neal, I was lost. But through him, I came to God and Jesus Christ. I was real confused, then one morning I woke up and realised I was going to spend the rest of time with the Lord. (*Beat.*) Oh boy. (*Beat.*) Now, when I have to make a decision, the Lord's right there to take it for me. Like Neal says, He's the boss, He calls in the plays.

Ruth   Yes. I see.

Amy   And until you get to know him, you don't know how kind and loving Neal can be. (*Beat.*) Marriage can be like that, not the way they always show it on TV and in the movies. (*Beat.*) And when I was in the hospital, he sent me roses every day. (*Beat.*) And ... I can't sleep in a South-facing room. So we never do. I don't like flying at night. So we don't. Or he lets me take a different flight ... (*Pause. She seems lost.*) Sometimes, it's like my whole life is a movie. Like I've just been watching it happen. (*Beat.*)

Ruth   I'm very sorry. (*Beat.*)

Amy   What? (*Beat.*) I picked these flowers. I hope that's OK. (*Beat.*)

Ruth   The lilies of the field.

Amy   Yes.

Gavin *comes out of the house.*

Gavin   Amy, Neal wants you. Something about the movie. He's with Felicia in the sitting room.

Amy   OK.

She goes as **Joanna** *comes out of the house.*

Ruth   Excuse me. (*She starts to go.*) Oh, how's your wife?

Gavin   She's gone into labour.

Ruth   Does that mean you'll be leaving us?

Gavin   No.

Ruth   Oh.

Gavin   And before you add male chauvinism to my many crimes, this is the first birth in five for which I won't be present.

Ruth   Five?

Gavin   Yes.

Ruth   My, what a fecund man you are. (*She goes, taking the manuscript with her.*)

Joanna   Sounds a bit rude: fecund.

Gavin   It means fertile.

Joanna   I know. (*Beat.*)

Gavin   What are you up to?

Joanna   Absolutely fat zero. Honestly, these people are getting me down. If it isn't Loony Lance sniffing round me every time I set foot outside my room, it's Felicia treating me like some sort of witch because I did a bit of topless sunbathing.

Gavin   You what?

Joanna   Oh, not you too . . .

Gavin   Joanna, you do not sunbathe half naked around Born Again Christians.

Joanna   Well, obviously, I know that now.

Gavin   Have a little thought. Show some restraint.

Joanna   What, like you? (*Beat.*)

Gavin   You want to go to the States, don't you?

Joanna   'Course.

Gavin   Well then. (*Beat.*)

Joanna   Do you feel at all guilty? (*Pause. He stares at her. Beat.* **Lance** *has come out of the house.*)

Lance   Gavin, Neal's shouting for you.

Gavin   Right.

He goes into the house. **Lance** *circles round* **Joanna**, *a strange look on his face.*

Joanna   If you're going to creep around like some lovesick stick insect, Lance, I'm off. (*Beat.*) Come on, Lance, have a bit of dignity. (*He chuckles.*) Look, you're neither moody nor mysterious. I am seriously unimpressed.

Lance   Two. Two mistakes. That I know of.

Joanna   Sorry, Lance?

Lance   You've made two mistakes, so far. (*Beat.*) Upsetting your co-star was one. I do believe that at this very minute she's pouring poison into Neal's ear. Poison to the effect that you're one very unchristian lady who prances around naked the minute our backs are turned, and ridicules the word of God, to boot. (*Beat.*) The other . . . well, how can I put this delicately? (*Beat.*) Just how long have you been fucking Gavin? (*Beat.*)

Joanna   Oh God . . .

Lance   Well, doesn't matter. Once is enough.

Joanna   You've been spying . . .

Lance   Funnily enough, yes. (*Beat.*)

Joanna   Lance, please . . . this film means everything to me. It means I get to go to LA. Gavin's arranged for me to see some agents. I might get a part in a soap or a mini-series. Please. It's everything I've always wanted. What option do I have if Gavin says he wants to go to bed with me? (*Beat.*) Please. It's my dream. (*Beat.*)

Lance   You're sort of like a prostitute really, aren't you?

Joanna   Not through choice. (*Beat.*) Please, Lance. (*Beat.*)

Lance   Well. Having you thrown off the film wouldn't do anything for *me*. (*Beat.*) Likewise, I don't see that I have very much to gain from blowing Gavin out. I'll go further with him than without him. So. (*Beat.*)

Joanna   You won't say anything? (*Beat.*)

Lance   No. (*Beat.*)

Joanna   Oh, Lance. (*She hugs him.*) Thank you. You've saved my life.

Lance   Yes. I have. However. (*Beat.*) There has to be something in this for me. Charity's not exactly my thing, really. (*Beat.*) What's Gavin like? You know. Is he any good? I assume he's very missionary, but you can never tell. Eh?

Joanna   What?

Lance   How does he do it? Wham bam? Huffing and puffing? That's what I imagined. Oh, well, tell me later. (*Pause.*) You know down by the river, there's that old boathouse? Yes?

Joanna   Yes.

Lance   Well, about fifty yards further on, there's a sort of shed. Go there. I'll follow you in a minute. (*Beat.*)

Joanna   Go there now?

Lance   Yes. And when you get there, strip. Take all your clothes off. (*Beat.*)

Joanna   Then? (*Beat.*)

Lance   Then . . . you stuck-up, middle class tramp, when I get there, I'm going to fuck the arse off you. OK. (*Beat.*) Say 'OK, Lance'. (*Beat.*)

Joanna   OK, Lance. (*Beat.*)

Lance   Right. Well, off you go. (*She hesitates then slowly moves off. She turns and looks at him.*) See you in a minute! (*She goes.*) Missing you already!

Fade

Scene Seven

The garden, about 9.00 pm. Centre stage is a trestle table from which dinner has been eaten. It has a white tablecloth, candleabra and flowers as well as the remains of dinner on it. There are nine chairs round the table. Standing to one side, holding his mobile phone, is **Gavin**. *He smokes a cigar, looking faintly upset.* **Lance** *comes on, a bit drunk, carrying a fresh bottle of brandy, which he waves in* **Gavin***'s direction with a smile.* **Gavin** *smiles back.*

Lance   Here we are. (*He pours two brandies.*) Did you get through?

Gavin   Yes. (*Beat.*) There's been a complication, they might have to do a Caesarean.

Lance   Bad news.

Gavin   Not especially. Sophie and the baby seem quite well, so . . . (**Lance** *raises his glass.*) Cheers. (*They clink glasses.*)

Lance (*indicating the table*)   They certainly know how to put on a spread.

Gavin   What, in my schooldays, we'd have called a slap-up do. (*Beat.*) Is there any sign yet of Joanna?

Lance   Funnily enough, no.

Gavin   As if she's not in enough trouble, silly girl. She's pushing her luck, you know. Her absence at dinner was noticed.

Beat.

Lance   The noble savage hasn't been around either.

Gavin   Freddy? You don't think . . . ? (*Beat.*) That's all we need.

Lance   Quite. Still, mustn't get jealous, eh? (*Slight frisson.*)

Gavin   You're rather keen on her, aren't you?

Lance   She's OK.

Gavin   You should ask her out. (**Lance** *shrugs.*) It's about time you thought about settling down, you know. You're, what, twenty six?

Lance   Twenty seven.

Gavin   Well, there you are. The ladies won't wait forever. Settle down. Get yourself a firm loving base. (*Beat.*) Children, they're the clincher. Nothing's ever the same again once you've had children. It really is a miracle, birth. Absolute miracle. When you've seen a child being born, you can believe anything is possible; that the material world has limits that can be overcome. (*Beat.*)

Lance I wonder if your wife sees it that way.

Gavin Oh, she does. She's as happy as I am.

Lance No, I mean right now. Now there's a surgeon standing over her in a mask, scalpel in hand, about to slit her belly open.

Gavin Lance, really . . .

Lance I expect that's one miracle she could probably do without. (*Beat.*)

Gavin I feel bad enough already about not being there. Please . . .

Lance I've seen it done. In Nicaragua. Except it wasn't a surgeon, it was one of our guys. And it wasn't a scalpel, it was a machete. (*Beat.*)

Gavin What are you saying?

Lance I'd have thought it was pretty clear.

Gavin I don't believe you.

Lance *leans forward and smiles.*

Lance I have photographs. (*Beat.*)

Gavin Are you talking about a pregnant woman?

Lance Yeah.

Gavin Dead? Alive? What?

Lance Half dead.

Gavin Half dead? Half dead is still alive.

Lance Not in that part of the world it isn't. (*Beat.*)

Gavin Is this the truth? Or are you just showing off?

Lance (*he smirks*) It's the truth. (*Beat.*)

Gavin I've never seen this side of you before, Lance. A word of advice, let's not see it again, eh?

Lance (*venomous*) Hey . . . we won. Yeah? (*Beat.*) You think we did it nice? You think we walked in with a Bible and a smile? (*Beat.*) We did whatever was thought necessary. I was there! Don't pretend you don't know. Enterprise Faith was one of the Foundation's biggest backers. (*Beat.*) Sure, our boys massacred civilians when necessary, they tortured and murdered prisoners. (*Beat.*) And *we* kept the photographs. We controlled the information because that's how you win wars. (*Long pause.*)

Gavin   I think you should pray to God . . .

Lance   You don't understand, do you . . . ?

Gavin   Pray for forgiveness . . .

Lance   It's all built on blood. Not love.

Gavin *starts to pray.*

Gavin   Heavenly Father, into whose care we commit our souls . . .

Lance   Oh, shut it . . .

Gavin   Look down with forgiveness on our unworthiness . . .

Lance *pulls* **Gavin**'s *hands apart.*

Lance   Don't include me in that. Fucking hypocrite.

Long pause as **Gavin** *gathers himself together. He takes a sip of brandy.*

Gavin   I don't like to have to say this to you Lance . . . I had hopes for you. I thought I saw some of me in you. I'd almost come to think of you as a son. (*Beat.*) I guess I was wrong. (*Beat.*) You realise . . . you can't go on working for me. I've no option but to let you go. You do realise that? (*Beat.*) Well. I'm very sorry.

Lance   No need to be.

Gavin   There is. I made an error of judgement.

Lance   You said it.

Gavin   It's as much my fault as yours. I take the blame.

Lance   Like I said, no need. (*Beat.*) Nobody's going to know any of this. You're not going to tell them. And you're not going to 'let me go'. Because I'm not going to tell anybody that you've been screwing Joanna. (*Beat.*) Gavin Driver, father of four, number five about to pop, the Lord's representative here on earth. Got caught with his dick in the cookie jar. (*Beat.*) But like I said, I'm not going to tell. OK?

Gavin   Do I have your word that this will never come out?

Lance   Yes.

Gavin   Your *word?*

Lance   Yes. I like this work. It suits me. Not going to queer my pitch, am I? (*Beat.*)

Gavin   I feel I want to punch you, very hard.

Lance   I can relate to that. It's guilt.

Neal *appears from the house.*

Neal   Gavin, there you are. What's the news?

Gavin   Sorry, Neal?

Neal   Holy smoke, man, your wife. I thought you came out here to call her.

Gavin   Oh, sorry, yes, there's been a complication. They're going to have to do a Caesarean.

Neal   I'm sorry to hear that.

Gavin   They were worried about the baby's heartbeat.

Neal   Later, we'll all pray. It's in the Lord's hands, there's nothing to fear.

From the grounds **Freddy** *and* **Joanna** *appear.* **Joanna** *looks upset but otherwise OK. Neither speaks. Beat.*

Gavin   Joanna, where the hell do you think you've been?

She walks past him to the house.

Joanna? (*Beat.*)

Freddy *stops and looks quizzically at* **Gavin** *and* **Lance**. **Joanna**'*s gone in. Beat.*

Have you two been off together somewhere?

Freddy *stares at him, then at* **Lance**, *then turns and goes. Beat.*

Neal   Lance. Maybe you could go inside, hustle everybody along.

Lance   OK. (*He goes.*)

Neal   He's a fine boy. Now, that actress. What sort of a contract do we have her on?

Gavin   Why?

Neal   Because we're going to have to lose her. (*Beat.*)

Gavin   It'll cost.

Neal   How much?

Gavin   I'm not sure . . . somewhere in the region of six thousand.

Neal   Dollars or sterling?

Gavin   Sterling. (*Beat.*)

Neal   OK. Call her agent tomorrow. And don't worry about a replacement. We'll get somebody in the States. (*Beat.*)

Gavin   May one ask why? (*Beat.*)

Neal   For this company to work properly, we must have the right personnel at every level. Every time. Just one person spreading doubt can infect the whole organisation. I need Christians, not backsliders. (*Beat.*) We're a happy company. And I won't tolerate anybody upsetting that.

Gavin   What has she done that's so terrible? (*Beat.*) Come on, if you're talking about a bit of harmless sunbathing . . .

Neal   I am not talking about anything harmless. I'm talking about deeply unchristian behaviour. I'm talking about ridiculing the Christian faith. (*Beat.*) And where was she tonight?

Gavin   She's a young woman Neal, I can't keep her under lock and key.

Neal   Well that's just too bad. You work for me, you have responsibilities. Being here for dinner was one of them. She struck out three times. She walks. OK?

Gavin   I think you're being hasty.

Neal   Gavin, you are supposed to be on my team. You're the one who told me he could handle this side of things. The Brit side. You're the one who told me what to look out for: the laziness, the lack of commitment, the slacking on the job. (*Beat.*) Now, if you're telling me that when it comes to it, you can't hack it, then I'll have to find myself somebody who can.

Gavin   I'm not telling you that. It's just . . . oh, yes, you're right. Yes. I suppose I was being soft. (*Beat.*)

Neal   Nothing else? (*Beat.*)

Gavin   I'm sorry? Could you clarify that for me?

Neal   The Devil lays traps for us all. Could be he laid one for you?

Gavin   I'm not sure I understand . . .

Neal   Heck, I'm only saying you might have got a little fonder of the girl than you intended. (*Beat.*)

Gavin   My wife is, at this very moment, lying on an operating table, about to undergo a Caesarean section. All I can think is that I want to be there with her. How many times today do you think I nearly got in the car and drove off to be with her? How many phone calls do you think I've made? (*Beat.*) I stayed for you. For Enterprise Faith. I put you first. (*Beat.*)

Neal   It wasn't really necessary. You know this weekend is largely ceremonial.

Gavin   What?! You wouldn't have lasted two minutes here with Ruth. I'm surprised, frankly, that she didn't tell you to leave after last night. Anybody else would have.

Neal   With two million on the table?

Gavin   You don't know her. They're perverse these people. She would get a real kick out of throwing that money right back in your face. That, for her, would be a moral gesture. (*Beat.*) I spent six months of my life setting up this deal. Do you really think I'd chuck it all in the bin for a piece of skirt? (*Pause.*)

Neal   Oh, Gavin. People do the strangest things. (*Beat.*) OK. Forgive me. Please. I shouldn't have doubted you.

Gavin   I don't have to forgive you, Neal. I know what a good man you are.

Lance *comes out of the house followed by* **Amy** *and* **Felicia**.

Gavin   OK, everyone, we're nearly ready. If you'd all like to take a seat.

Amy, Felicia *and* **Lance** *sit.* **Ruth** *comes out of the house, carrying the contracts and a typewritten manuscript.*

Gavin   Ah, the guest of honour. (*He ushers* **Ruth** *to the centre chair at the table.*)

Ruth   First time I've ever been a guest in my own house.

Gavin   That's it, Ruth, let's have you at the head. (*She sits.*)

Neal   OK. Let's get on. (*He sits at the opposite end of the table to where* **Gavin** *is standing.*)

Gavin   Firstly, as you know, we're here to witness an historic moment. This building, these grounds, hold a very special meaning for us at Enterprise Faith. To be able to establish our ministry here has been a dream we have long cherished. A dream which is about to come true. (*Beat.*)

Where did that dream originate? It springs, of course, from
the miraculous events of forty years ago, but equally, it
springs from the man who made this achievement possible.
The man who so reveres the word of God that he has
devoted his whole life to bringing the word to the people
of the world. The man opposite me, who I am proud to
call colleague, friend and mentor, the Reverend Neal
Hoffman.

He taps the table, as does **Lance**. **Felicia** *claps and does a
whoop. Beat.*

Neal, I know what Hartstone means to you. It's a dream
I've lived with for many years. All I can say is, I'm thrilled
to be here, to be able to see the fulfilment of the dream
and to see a piece of God's kingdom established here on
earth.

He sits. The Enterprise Faith people clap. **Neal**, *looking very
pleased, slowly gets to his feet.*

Neal   Well . . . uh . . . I thank you. From the bottom of
my heart, Gavin, I thank you. Forty years ago, a
missionary family returned from Africa to Britain, their
work, for the time being, done. They were a pious and
energetic family. Through their calling they converted and
healed many thousands. They brought light to the darkness
that was that great continent, and brought many souls to
Jesus Christ. On their return, they were struck with a great
affliction; their elder daughter had contracted a fatal
disease. Conventional medicine could do nothing for her, so
the family prayed day and night. There was some relief,
but in time it became clear that the Lord's will was that
she should be with Him. The family trusted in God's
purpose for their daughter and waited for her time to
come. During this time, as her mother shows so movingly
in the memoir she wrote a little later, the daughter became
an inspiration to them all. Her spirit and her faith
strengthened them all. Nobody was not touched by her
immense courage. All were impressed by the resolution and
wisdom this fifteen year old girl showed in the face of

death. She was living proof that death is only the
beginning of our journey to everlasting life. (*Beat.*) When
her time came, the family gathered not sadly but gladly, to
witness her final triumph over death. And a miracle
happened. As she breathed her last in prayer, the Lord
Jesus Christ appeared to them all, smiling down on his
charge. And taking her hand gently, he led her soul to
Heaven. (*He is moved by his telling of the story.*) When I first
read that book, I made a promise. I said to myself, we will
take our ministry to this miraculous place, and from there
we will spread the word of God right across the globe.
(*Beat.*) Well, here we are! (*The Enterprise Faith people applaud.*)
Here we are, Lord! (*Beat.*) Let all our efforts be for the
glory of God, that we may in time establish on this earth
His one true universal kingdom!

The Enterprise Faith people 'amen' and applaud.

Now . . .

Neal *motions to* **Gavin***, who gets up and starts to spread the
contracts out in front of* **Ruth***.*

Gavin   OK, Ruth. We'd like you to sign here.

He holds a pen out to her. Beat. She takes it. Beat. **Freddy** *comes
out of the house.* **Ruth** *looks at him. She gently puts the pen down.*

Ruth   I hope you don't mind . . . (*She stands.*)

Gavin   Of course not.

Neal   Say a few words, Ruth. (*Beat.*)

Ruth   A few words . . . (*Beat.*) Yes. You're right, Freddy. I
ask you to forgive me. (*Beat.*) In all the Christian
vocabulary, the word which means most to me is probably
the simplest, yet the most problematical. It is a word
which, whenever I hear it, chimes in my heart with a force
I imagine the scriptures do in yours. That word is truth.
(*Beat.*) I don't pretend to know any one big truth, I leave
that to the men of God. But I have always believed that
the truth protects us from pain. Without the truth, we will
believe anything. When we believe anything, we become

victims of the cruel and the greedy. (*Beat.*) I said I don't
know any one big truth. That's not strictly, er, true. The
truth is: I have lied to you. And now, I just want to tell
the truth. (*Beat.*) I have written a book, an autobiography. I
have told the story of my family, and of my sister Grace in
particular. Perhaps it would have been more honest of me
to have told you this earlier, but I'm afraid I lacked the
courage. Or perhaps I was just being greedy. Well. (*Beat.*)
The book my mother wrote is pure fantasy from beginning
to end. To begin with, our time in Africa was a miserable
failure. We bribed many, we converted few. And thanks to
my father's only slight grasp of matters scientific, his
pioneering irrigation techniques led to many, many deaths.
We didn't arrive back in England our work done, we were
ordered back in disgrace. Luckily, my grandfather had a
better grasp of reality than my father, and he left us
Hartstone to come back to. Otherwise we would probably
have starved. What an irony that would have been. (*Beat.*)
My mother . . . my mother was a devoted Christian, who
liked to think she had dedicated her life to God. In actual
fact, she dedicated her life to a series of fantasies. She
fantasised my father's greatness, she fantasised their
achievements in Africa, and most of all, she fantasised my
sister's death. (*Beat.*) Grace was not in the grip of a
terminal illness when we returned from Africa. When we
returned, she was, in fact, six months, or thereabouts,
pregnant. (*Beat.*) It was too late by the time my parents
found out to do anything about the baby. And believe me,
they would have. Anything rather than live with the truth.
Instead, we came back here, and Grace was confined, a
prisoner in that tiny room upstairs. From the day we
returned, my father never spoke to Grace. As far as I
know, he never saw her again. (*Beat.*) She died giving birth.
There was no doctor, my mother didn't believe in doctors.
I think they hoped the baby would die too, but he was
strong, very strong. But poor Grace died in more agony
than you will ever be able to imagine. A frightened,
tortured fifteen year old girl, left in unbearable pain for
hours, to die. (*Beat.*) I like to think that Christ would have

appeared and gently led her to heaven, but I heard her screams, and I can tell you: they came from hell. (*Beat.*) My poor dear sister. (*Beat.*) The child, of course, is my darling Freddy.

Amy *is quietly sobbing;* **Felicia** *is looking urgently at* **Neal**, *who is staring fixedly at* **Ruth**. **Gavin**'s *head has dropped.* **Lance** *pours a drink.*

Ruth   I'm sorry. My stupid mother's book . . .

Amy   WHY!?

Ruth   Because it's the truth! (*Beat.*) I'm sorry. (*Long pause.*)

Neal   Ruth . . . you didn't sign the papers. (*Beat.*)

Ruth   I don't intend to. (*Beat.*)

Gavin   Neal . . . don't you think we should talk?

Neal   Not right now, Gavin, no. Please . . . Ruth. I thought we had a deal here. I've spent a lot of time, invested a lot of money. I really think you should sign.

Ruth   Are you deaf?

Neal   Oh, I hear you fine. (*Beat.*) You want to up the price? Is that what this is all about?

Ruth   No . . .

Neal   OK. Two point two five. (*Beat.*) Two and a half. That's the best I can do.

Amy   Neal . . . didn't you hear? What she said?

Neal   This is business, honey.

Amy   What if it's true!?

Neal   True? This woman doesn't know the truth. She only knows what Satan tells her.

Amy (*distraught*)   But what if it's not Satan?!

Neal   It is.

Amy   How do you know?!

Neal   Because I know!! (*Beat.*) Felicia, be so good as to take my wife inside, will you? Thank you.

Amy   I don't want to . . .

Neal   You're all upset . . .

Amy   But I don't want to.

Neal   Go. Inside. Now.

Beat. **Felicia** *takes her arm and stands her up.*

Amy   What if it's true . . . ?

Beat. **Amy** *turns and starts to go.* **Felicia** *puts her arm around her and takes her off.* **Ruth** *holds up the manuscript.*

Ruth   I have a publisher for this.

Neal   I don't doubt that. (*Beat.*)

Ruth   I don't want your money. I thought I could go through with it. Take the money and run. The prevailing wisdom. Well, I can't. I don't care if I die here, poor and cold and hungry. Anything . . . anything rather than see you profit from a lie.

Neal   I suppose you think that's principled.

Ruth   I don't know, but I damn well hope so.

Joanna *appears from the house carrying* **Freddy**'s *shotgun. She walks straight up to* **Lance** *and points it at his head.*

Joanna   You! (*They all turn.*) Get up!

Gavin   What the devil . . . ?

Joanna   I said get up!

Lance (*rising, frightened*)   Look, for Christ's sake . . .

Gavin   Put that bloody thing down.

Joanna (*to* **Gavin**)   And you. You get up too.

Neal   Put the gun down, young lady.

Joanna   Oh shut your great fat face. (*She motions* **Gavin**

and **Lance** *to one side.*) OK. Kneel down. Come on, kneel down, hands behind your heads. Let's do this right.

They kneel, **Gavin** *upright,* **Lance** *low and cringing.*

Ruth   What exactly are you going to do, dear?

Joanna   I'm going to do to them what they did to me. Only I'm going to do it with this.

Ruth   You don't really want to do that.

Joanna   No? Why don't I? Why should I have to take it all in silence?

Ruth   Freddy . . . (**Freddy** *raises his hand a little.*)

Lance   Please . . .

Joanna   Please!? That's not what you said a few hours ago, is it? No please then. No fucking please then!

Ruth   We get the point, Joanna. Put the gun down. Please.

Joanna (*pointing it at* **Gavin**)   And you . . .

Ruth   You'll hurt someone.

Joanna   Why should I care? *They* hurt people. They don't care.

Ruth   But you're not them.

Freddy *walks calmly up beside* **Joanna**.

Freddy   It's OK. It can't be loaded. I keep the cartridges locked away.

Pause. **Joanna** *starts to laugh.* **Lance** *suddenly leaps up to attack her.* **Freddy** *grabs him in a headlock.*

Freddy   I could break your neck.

Lance *struggles and* **Freddy** *tightens his grip.* **Lance** *squeals.*

Freddy   Just don't move. (*Pause.* **Freddy** *slowly relaxes his grip.*) Now. Sit.

Lance *slowly sits at the table.* **Gavin** *is kneeling upright, his hands over his face.* **Ruth, Neal** *and* **Lance** *sit at the table.* **Freddy** *stands over* **Lance. Joanna** *stands to one side, quietly laughing. Pause.*

Ruth   Right. Has anybody got any idea what we do now?

Scene Eight

The garden, 10.00 a.m. Monday morning. It is as it was, with the garden furniture back in place. **Felicia** *is sitting at the table strumming her guitar and singing. Upstage,* **Lance** *carries suitcases from the house to the car.* **Amy** *appears.*

Felicia   'Softly and tenderly, Jesus is calling.'

Amy   Felicia? Honey? You all packed?

Felicia   Uh huh. It's in the limo.

Amy   OK.

She goes back in. **Lance** *comes for more cases as* **Neal** *comes out. He comes down to* **Felicia,** *puts his hand on her head and smiles.*

Neal   That's very pretty.

Felicia   Sir? What's going to happen now? Are you still going to make the movie?

Neal   I doubt that. (*Beat.*) Don't worry, there'll be plenty more movies.   •

Felicia   Why would Miss Hartstone make up something like that? Why?

Neal   Too many questions, young lady. There's only one question you should ask: 'Do I love the Lord?' Answer that correctly, and you won't need to ask any more.

Felicia   But there's . . .

Neal   Hmm? (*Beat.*)

Felicia   Sir.

Gavin *comes out of the house.*

Gavin   Well. Number five, at last.

Neal   Gavin, that is wonderful.

Gavin   A little girl. Seven pounds ten ounces. Mother and daughter both doing fine.

Felicia   Congratulations.

Gavin   Thank You.

Neal *(he shakes* **Gavin**'s *hand)*   You have a name for the little lady? *(Beat.)*

Gavin   What else? Grace.

Neal *beams and throws his arms around* **Gavin** *as* **Freddy** *comes up from the grounds.*

Well, it's the Lord of the Manor. Any sign of Ruth? (**Freddy** *shakes his head.*) I guess she's avoiding us.

Freddy   Probably.

Neal   Felicia, do you think you could fetch Amy for me? I think we're just about ready to leave.

Felicia   OK. *(She goes.)*

Neal   When you see Ruth . . . tell her, the manuscript, whatever she's been offered, I'll pay double. However much it is, I'll double it. OK?

Freddy *(he smiles and shakes his head)*   It's not about truth, is it, for you?

Neal   Young man, it is about God's will.

Freddy   Yeah.

Neal   It is about those millions of people who believe in Him, whose lives are given meaning by the fact of His existence. Those people I exist to serve.

Gavin   Praise the Lord.

Freddy   Oh, man . . . save it.

Neal   Never, ever, ridicule faith.

Lance *enters. Beat.* **Amy** *and* **Felicia** *come out of the house.*
All set, honey?

Amy   Yes. I just called Houston and left a message for
Kimmy. I said I'll be home tomorrow.

Neal   But we have to go see some more properties.

Amy   I'm going home, Neal. *(Beat.)*

Neal   Yeah. Sure, OK.

Amy   Fine. *(Beat.)* We'll wait in the car. *(She and* **Felicia**
go.)

Neal   Well. A setback, that's all. We'll find another
location. I have a mission, and nothing deflects me from
that. It's why I was put on this earth. We have the money
and we have the will. Sooner or later, God's truth will
prevail. *(Beat.)* Tell Ruth from me . . . she changes her
mind about selling, she has my number.

Freddy   She won't change her mind.

Neal   Then that is God's will. *(Beat.)* Well, let's roll.

Gavin   I'll be with you in two seconds, Neal.

Neal   Sure. Don't be long now. *(He goes.)*

Gavin   Ruth's book won't hurt us. If you attack us, it
only strengthens our faith and brings us more followers.
The faithful will still believe, whatever. That's why they're
the faithful. *(Beat.)* You can send us a bill to cover any
expenses for Joanna.

Freddy   I'll do that. *(Beat.)*

Gavin   Right. Well, goodbye. *(He offers his hand.* **Freddy**
doesn't take it.) In two months' time, this would have been
my home.

Freddy   You don't deserve it.

Gavin *(going)*   One day, Freddy . . . one day.

He's gone. We hear the car engine start. The car pulls away. As the sound dies, **Ruth** *and* **Joanna** *come from the garden.* **Ruth** *has a basket of vegetables,* **Joanna** *has a handful of herbs. They watch the car go.*

Ruth　Gone?

Freddy　Yes.

Ruth　Thank God. Or not, as the case may be.

Joanna　I wish I'd killed them.

Ruth　No, you mustn't wish that. (*Beat.*)

Joanna (*taking vegetable basket from* **Ruth**)　Shall I take those in?

Ruth　Thank you.

Joanna *goes in.* **Ruth** *sits at the table.*

Freddy　He says he'll double the price for the book.

Ruth　He would, wouldn't he?

Freddy　And I expect he'd offer more if you pushed.

Ruth　The only thing I want from Reverend Hoffman is his presence elsewhere. Preferably in another hemisphere. (*Beat.*) Well. You got what you wanted. (*Beat.*) Are you still set on Africa?

Freddy (*he nods*)　So long as I stay here, I'll never really know who I am. (*Long pause.*)

Ruth　We'll still have to sell, you know. Only this time it'll probably be a fat property developer or some ghastly pop singer.

Freddy　At least we beat that lot off.

Ruth　Yes. God knows why. They'll just keep coming. (*Beat.*) I wish I knew what the point of it all was. (*Beat.*) You know, when Brian, my lovely plumber, ran off . . . well, I make a joke of it now, of course . . . but I was truly heartbroken, you know. I thought I'd found real happiness,

but he went. He just went. And what was the point of it?
The pain, the disappointment, loss . . . (*Beat.*) Mind you,
sometimes I just remember the way his lovely black hair
used to brush his jawline . . . and that makes me feel nice.
So it's not all been bad, I suppose. (*Beat.*)

Freddy   I'm going in. Need anything?

Ruth   A hug. (*She stands and they gently hug. They let go and
she sits again.*) Put the kettle on, will you, darling? I'm
parched. (**Freddy** *smiles and goes.*) Absolutely parched.
(**Ruth** *stares out at the grounds.*)

Fade

Gaucho

Gaucho was first performed on 20 October 1994 at
Hampstead Theatre, London, with the following cast:

Stephanie	Phyllis Logan
Murph	Grant Masters
Declan	Tim McInnerny
Louise	Kate Fahy
Yana	Julia Lane
Spencer	Dominic Jephcott

Directed by Doug Lucie
Designed by Geraldine Pilgrim
Lighting by Chahine Yavroyan
Sound by John Leonard
Artistic Director Jenny Topper

Scene One

An open patio area in a large Mediterranean-style house high in the hills overlooking the sea. Upstage to one side is the top of a flight of steps leading up from the hill. On the other side of the stage is the open doorway into the house. There is a large table and chairs upstage centre. As the lights come up, **Dec** *is standing in the early morning sunshine staring out front through a pair of binoculars. He wears Levi shorts, climbing boots and a grubby white T-shirt, and has the slight beard of a man who has been up all night. He has his foot up on a chair, on which is an automatic sub-machine gun and an ashtray with a joint smoking in it. Resting against the chair is a smart black briefcase. Without taking the binoculars from his eyes, he reaches down for the joint, takes a deep hit and returns it to the ashtray.* **Yana** *enters from the house. She is dishevelled but beautiful. She wears just a long T-shirt and unlaced trainers. She shields her eyes from the sun and puts on her sunglasses. She has only just got up. She saunters across and picks up the joint.*

Yana   What time is it?

Dec   It's about half six.

She yawns.

Yana   Did it go OK?

Dec   Fine. Except some bastard helped himself to twenty kilos somewhere between here and Karachi. (*Beat.*)

Yana   Did Mickey get my smack?

Dec   In the case.

She reaches down for the case and notices something on the gun.

Yana   The catch. You left the catch off.

Dec   Sorry. Forgot.

Yana *slips the safety catch on the gun.*

Yana   Anybody would think you wanted to use the bloody thing.

She takes the case to the table and opens it. She takes out a bag of pure heroin. Throughout the following, she prepares the heroin for smoking. **Dec** *continues looking through the binoculars.*

Dec George was late showing last night. Something wrong with his engine.

Yana Yeah? He's crap, George. (*Beat.*) Who are you watching?

Dec No one.

Yana Why are you watching no one?

Dec *holds his hand up. She shrugs, walks down to him and puts the joint between his fingers.*

Dec Thank you.

Yana You get paranoid, you smoke grass this early. (*She laughs.*) Hah. You stand there with your spyglasses glued on your eyes, watching no one, and I say you *get* paranoid. Some joke. (*She sits at the table again.*) Maybe in the old days, back home, the guards they sat in their towers smoking dope all day and then they couldn't get their spyglasses off their noses because they were all stoned into the middle of last week –

Dec Next week –

Yana *Next* week. (*Beat.*)

Dec It's a theory. (*Beat.*) Any calls last night?

Yana Uh ... yes, your friends from London, they are arriving one o'clock.

Dec Right. (*Beat.*) We'd better have some lunch ready.

Yana Why are they coming here?

Dec Search me. (**Dec** *raises the binoculars slightly and looks at his watch.*) Early risers. Unless they've been up all night.

Yana The no ones? (*Beat.*)

Dec The two men and a woman who moored their boat off the point yesterday. (*She comes and stands next to him. He* *hands her the binoculars.*) Here. (*She looks out to sea.*) What d'you think? French? Italian?

Yana   The woman's clothes are French . . . but she doesn't look French. Not the hair. I don't know . . .

Dec   I can't place them . . .

Yana   There is a man now.

Dec   Which one?

Yana   He wears swim-shorts.

Dec   Tattoo?

Yana   Yes.

Dec   That's the sailor. Seems to know his way round the boat a bit better than the others. Could have some Arab in him.

Yana   I don't think so. (*She passes him the binoculars.*)

He looks and realises something.

Dec   Shit. American?

He hands the binoculars back to her. She looks.

Yana   Another man has come on deck.

Dec   What's he doing?

Yana   He's brought them breakfast on a tray. (*Beat.*) Shitfuck Americans.

Dec *takes a mobile phone from the case and punches up a number.*

The woman is taking photographs. Now the men have gone below.

Dec (*into the phone*)   Mickey? Dec. (*Beat.*) Fine. Get all your chores done? (*Beat.*) Good. Listen –

Yana   She's taking one this way –

Dec   That dog we were talking about yesterday –

Yana   She's focusing –

Dec   Is it friendly? Or?

Yana   She's seen me. She's turning the other way.

Dec   See if you can find out for me, then. Yeah. (*Beat.*)
Appreciate it. OK. (*He turns off the phone and puts it back in the case.*)

Yana   The men have come back on deck.

Dec   Mickey's going to check them out. (*Beat.*) I mean,
tourists moor off there all the time . . . (*Beat.*) Yeah, tourists,
probably.

Yana   OK, I think they are tourists also. (*She goes back to the table and the heroin.*)

Dec   Let's go to the Far East next month.

Yana   OK, why not?

Dec   I want some humidity. I need to sweat. We could
visit Tommy on his island.

Yana (*not keen*)   Yeah . . .

Dec   What?

Yana   Tommy . . .

Dec   Yeah, what? (*Beat.*)

Yana   A dangerous man, that's all.

Dec *laughs.*

Dec   We're all dangerous men.

Yana   And I think he's a grass.

Dec   Never say that. (*Beat.*) Unless you've got a gun in his
ear, and you're about to blow his head off, never say that.
(*Beat.*) Tommy's in business, like I'm in business, and in
business we have to trust dangerous men. If he's grassed
anyone, it's for a reason, not for profit. Sure, I have my
doubts about Tommy. I have my doubts about everyone.
But we've been doing business for fifteen years, and hey,
I'm still here. We lost a few shipments. In fifteen years, we

lost a few shipments . . . accidents, fuck-ups, tip offs. But
Tommy never grassed, not as far as I know. (*Beat.*) If I find
that he has, I'll personally stick a piece in his ear. But if I
find he has, it'll already be too late. I'll be in prison.

Yana   Yes. And Tommy will laugh while you are in
prison.

Dec   Who cares? Prison is simply a state of mind. (*Beat.*)
Like I say, the Far East. Next month, after Zurich. Real
heat. I want to sweat.

Yana   And you want more business.

Dec   Yeah, why not?

Yana   Because you have enough money for a thousand
lives.

Dec   It's not the money. It's never been the money. The
money is purely metaphorical.

Yana   Whatever that means.

Dec   It means I don't have to explain myself.

Yana   Because you can't. The person who explains you,
he will be one very rich man.

Dec   No doubt. (*Pause.*)

Yana   I missed you last night.

Dec   Yeah?

Yana   Well, I turned over and you weren't there. And I
thought, oh, he's working. And it was like you were never
there.

Dec   So you didn't miss me. (*Beat.*)

Yana   Who knows *what* I miss?

Dec   Whatever that means.

Yana   It means *I* don't have to explain myself. (*Beat.*) Last
night I wanted to chain you up. If you were there.

Dec That would have been nice.

Yana Yes, but you weren't there.

Dec I'm here now.

Yana You want that I hurt you?

Dec If that's what you want.

Yana It's what *you* want. I'm neutral. The United Nations of sex. (*She smiles as she smokes the heroin.*)

The mobile phone rings. **Dec** *is looking through the binoculars.*

Dec Ah, our two friends go below again. (*He picks up the phone.*) Moss. (*Beat.*) Mr Halstein, hi. Long time. (*Beat.*) No, I've been up for hours. (*He laughs.*) Right, Bob, I never stop. That's how I keep the devil at bay. (*Beat.*) Yeah, that'd be very interesting. (*Beat.*) Well, I'll be in Zurich the week of the twelfth. Talking to my bankers. (*Beat.*) Yeah, I'll have all my marketing people with me, so . . . (*Beat.*) Great. I'll look forward to it. (*Beat.*) Here? Oh, the sun is shining, the sea is shimmering, the boats are bobbing. If you close your eyes, you can smell God. (*Beat.*) Oh, she's fine. (*He glances at* **Yana***, who is sitting back, eyes closed.*) She loves it here. (*Beat.*) Fine. Great, yeah, see you then. (*He puts the phone down, still staring out to sea.*) And now they come back on deck.

Yana *stands.* **Dec** *puts the binoculars down.*

OK?

She smiles dreamily and nods.

Where are you going?

Yana Somewhere nice . . . and safe. I get the handcuffs?

Dec Hmmm.

Yana And one day, I throw away the key.

She walks off into the house. He looks through the binoculars.

Dec More photographs? Well, stick this in your album . . .

He picks up the machine gun and brandishes it in the air while he holds up his left arm making a victory sign. He flashes a huge smile.

Blackout.

Scene Two

The patio. **Murph** *appears from the steps leading up to the patio. He carries two large cases and has a backpack on. Around his neck are two cameras and over one shoulder is a camera bag. He wears shades and a baseball cap. He puts the bags down, turns his cap back to front, pushes his shades up and starts taking pictures. From offstage,* **Spencer** *calls.*

Spencer   Murph! Murph, can you grab this case?

Murph *takes two more pictures then puts his cap and shades back in place.*

Murph?!

Murph   Yeah, I got it. (*He goes to the steps and grabs a case from* **Spencer** *as he appears, struggling.*) OK, there you go.

Spencer *comes on, panting and tired. He wears a white linen suit, shirt and tie and a Panama hat. He manages to look a bit seedy.*

Spencer   Christ, I didn't know they lived on a fucking mountain. I'd have brought oxygen.

Murph   Where are the girls?

Spencer   Stopped for a rest by that tree thing.

Murph *has gone downstage and is staring out to where the boat is moored.*

So. Crime *does* pay. Obviously.

Momentary pause, then **Murph** *turns to him and gives him a totally insincere smile.*

I must say, though, the au pair's something of a delight to the eye. What d'you say?

Murph   Well scrumptious.

Spencer *puts his hands on his hips and gazes around.*

Spencer   You've come a fucking long way, Moss, you
bastard. (*He takes out a cigarette and lights it.*) How much d'you
suppose this little lot set him back?

Murph   Oodles, at a guess.

Spencer   And some. Mind you, in this part of the world,
it's six to four on the plumbing doesn't function properly.
(*Beat.*) He might have millions in the bank, but I bet his
khazi's buggered. (*Beat.*) I've often comforted myself in the
wee small hours, when I'm lying there incapable of sleep,
that somewhere half a world away, the richest man on
earth may have just taken a dump, only to find the
cistern's fucked. He rattles the handle and gets only an
insolent little trickle. And a hand that controls billions
cannot flush the porcelain clean.

Murph   Usually drop off after that, do you?

Spencer   Sadly, no. (*Beat.*)

Murph   You should try yoga.

Spencer   What? Bugger me, no. That's the wife's
territory. Mumbo jumbo legs akimbo. I had a go once . . .
total bollocks. No, a double malt usually does the trick. (*He
picks up a bottle of wine and looks at it thirstily.*)

Murph   Where is he then? Where's the infamous,
enigmatic Declan Moss?

Spencer   Counting his dosh, probably.

Murph *purses his lips.*

No, I mean, talk about bloody irony. When I knew him he
never had two shekels to rub together. Used to sponge off
me rotten. (*He takes out a hip flask and drinks.*) We were at the
same college, you know. Dec had the room below me on
my staircase. Not quite what I had in mind when I got my
scholarship, sharing staircase space with a provincial

Grammar school yob. He was wearing a bloody donkey
jacket the day he arrived, a workman's bloody donkey
jacket. I honestly thought he'd come to inspect the drains
or something. But no, he squeezed past me on the stairs,
I'll never forget it, and he said 'All right? Dec Moss.
English'. And he winked, you know how they do. I
thought, you might very well be English, old son, but what
the buggery are you doing on my staircase? Then the
penny dropped. Oh my God, I thought. (*Beat.*) And the
other chap on the staircase was a sort of nondescript,
Midlands bank clerk, trainspotting type. Mercifully, we lost
him after the second term. Went walkabout and took a
dive off Beachy Head for some reason no one ever
fathomed. Things brightened up after that. They moved
Paul Merchant into his room. You know Paul?

Murph   No.

Spencer   He's something high-powered in the treasury
now. 'Course, he was a lefty then. Most people were, even
Wykemists. (*Beat.*) And there we were: the toff, the Trot
and the yob. Got on like a house on fire eventually. I
remember the three of us once, sprawled on bean bags in
Merchant's room, having a puff, and someone used the
word cosmic. And Dec looked around and he said: micro-
cosmic! Nearly died laughing, silly bugger. (*Beat.*) How the
fuck is it that someone can turn up at Oxford one day in a
donkey jacket, and twenty odd years later, they've got all
this? That's what I'd like to know.

Murph   Wouldn't we all? (*Beat.*)

Spencer   Still, be good to see the old bastard again. If he
ever puts in an appearance.

The women appear at the top of the steps. **Yana** *comes first, carrying
someone's case, which she immediately puts down. Then* **Stephanie**,
then **Louise**, *both carrying bags.* **Yana** *is subdued,* **Stephanie**
is tired but bubbly, while **Louise** *is centred.*

Murph   Ah, you made it.

Steph   No thanks to you. Why didn't you come back

down and give us a hand?

Murph   Give us a chance, I was just getting my breath back.

Spencer   Welcome to base camp one. Next, we tackle the summit.

Steph   Please, don't, not even in jest. I am spent. It's varicose vein surgery if I have to do that again.

Yana   Maybe we put in a ski-lift.

Steph   Good idea.

Spencer   Louise, darling? All right?

Louise   Mmm. (*She looks out to sea.*) It's so fabulously . . . sort of . . . *here.*

Spencer   Oh yes, it's definitely here.

Louise   I mean . . . oh, sense of place . . . (*Beat.*) What's the use?

Spencer   Quite.

Yana   There is food and drink . . .

Steph   Thank you, I am famished . . .

Spencer   D'you have any meat?

Yana   Meat?

Spencer   Yes. Dead animal. You know, to eat. (*Beat.*)

Yana   Yes, of course we have meat to eat.

Spencer   Splendid. (*Beat.*)

Yana   You want meat?

Spencer   Well not, y'know, I mean . . .

Yana   You want I get you some meat.

Steph   Only if it's no trouble.

Spencer   Absolutely. Only if it's no trouble. That would be lovely.

Yana   OK. No trouble. (*She starts to go.*)

Steph   Do you know where Dec is?

Yana *stops, thinks, almost smiles, shrugs, then goes.* **Steph** *collapses onto the bench behind the table.*

God, I am *so* hot.

Murph   The weather? Or the beefcake who brought us over from the mainland?

Steph   Don't. He was seriously native. Never on a Sunday my arse.

Spencer   Anybody for a glass of the old vino?

Steph   Oh, please . . .

Louise   It's far too early.

Spencer   Murph?

Murph   Nah. Far too early. (*He smiles at* **Louise**.)

Spencer   Well, bugger that. My body clock's on pub time, and they're *open*. (*He uncorks the bottle and pours two glasses. He hands one to* **Steph**.) Cheers, m'dear.

Steph   May your laptop never wither.

They clink glasses and drink.

Spencer   Fuck me, the yob's got taste. This is very good stuff.

Steph *has taken a large gulp.*

Steph   Second opinion . . .

She holds out her glass. He refills it and she drinks.

Yup . . . it's definitely . . . red.

Louise *is picking at the salad bowl.*

Spencer   Don't nibble, darling. Have a proper plateful.

Louise *stops picking and moves away from the table.*

Steph   God, when I wake up, somebody remind me I'm here to work.

Murph *lifts his camera and points it at her.*

Murph   Here you go. One for the editor.

Steph   No!

He snaps.

You bastard, if that ever surfaces at the paper, I'll kill you.

Murph   Chill, Steph, I don't think 'Journalist drinks glass of wine' is exactly hold-the-front-page material.

Steph   Just don't, that's all.

Louise   Don't the waves breaking look like little horses? Like horses, sort of . . . dancing.

Spencer   Horses don't dance.

Louise   How do you know?

Spencer   Well of course horses don't fucking dance.

Louise   Not literally, no.

Spencer   What other bloody way is there?

Louise   Ah.

Spencer   Ah. There you go, ah. As if that proves a damn thing . . . (*Beat.*)

Steph   I wonder if Dec's changed much?

Spencer   We all have.

Steph   Mmm. Be a shame if he has.

Spencer   Be a miracle if he hasn't.

Murph   All that running from the law's probably kept him in shape.

Steph   You clever thing. Been working on that one long?

Spencer   Well I know what *I'd* do if I lived here with all his money. I'd get tanned and fat. I'd stretch out in the sun and watch myself grow quite huge, until one day I just popped with satisfaction.

Yana *enters with a plate of meat and sausage. She puts it on the table.* .

Oh, so kind . . .

Yana   Some meat for you.

Spencer   Yes, thanks.

Steph   Is Dec . . . around . . . or . . . ?

Yana   Yes he is somewhere. (*She starts to go.*)

Steph   You must let me have the address of your charm school, dear. I'll arrange a firebombing.

Yana *'s gone.*

Spencer   D'you suppose she's his, er, piece?

Steph   Piece of what, Spencer?

Spencer   His, you know, amour.

Steph   God knows.

Spencer   I mean, am I supposed to treat her as the help or as the lady of the house?

Steph   Tell you what, why not go out on a limb and try treating her as a person?

Spencer   Because I can't. I have to know her . . . status . . . before I can interact, as it were.

Steph   Christ, you're weird sometimes.

Spencer (*uncomprehending*)   What?

Louise   I think Stephanie means that she's surprised by the rigidity of the social construct by which you live your life.

Spencer   Well, I can see that, obviously. But a chap has to know where he stands . . .

Steph   And weirder . . .

Spencer   OK. So. I treat her like a 'person', and then tomorrow morning she comes into my room to collect the dirty sheets . . . I mean . . .

Steph   Well, obviously, the world comes to an end . . .

Spencer   Think of the embarrassment . . .

Steph   Empires crumble . . .

Spencer   It helps to know where you stand, that's all.

Steph   Can't you get him some treatment, Louise? You're the shrink.

Louise   Therapist. No, I wouldn't touch him with a whatsit.

Spencer   Bargepole.

Louise   That's the one.

Spencer   Look, can we, you know, perhaps find some other poor bastard to tear to shreds? Please? For fuck's sake?

Steph (*to* **Murph**)   Hard to believe, but this man was president of the Oxford University Oscar Wilde Society.

Spencer   Oh, God . . .

Steph   Where did all the witty ripostes go, Spencer, old fruit?

Spencer   Fuck off.

Murph   Oscar Wilde Society? Boys' club, was it?

Spencer   No.

Steph   Yes it was!

Spencer   I know, but not in the way he means.

Steph   We used to call it the cravat, cummerbund and

corkscrew club. (*She and* **Louise** *laugh.*)

Spencer   For God's sake . . .

Steph   It was a lot of public school sodomites with their fingers up each others' bums . . .

Spencer (*angry*)   OK! Thanks! Right, good, yes. OK?

Louise   I so wish I could paint.

Spencer   I don't think there's much of a market for dancing bloody horses.

Suddenly **Dec** *appears from the house, rubbing his wrists. He wears expensive white clothes but still manages to look casual and hippyish.*

Dec   Hey!! Sorry, everyone, I've been tied up all morning. Stephanie, look at you . . . (*They hug.*)

Steph   You look great.

Dec   You too. And Louise, God is that really you?

Louise   Dec . . . (*They hug.*)

Dec   Ah, you *feel* good, too. Hey, listen, are you still married to that tight-arsed property developer?

Spencer   Mind your lip, bloody yob.

Dec   Christ, what's that smell? (*He turns to* **Spencer** *with a huge grin.*)

Spencer   You old bastard!

They have an extravagant man's hug.

Dec   How you doing, you noxious old Tory?

Spencer   In the pink, old chap.

Dec   I thought you'd be running the country by now.

Spencer   What, and miss out on the *real* money?

Dec   Same old Spencer. (*Beat.*)

Steph   Dec, this is my photographer, Murph.

Dec   Nice to meet you, Murph.

They shake hands.

Murph   Same here.

Dec *takes a step back and looks at them all. He smiles and shakes his head.*

Dec   Whoah . . . I can't get my head round this at all. It's been *so* long. Well, what can I say except welcome? (*Beat.*) Welcome to my island! Uh . . . (*He looks at the cases.*) Yana hasn't shown you your rooms yet?

Steph   Is Yana the young . . .

Dec   Yeah, that's her.

Spencer   No, she hasn't.

Dec   Ah, hang on. (*He shouts off into the house.*) Yana! (*Beat.*) Yana!? (*He turns back to them.*) You just can't get the staff these days . . .

Spencer *glances at* **Steph**.

Darling!?

Steph *returns* **Spencer**'s *glance.*

Yana (*off*)   Yes, I hear you!

Dec   OK.

Spencer   This place really is magnificent. Absolutely first class.

Dec   We like it.

Louise   Superb view.

Dec   Magic, isn't it?

Louise   Yes it is. Magic.

Yana *appears.*

Dec   Right, well let's get your gear stowed, shall we? Spencer and Louise are in the double.

Yana   Yes, I know.

They start picking up their gear. **Yana** *leads* **Spencer**, **Louise** *and* **Murph** *off.* **Steph** *hangs back.*

Dec   The bedrooms are through the house, across the courtyard OK. Move along the bus. Please no standing on top. OK?

Steph   Mmm. (*She gives him another hug, which surprises him.*) Listen, I know it was a long time ago, but I just wanted to say how sorry I was about Susanna . . .

Dec   Thanks.

Steph   It was tragic. I wept for days when I heard. I just couldn't believe it.

Dec   No.

Steph   Those . . . bastards.

Dec   Yeah. (*Pause.*)

Steph   But. Life goes on.

Dec   With a vengeance. (*Beat.*)

Steph   Yana . . . is she your current?

Dec   Certainly is.

Steph   She seems . . . nice.

Dec   No, I don't think nice is the word.

Steph   Perhaps not. Still, you're happy?

Dec   Very. (*Beat.*)

Steph   God, I am so pleased to see you. (*Beat.*) Thanks for agreeing to the interview, by the way.

Dec   How could I possibly refuse *you*? We go back a long way.

Steph   Frightening how long a way it is now.

Dec   Frightening?

Steph   Yes. Age, wrinkles . . . I mean, I can't imagine us jumping into bed with each other any more, can you?

Dec (*beat*)   Did we?

Steph   What?

Dec   Jump into bed with each other? (*Beat.*)

Steph   Did we ever? Christ, don't you remember?

Dec (*beat, then he laughs*)   Of course I do. Just winding you up.

Steph   You had me worried there for a minute. That'd really blow my cred. God, I've dined out on my 'I slept with Declan Moss' story.

Dec   Really?

Steph   Really.

Dec   I didn't know anyone was interested.

Steph   Christ, sex is about the only thing people talk or write about these days. I suppose I ought to find it tawdry, really, but actually, it's rather fun.

Dec   Fun.

Steph   Yes.

Dec   And is there a lot of fun being had in London these days?

Steph   Oh yes.

Dec   Lucky London.

Steph   Nothing wrong with having a good time.

Dec   But is it being had by all?

Steph   Well, it's definitely an advantage if you've got a good job and a bit of disposable income . . .

Dec   And if you haven't? (*Beat.*)

Steph   Tough titty, darling. (*Beat.*)

Dec The last time I was back –

Steph Which was when?

Dec Can't say –

Steph Just looking for a scoop.

Dec The last time I was back, I was in the car, and I tuned the radio to the pop station, the BBC one, for old times' sake, and there was a woman on doing the weather forecast. This would have been November time, and she started apologising to the listeners for the fact that there was no sunshine. I mean, she was really *sorry*, like she was personally very depressed by the news that in England in November there was a distinct lack of sunshine. I just thought: where does the silly cow think she is? Florida? Of course there's no bloody sunshine. There never is in November. This is England. (*Beat.*) Then I realised that there must be thousands, millions of people out there who hate the fact that they're in England and that there's no sunshine in the winter.

Steph One of the broadsheets did a poll last year which showed that about three quarters of under twenty-fives would emigrate tomorrow if they could.

Dec God, that's sad.

Steph Nearly all to the States, of course. California.

Dec They don't appreciate the cold any more.

Steph Who ever did?

Dec Me. I used to love it.

Steph Which is why you live here . . .

Dec I don't really have much of a choice where I live.

Steph You'd swap this for grotty old England?

Dec Yes, I would.

Murph *comes on.*

Like a shot.

Steph   Murph, where would you rather live? Here or in England?

Murph   Australia.

Steph   Ask a photographer a simple question . . .

Murph   It's a wave thing.

Steph   Of course. Tell Dec what you do when you're not snapping the rich and famous.

Murph   I hit the surf.

Steph   That's it. He goes surfing. He travels all over the world and all he can think of to do is skid around on top of the sea.

Dec   Hey, don't knock it. Surfing is serious Zen, right.

Murph   Yeah, right. (*He claps* **Dec** *on the shoulder.*)

Steph   Well, if you two are going to bond, I'll go and unpack.

Dec   It's the third bedroom . . .

Steph   I'll find it. And if I end up in yours, I'm sure you'll put me right.

She goes. **Murph** *watches her.*

Murph   Man, you'd think sex had just been invented. It's all she thinks about.

Dec   Are you two, er . . . ?

Murph   Fucking? Yeah, sure. Why not? She's wild.

Pause. **Dec** *looks at him, sizing him up.*

Mind you, you gotta handle that one with kid gloves. She's like a piece of china. One slip and . . . crash.

Dec   Oh?

Murph   Yeah. (*Beat.*) She's got quite a thing about you, y'know.

Dec   How d'you mean?

Murph   Hey, get up to speed, man. She is totally rapt in you.

Dec   Meaning?

Murph   Meaning: forget torches, she's got the eternal flame lit for you. (*Pause.*)

Dec   Been a photographer long, Murph?

Murph   Nearly ten years now.

Dec   Good living?

Murph   Good enough.

Dec   Just do celebs, do you? Or do you get out and about?

Murph   What, war zones and shit?

Dec   Yeah.

Murph   Not any more. I did a bit, a few years ago . . .

Dec   Whereabouts?

Murph   Oh, Afghanistan, South Africa, Baltic republics . . . (*Beat.*) Seen one brain splashed on the ground, you've seen them all, really.

Dec   I suppose you have. So, who are you working for? (*Slight frisson.*)

Murph   I'm freelance.

Dec   Go where the work is.

Murph   You got it.

Yana *enters in a bad mood.*

Yana   Dec, that man, he is horrible.

Dec   Who?

Yana   You know who. With the stupid hat.

Dec   Spencer . . . well, I did warn you.

Yana   He is like a big thing, you know, in the garden . . .

Dec   A tree?

Yana   Slimy . . .

Dec   Ah. Slug.

Yana   Slug. Yes.

Murph *smiles.*

Dec   Darling . . . we have guests.

Yana (*looking at* **Murph**)   No, I can see by his clothes that this man would not like this Spencer.

Dec   His clothes?

Yana   Yes.

Murph   I gotta tell you, she's spot on. (*Beat.*)

Dec   My friendship with Spencer could probably be seen as emblematic of the post-war British consensus which, for a time, enabled the country to navigate difficult periods of change without the sort of upheavals seen in other comparable nations. (*Beat.*) That said, I've always thought he was a total cunt.

Murph *laughs.*

Yana   No.

Murph   I wouldn't mind a bit of blow.

Dec   You smoke, do you?

Murph   Sure.

Dec *sits and starts to roll a joint.*

I suppose you must get it wholesale.

Dec *smiles.*

I try to lay off the booze. My old fella drank himself to death and I don't want to find out if it runs in the family.

Dec Yeah, booze, it's a killer. (*Beat.*) Murph . . . that's short for Murphy, yeah?

Murph That's right.

Dec Irish.

Murph The old fella. He drifted over after the war.

Dec Where from?

Murph Kerry. (*Beat.*) Should never have left.

Dec Someone should have told him. There's no escape.

Murph He found that out.

Dec Emigration, booze, whatever . . . we end up at the same place. Always.

Murph He ended up with no legs and a liver the size of a football.

Dec Poor guy. (*Beat.*)

Murph You've got a touch of the Green in you as well, yeah?

Dec My mother was irish. Hence Declan. (*He lights the joint and hands it to* **Murph**.)

Murph Thanks. (*He looks out at the view.*) Well, this is very nice, eh? (*He hands the joint back.*) Hey, tell me if I'm, you know, out of order, but you got involved with the boys, is that right, back in the seventies.

Dec The boys?

Murph The Provos.

Dec Ah. Well, that's the myth.

Murph It's just, Steph was saying . . .

Yana Do we eat here tonight, or on the mainland?

Dec   I thought we'd go over to Pete's Bar.

Yana   Good I Like Pete's.

Dec (*to* **Murph**)   It's a nice place. Great seafood.

Murph   Look forward to it.

Dec   Right. I have to make a call. Catch you later.

Murph   Sure.

Dec *goes.*

Nice guy. Hard to believe he's what they say he is.

Yana   What's that?

Murph   Well . . .

Yana   No, what?

Murph   'They say' . . . that he's a big time drug smuggler. Perhaps the biggest. That's what they say.

Yana   Who say?

Murph   The press . . .

Yana *snorts.*

Yeah, well . . .

Yana   Do you have a girlfriend? A wife?

Murph   Uh, no, not really.

Yana   Why not? (*Beat.*)

Murph   I'm never in one place long enough.

Yana   Or perhaps you are too . . . slippy.

Murph   Could be.

Yana   But you're not a faggot.

Murph   No.

Yana   Good. These days, too many men are faggots.

Murph *smiles.*

Murph   Where are you from?

Yana   I am from Romania.

Murph   Ah.

Yana   Where the vampires come from.

Murph   Yeah. So how'd you end up here?

Yana   I was in Brussels, working as a whore, and I meet some people and they know Dec, and I meet Dec and I end up here.

Murph   Very romantic.

Yana   No, I don't think so. (*Beat.*)

Murph   And Dec knows about your, uh, profession?

Yana   Sure.

Murph   Broadminded kind of guy.

Yana   I'm sorry?

Murph   Nothing.

Yana   Dec says we are all whores, but we must keep that little piece of us which is always us. We must keep that safe.

Murph   And do you?

Yana   Yes.

Murph   That's good. (*Beat.*)

Yana   You want sex with me? (*Beat.*)

Murph   Is that a come-on, or an innocent question?

Yana   It's just a question.

Murph   Then just an answer would be yes, why not? (*Beat.*) I wonder what Dec would say about it, though?

She shrugs.

Yana   He might not care or he might shoot you.

Murph   Does he have a gun?

Yana   Yes. (*Beat.*)

Murph   Let's put that idea on hold then, shall we?

Yana   You're scared?

Murph   I don't want to be shot for a fuck.

Yana   You're scared.

Murph   Just interested in staying alive.

Yana   Why? What is so good about life?

He looks puzzled.

Murph   Well, it passes the time . . .

She gives him a disdainful look then gets up and stands looking at the view. He stares at her.

Yana   You think that here, it must be like paradise. That it is impossible not to be happy. But for me, this is nowhere. When I am not where I belong, the time is like always and never, both at once. Like dead and alive at the same time. When I wake up, it is a new day and it is still yesterday.

Murph *stands and comes and stands behind her. She turns, looks at him long and hard and then kisses him on the lips.*

Murph   I'm not understanding this.

Yana   I am.

She goes off into the house. **Murph** *watches her go then faces out towards the moored boat and smiles.*

Fade.

Scene Three

Night. Light from the house spills onto the patio. From offstage we hear the sound of people noisily approaching. **Dec** *and* **Murph** *appear, carrying* **Steph** *between them. As they come onto the patio, she lets out a cry of triumph and they exhaustedly put her down.*

Steph   It's the only way to travel!

Dec *and* **Murph** *are out of breath and tired.*

Come on, two big strong men like you . . .

Dec   I'm too old for this . . .

Steph   Rubbish, darling. (*She goes to him and puts her hand to his face.*) You have a light dew upon your forehead and it's very becoming. (*She kisses him lightly.*) Now, where's that Scotch you promised me?

Dec   It's inside. I'll get it . . .

Steph (*as he goes*)   Cor, look at the arse on that . . . (*He's gone.*)

Murph   You shouldn't make it so obvious.

Steph   What?

Murph   You're embarrassing the guy. You're all over him . . .

Steph   Mind your own fucking business.

Murph   It's pathetic. *And* you're pissed . . .

Steph (*advancing on him*)   Who do you think you are? (*She slaps him round the head.*) How dare you criticise me? You little shit!

She launches a flurry of slaps at his head. He fights her off then grabs her hands and stares into her face.

Murph   All right! That's enough.

He lets go of her. Chastened, she flounces off and sits down.

Steph   You're just a poxy papparazi, that's all. A tiny little name next to the photo, that's all. I'm the one with the byline and her photo at the top of the column.

Murph   Well, cue fanfare.

Louise *appears.*

Steph Where's the beast, Lou, what have you done with him?

Louise Last I saw, he was having a piss.

Dec *comes back on with an oil lamp, which he lights, a bottle of Scotch and a bag with dope rolling gear in it.*

Dec Who's for Scotch?

Steph Me.

Dec *puts the bottle down in front of her and fetches a glass.*

Christ, it's a good thing I haven't got a hang-up about drinking alone. (*She laughs self-consciously then opens the bottle and pours a drink. She sips.*) Cheers.

Dec *has started rolling a huge joint.*

I suppose you're all going to look all squinty at me for having a drink, while you get silly on that stuff.

Dec It's cool, Steph, no one cares. Each to his own.

Steph Quite. (*Beat.*) Oh, stuff it. (*She drains her glass and pours another one.*) Remember what we used to be like? Remember finals?

Dec *Do* I . . . ?

Steph What a night.

Dec Incredible.

Steph You were fucking that nurse in the pub . . .

Dec Was I?

Steph 'Was I?' Underneath the dartboard. She was on your lap . . . she had one of those gypsy dresses on, billowy great thing . . . and you were sat there drinking champagne from the bottle while she was bobbing up and down on your lap.

Dec Yes, it's all coming back . . .

Steph   I should think so, too. And then we had that monster clusterfuck round at Jerry's, d'you remember? About twenty of us, all over the floor . . . (*She starts to laugh.*) . . . and Lou, d'you remember? You went strolling off up the road in your birthday suit. We sent out a search party.

Louise   I woke up in someone's bed and realised I wasn't at home. So I thought I'd better go there.

Steph   Stark bloody naked.

Louise   Well, I was drunk.

Steph   I bet you don't remember who you woke up in bed *with*.

Louise   (*beat*)   No.

Steph   Well *I* do, because I came and sat at the end of the bed at some point. I was all weepy over some man and I needed a shoulder. And all I got was you giving blow-jobs to Jerry and that actor bloke, both at the same time . . .

Murph   Yeah, look Steph . . .

Steph   I'm going 'Lou, what am I going to do?' and you're going . . . (*She makes a gobbling noise and collapses in hysterics.*)

Louise   It was all a long time ago . . .

Steph   And besides, the actor bloke is dead. (*Beat.*)

Louise   Is he?

Steph   Yes, about three years ago. Didn't you read about it?

Louise   No. (*Beat.*) Michael.

Steph   Yes, Michael.

Louise   Rest in peace. (*Beat.*)

Steph   Remember that huge dinner party Spencer had after finals?

Dec   Out at the cottage.

Steph   That's the one. We were all sat round that enormous table, loads of us, and I remember looking round and thinking: Dec Moss has had every woman at this party.

Dec   Never . . .

Steph   Yes! Every single one. There was you, Lou, Mel . . . Josie, Sarah . . . Both Sarahs. And Chloe, and . . . God I can see the faces, but I don't remember the names. But you had slept with *all* of them.

Louise   When *I* think back to those times, all I feel is abused.

Steph (*beat*)   Christ, it's not as if anybody was forcing you.

Louise   Yes it is. That's exactly what it was like. I mean, what rational young woman with *any* self-esteem is going to voluntarily perform oral sex on two drunken undergraduates.

Steph   I think you're exaggerating. It was fun, that's all.

Louise   But that's what I'm saying. It *wasn't* fun.

Beat, then **Spencer** *appears from the steps. He is very drunk. He hasn't done his flies up properly and has a wet stain all down the front of his trousers. His shirt is half-undone and hanging out, and his hat is only precariously balanced on his head.*

Spencer   Did somebody say fun?

Steph   Pull up a glass, Spencer.

Spencer   Don't mind if I do.

He lurches over to the table. **Dec** *passes him a glass.* **Spencer** *pours a Scotch and drinks.*

Oh, by God, that's good . . . (**Dec** *is lighting his huge Countryman style spliff. He hands it to* **Spencer**.) I shouldn't really, it makes me go funny, that stuff, always has . . .

He takes a couple of big puffs and hands it to **Louise**, *who smokes it very calmly.*

Steph   We were just talking about the good old days.

Spencer   Oh yes? When were they?

Steph   Oxford.

Spencer   Ah, great days, great days. (*He sits, suddenly looking sad.*) Where'd it all go, eh?

Dec   Oh, no, please . . .

Spencer   I mean . . . one minute you're there, doing it . . . and the next, it was a thousand years ago. I don't think the human animal is a sophisticated enough beast to cope with this passage of time lark, do you? No, I don't. See?

Steph   Earth calling Spencer, are you receiving us, over?

Spencer   We should be like goldfish. Eight second memory, that's the answer. Take a spin round the bowl? Why not? Swim, swim. Eight seconds later, that was nice. What was? Take a spin round the bowl? Why not? Swim, swim. And on and on, until one day your fins rot and they flush you down the bog. No regret in the life of a goldfish, y'see. No time for regrets.

Dec   What have *you* got to regret?

Spencer   Me? Absolutely bloody everything. The whole fucking works . . . (*He stands and staggers off into the house.*) And now, I do believe I may be about to upchuck . . . seafood and pot, God help me . . . (*He's gone.*)

Dec   Is he all right?

Louise   He'll survive. He always does.

Dec   Is everybody like this at home now?

Steph   Like what?

Dec *thinks.*

Dec   Sad. (*Beat.*)

Steph   Sad?! (*She bursts out laughing.*) Oh, Dec, you're so naive. You're such a romantic old thing. Like a little boy. We're not sad. Least, *I'm* not. I'm having the time of my life. Really. It's just nice to remember the good times, that's all. People do that when they get older.

Yana *comes on from the house. She has smartened up and looks stunning.*

Yana   Hello everyone. (*She kisses* **Dec**.) I missed you. How was Pete's Bar?

Dec   Great, as always.

Yana   I'm sorry I wasn't feeling well.

Louise   Are you better now?

Yana   I am wonderful now, thank you.

Louise   Good. (*She offers* **Yana** *the joint.*)

Yana   Thanks. Your husband inside, I don't think he is very wonderful.

Louise   No. (*Beat.*)

Yana   Did you dance at Pete's?

Dec   No, it was too crowded.

Yana   You didn't dance? We always dance at Pete's.

Dec   Not tonight.

Yana   Well, I dance now . . . (*She goes off into the house.*)

Dec   Darling, everybody's tired . . .

Steph   And emotional.

Dec   Sorry, guys, she does this.

Steph   Don't apologise, Dec, I wouldn't mind a bit of boogie. Whatd'you say, Murph?

From the house, the opening bars of 'Babylon Sisters' by Steely Dan

begin playing. **Yana** *comes back on, grooving to the music.* **Steph**
gets up, glass in hand and starts gyrating to the music. She grabs
Murph*'s hand and yanks him up. He very reluctantly goes through*
the motions of dancing with her. **Yana** *stands in front of* **Dec** *and*
takes a long drag of the joint, then, as if kissing him, blows the smoke
into his mouth. He closes his eyes and breathes out. **Yana** *laughs*
and dances across to **Murph** *and blows smoke into his mouth. He*
has become less reluctant now. **Yana** *turns to* **Steph***, who waves*
her hand.

Steph   No, no, I've got this . . .

She holds up her glass, but **Yana** *persists. Very uncomfortably,*
Steph *accepts, then turns away, spluttering the smoke out.* **Yana**
grooves towards **Murph** *as* **Steph** *leans against the table, watching*
them. As they dance, the other three watch as if hypnotised, fascination
and regret on their faces. Suddenly, from inside the house comes the
sound of a crash, and the music stops. **Spencer** *calls out from*
inside.

Spencer *(off)*   Ouch! What the fucking hell . . . !?

The others are frozen. **Spencer** *staggers on, rubbing his leg.*

Who put that bloody junk in the middle of the room? For
fuck's sake, a man could hurt himself . . .

Dec   It's a midi system on wheels, Spencer.

Spencer   It's a bloody death trap.

Dec   We find it very convenient.

Spencer   Well the best of luck to you, old fruit . . .

He goes to pour himself a Scotch. **Yana** *suddenly turns on him.*

Yana   You stupid fucking ugly imperialist bastard fucking
cunt!

Spencer *(beat)*   I'm sorry?

Yana   You're not sorry! You're fucking an asshole.

She storms off down the hill. **Spencer** *stands with the mock-guilty*
look of a drunk who couldn't care less.

Spencer   The perfect hostess.

Louise   And what are you? The perfect guest?

Murph   Man, what is she *on?*

Dec   She's very emotional. Sorry.

Murph   Whatever it is she took, I want some.

Dec   She didn't take anything. (**Dec** *stands.*) I'll be back in a minute. Enjoy yourselves. (*He goes.*)

Steph   Spencer, you are a prat. Honestly . . .

Spencer   Look, there's a bloody great . . . thing . . . in the doorway that wasn't there when I went out. So I collided with it. So what an absolute fucking tragedy.

Louise   Can't you ever say sorry?

Spencer   For *what* ?!

Louise   For being the most self-involved, egocentric thing on the face of the planet. For being ignorant and rude. For being you!

Spencer   Well, I'm sorry I'm me. Do accept my most sincere apologies for not being someone else. OK? I'm sorry I'm not Dec Moss. I realise I've committed an unforgivable crime, but I hope you can find it in your hearts to forgive. Go to fuck, the lot of you. (*He pours a drink.*)

Murph   D'you suppose he's, like, hands on with the drugs, or does he do it all from a distance?

Spencer (*pointing at* **Murph**)   Now *that* is a rude man. You don't pry into another chap's business actually, Murph.

Murph   Why not?

Spencer   A little thing called discretion.

Murph   Hey, the fact is the guy's a major dope dealer. That's cool, yeah? I'm not prying, I'm just interested.

Spencer   Business is business. If they clap him in irons and bang him up for the rest of his natural, then perhaps we have a legitimate right to inquire into his affairs. But until that happens, it's shtum, matey. All right?

Murph   Steph?

Steph   What?

Murph   You go along with that? (*Beat.*)

Steph   Dec . . . Dec is a friend.

Murph   Oh, sorry, I thought you were here to write a feature on him. I thought you were going to dig the dirt, expose him.

The others look at **Steph**, *who looks flushed and guilty.*

Steph   I'm here because I'm the only bastard in the entire British media that Dec will speak to. Because we're old friends.

Murph   Yeah, sure.

Steph   If Dec's a criminal, let the police catch him. It's not my bloody job.

Murph   There speaks a British journalist.

Steph   I write features, middle-brow gossip, I do celeb interviews. If, in my considered opinion, the celeb's a shit, I say so. If he's nice, I say so. In Dec's case, I already know what he is.

Murph   OK, fine. I misunderstood.

Steph   Anyway, who did cannabis ever kill? You'd have a better case arresting the men who own Guinness.

Spencer   No, they tried that.

Steph *laughs.*

Steph   Exactly. (*Beat.*) I'm here to do an interview, not to judge. I'm not qualified to judge, who is?

Louise   Well, we all have our own belief systems from

which we evaluate other people's actions in a moral
sense . . .

Murph   That's right, in a moral sense . . .

Steph   Christ, who *are* you? Moral sense my arse. You're
a little boy with a camera and a big dick, what do you
know about my moral sense?

Murph   Nothing, obviously.

Steph   Good. Now fuck off. Sermon over. Christ. (*She
pours a drink.*)

Louise   But Steph, if you don't have a belief system, a
moral sense, what's to stop you betraying an old friend?

Beat. **Dec** *and* **Yana** *come back on. He has his arm around her.*

Dec   Everyone OK?

Yana *goes to* **Spencer**.

Yana   Spencer, I am sorry that I shouted, and for what I
called you.

Spencer   Not at all, old thing.

Yana   Dec says they were rude things I said to you, but it
is acceptable for me to call you a . . . Tory wanker. Yes?

Spencer   No problem with that at all, my dear, for that,
most definitely, is what I am.

Dec *sits and starts to roll another joint.*

Dec, did you know I was nearly adopted as a Conservative
candidate?

Dec   No, I didn't.

Spencer   Didn't get it, though.

Dec   Why not?

Spencer   Gave it to a fucking coon, didn't they.

General outrage.

Steph Spencer!

Murph For Christ's sake . . .

Spencer What? Upset the politically correct apple cart, did I?

Murph It's racist, man.

Spencer Of course it is! *I'm* racist. So's the Tory Party. That's one of the reasons I joined. That's one of the reasons millions of upright Englishmen vote for them. But Christ, you don't expect the Tory Party to come over all PC and go and select some twerp who only came down out of the trees last week, just because it's good PR.

Steph Look, shut up, will you?

Louise He's trying to shock. He's in his little boy phase. The trousers will probably come off next.

Spencer You want my trousers off?! (*He tugs at his belt.*)

Louise No, I don't want your trousers off. That's the very last thing I want.

Spencer Too late! (*His trousers drop to the floor.*) There. Satisfied?

Yana *giggles.*

Steph Oh *do* put them back on.

Spencer No. My good lady wife has asked that I divest myself of my trousers. And I always do as I'm told, don't I dear?

Louise *folds her arms on the table and drops her head onto them.*

Anyway, where was I? Yes. There I was, I'd got through all the stages with flying colours, had the constituency blue rinses eating out of my hand. It looked like a shoo-in. I'd stood for hours on end, precariously balancing wine glass and vol-au-vent-filled paper plate, discussing the urgent matters of the day with the old fools . . . Maastricht, sound finance, single mothers, housing queues, uncivilised delinquents, bring back the birch, bring back hanging, privatise everything lean, fit, competitive, zero inflation, lower taxes, delivering services at the point of need, dependency culture, let managers manage, advertising on the BBC, new world order, choice, charters, recovery, green shoots, world recession, uniquely poised to benefit, back to basics, the market rules in perpetuity OK. I could see myself already on the evening news. Spencer Taplow MP, being interviewed outside the House, presenting his always loyal but loveably maverick spin on events, buttonhole on expensive double-breasted suit defiantly and rakishly in place. Oh, I was sound.

Dec *hands him the joint, which he takes without thinking.*

God, I was so fucking sound. (*Beat.*) And what did the old bastards do? Central Office said jump and the geriatrics turned somersaults. And they selected a fucking black man. (*Pause.* **Spencer** *stands there in tears, trousers round his ankles, hat nearly falling off his head, puffing on the joint.*) My birthright, and they gave it away to . . .

Pause, then **Murph** *bursts out laughing.* **Spencer** *drains his glass and stands unsteadily staring into space.*

Dec   Hey, don't hog the joint, man.

Spencer   Sorry.

He turns to hand the joint to **Dec** *and trips over his trousers. He crumples to the floor. Nobody moves to help.*

Steph   Get him up, somebody. (*Beat.*)

Dec   I am not my brother's keeper.

Louise *lifts her head, looks at* **Spencer** *and stands up.*

Louise   See? Little boy phase. (*She goes to him.*) Come on. Up. (*She helps him up.*) That's it.

Spencer   I'm sorry.

Louise   Yes . . .

Spencer   No, I am, really. I'm sorry I'm me . . .

Louise It's all right. (*She pulls his trousers up and gently leads him into the house.*)

Dec Plus ça change . . .

Murph What a sleaze.

Steph He's always been like that. He's perfectly harmless.

Dec That's what *I* used to think. That whole class of people who think and behave like Spencer, I used to think, well they're offensive but harmless. A lot of unpleasant noise on the surface, but underneath, tolerant and kind. One day we'll wake up and they'll have simply withered away. That's what I used to think. I always assumed their Englishness was a guarantee that they were incapable of genuine cruelty. After all, what harm did green suburbs, warm beer and cricket ever do anybody? But now, I think we know that deep down they have cruel, hateful little souls. And I suppose they always did have, I don't know. But that was just me making the same old mistake. Something I grew up with. If you're going to oppose in Britain, it's vital that you're 'good' about it. It's essential that you're well-behaved and decent. That way, the story goes, they'll give you a fair hearing. And by the time you're allowed to drag yourself in front of them with your reasonable petition, you look down and realise that you've hacked your own balls off. You've been fair and reasonable, but it's too late. You've done their dirty work for them. There you are, feeble and useless. And there they are. And they don't even look at you, they don't listen. They just ignore you. And this isn't what you were led to expect. It was all a fucking great con. (*Beat.*)

Murph So *then* what do you do?

Dec *smiles.*

Dec You get the hell out of it. (*He stands and looks out at the view.*)

Murph Couldn't you do something more positive?

Dec Such as?

Murph I don't know . . .

Dec You do what you can. But not nicely and not with tolerance. (*Beat.*)

Murph Like . . . arming the IRA?

Steph Look, for Chrissakes, can it, will you, Murph?

Murph I'm sorry, but, you know, I have a legitimate interest. I *am* Irish.

Steph Half-Irish.

Murph OK. But I have a legitimate interest.

Dec Sure you do. (*Beat.*)

Murph So, is it true?

Dec Is what true?

Murph The stuff about you and arms shipments . . . ?

Dec Oh. It might be. Who knows?

Murph Well, I figured *you* might . . .

Dec Why? You seem to be labouring under the misapprehension, Murph, that I know what I do.

Beat. **Murph** *laughs.*

Murph You got me, man . . .

Dec The nature of my business can be . . . inexact. I export, I import. Now, there are plenty of dodgy characters out there looking to hitch a ride. I have eyes and ears out there, but, hey . . .

Murph So you don't know anything about it . . . ?

Dec *laughs.*

Dec You don't get it, do you. You believe that every question has an answer. (*Beat. Icy.*) That is very simplistic of you.

Murph I'm a simple guy.

Steph   Seconded.

Dec   The only question worth asking me is: do I care? (*Beat.*) But somehow, I don't think you'd really be interested in the answer to that.

Dec *gets up and goes into the house.* **Yana** *follows.*

Steph   Are you deliberately trying to fuck this up for me? Did someone send you here as a spoiler, or what?

Murph   I just asked the guy a question.

Steph   Bullshit. You're trying to pull something.

Murph   Steph . . .

Steph   Don't get clever, sonny. I only have to phone London and you're on the first flight out of here, OK? (*Beat.*) OK?

Murph   Go on then. Do it.

Steph   Don't push me.

Murph   Do it. (*Pause.*)

Steph   Look . . . I thought we were getting on. I don't need this. We were having fun. Weren't we? What's changed? (*Beat.*) I can do without the moody, thank you. (*She pours a drink.*) I mean, we've had some laughs . . . can't we just leave it at that?

Murph   You don't know me, do you?

Steph   What's to know?

Murph   And it doesn't bother you even a little bit.

Steph   Why should it? In two days' time I'll be back in London, and you'll be God knows where. I'm too bloody long in the tooth to go falling for you, if that's what you want. I have a life. I have a job, a car, a nice house, a nice garden, two cats, a kitchen where I cook and entertain friends. I have a life. I don't need anybody . . . disrupting that. Least of all you.

Murph   Fine.

Steph   Fine. (*She drinks.*) However, if you want to come to my room and fuck me later, that's fine too. (*Beat.*) Come on. I'm hardly being clingy. I have needs, that's all.

Murph   So do I.

Steph   Yes . . .

Murph   And they don't necessarily coincide with yours. (*Beat.*)

Steph   Well I'm not exactly going to die of a broken heart, if that's what you want to hear.

Murph   No.

Steph   Christ, I can get a fuck anywhere.

Murph   Congratulations.

Steph   I mean, I've got American Express.

Murph *laughs.*

Murph   I don't think you can buy what you need.

Steph *laughs.*

Steph   I don't need. I *want.* There's a difference.

Murph   We all need.

Steph   Fuck me, you sound like Oprah Winfrey.

Murph   Big fan, are you?

Steph   Features are trying to set me up for an interview. So far, I've sat through twenty-seven hours of videos of the damn woman fiddling with the innards of the stupid, dysfunctional American psyche. Twenty-seven hours of bloated stupidity staring gormlessly at its own reflection, wondering why it's bloated and stupid. I tell you, you can get seriously lost in Oprahland, if you're not careful.

Murph   So why write about her?

Steph   She is apparently, a phenomenon. You know she's

been trying to set up an interview with Diana? Pathetic, isn't it? I chase Oprah, Oprah chases Di. Like a celebrity food chain. (*Beat.*) It might be nice to write about people for a change. The trouble is, people don't want to read about people. They want to sit back, mouths open, drooling at the stars in the sky. And why should I presume to know any better?

Murph   'Cause it's bad for your soul?

She laughs and pours a drink.

Steph   My soul turned to shit a long time ago. (*She stares morosely into her glass. Pause. She sings quietly.*) 'Oh hello Mister Soul, I just dropped by to pick up a reason . . .' (*Beat.*) Who sang that?

Murph   Pass.

Steph   'Oh hello Mister Soul, I just dropped by to pick up a reason'. (*She hums the next line.*) God, why do I know that?

Dec *and* **Yana** *come back on.* **Dec** *holds a large spliff.*

Dec . . . 'Oh hello Mister Soul, I just dropped by to pick up a reason . . .'

Dec (*sings*)   'For the thought that I caught that my head is the event of the season'.

Steph   Ha! Yes, who is that?

Dec   You don't know?

Steph   I know, I just can't remember

Dec   That is the godlike genius of Neil Young.

Steph   Neil Young! Of course. Parties, Neil Young records. It all comes flooding back.

Dec   I read that he played Finsbury Park last year.

Steph   Finsbury Park? What for?

Dec   Well, because that's what he does.

Steph   Is he a phenomenon? Should I interview him?

Dec   He is a phenomenon. But I don't think you should interview him.

Steph   But he's part of my past.

Dec   Then let him rest there.

Steph   *You're* a phenomenon. *You're* a part of my past. I'm interviewing *you*.

Dec   Only if you're nice.

Steph   I'm always nice to you.

Yana   What's . . . phenom –

Dec   Phenomenon. It's . . . something special.

Steph   Or some*one* special.

Dec   Or some*one*.

Yana   That's you?

Dec   Apparently.

Yana   My ass.

Dec   That too. (*He goes to* **Murph** *and hands him the joint.*) Here.

Murph   Oh, man . . .

Dec   I thought you liked a bit of blow.

Murph   Yeah, but –

Dec   Go on, it's good stuff.

Yana *comes over and takes it.*

Yana   Here. (*She lights it, takes a drag and hands it to* **Murph**.) Now you.

He takes it.

Murph   What is it?

Yana   Just cannabis.

Murph   *Just* cannabis? (*He takes a drag and screws his eyes up.*) Man . . . *just*?

Dec   It's skunk.

Murph   Ah, shit . . .

Dec   It's fine.

Steph   What the hell are you lot on about? Why are you smoking a skunk, Murph?

Murph   Because it would be impolite not to.

Dec   Correct.

Steph   Smoking a bloody skunk, what next?

Dec   It's not *a* skunk. It's a name we have for a new, stronger strain of cannabis. It's grown indoors, without soil, using nutrients and intensive watering. The THC level in skunk can be anything up to thirty times as strong as in normal cannabis.

Steph   The *what* level?

Murph   Delta 9 tetrahydrocannabinol. THC. The main psychoactive ingredient in cannabis.

Dec *looks at him.*

Like I said, I like a bit of blow.

Steph   So what's so good about this skunk, then?

Murph   Hallucinations, right?

Dec   Right.

Murph *hands him the joint.*

Steph   Hallucinations? Oh, bloody wonderful, my photographer's about to make a moonshot.

Dec   No, this one's not really strong enough. Not quite.

Murph   So, is this the new product?

Dec   Hmm?

Murph   Your latest market venture.

Dec   Purely recreational, old son.

Steph   Oh, come on then. (*She gets up very shakily and goes to* **Dec**.) Hit me with the skunk, man.

Murph   I don't think –

Steph   I want to get high as a kite.

Murph   – that's a good idea.

Steph   Yeah, great idea.

Dec *holds the joint away from her.*

Come on, Dec.

Dec   It doesn't mix with booze.

Steph (*putting her arms around his neck*)   Who cares? Everybody must get stoned, eh? Come on. We'll go for a walk in the sea. Go for a paddle. Splish splosh in the briny. Hold hands in the surf. Screw on the shingle. Let's do it.

Dec   I'm spoken for. (*He nods towards* **Yana**.)

Steph   Only in pidgin English.

Dec   That's not nice.

Steph   Fuck her. Come on. Let's, please. *Please.*

She's staring imploringly into his eyes, her arms round his neck. He slowly lifts the joint to her lips. She takes a long drag and kisses him heavily on the lips, the smoke wreathing their faces. He responds to her kiss. **Yana** *plucks the joint from* **Dec**'s *fingers and goes to* **Murph**. *She takes a drag and kisses him. Pause while both couples kiss heavily.* **Steph** *stops kissing and slowly sinks to her knees, arms around the back of* **Dec**'s *legs, her face pressed into him.* **Murph** *looks across and sees what's happening. He breaks away from* **Yana**.

Murph   Whoah, that is some stuff! Yeah? Steph? How you feeling?

The mood is broken. **Dec** *moves away from* **Steph**, *who remains, blearily, kneeling.*

Steph   What?

Murph   Has it hit you yet?

Steph   What?

Murph   You got a winner there, Dec.

Dec   Yeah.

Murph   Man . . .

Steph   Gimme a drink.

Murph   Drink . . . (*He gets her glass for her.*)

Dec   Were you somewhere nice there?

Steph   Mmm.

Dec   Good.

Yana   I want to party.

Dec   It's late.

Yana   Yeah, it's always late. (*She sits.*)

Steph   'Oh hello Mister Soul, I dropped by to pick up a reason'

Dec   (*beat*) 'Is it strange I should change? I don't know . . .'

Murph   Man, I feel . . . I feel like I'm in a fast car, y'know?

Dec   Yeah, that's the feeling. It's good. Hey, you like fast cars, Murph?

Murph   Sure.

Dec   Little ones? About that big?

He gestures. **Murph** *looks puzzled.* **Dec** *makes a racing car noise and mimes pressing a hand control set.*

Murph   Not Scalextric? You don't have a Scalextric?

Dec   In the games room. It's three sets put together. It's huge, man.

Murph Oh, wow, I could get into that.

Dec Yeah?

Murph For sure.

Dec OK.

Yana *stands.*

Yana . . . we're just going down the games room . . .

Yana And what about me?

He goes to her.

Dec Oh, honey, it's boys' stuff. (*He nods towards* **Steph**.) Yeah? (*He kisses her.*)

Yana OK.

Dec See you. (*He turns.*)

Murph So what cars have you got?

Dec Uh, two Ferraris, a Jag, Porsche, Williams Formula One . . . ·

They've gone. **Yana** *stands grumpily, looking at* **Steph** *kneeling on the floor. Then she picks up the Scotch bottle and takes a swig.*

Yana So. You want to fuck my husband?

Steph What?

Yana You want to fuck Dec?

Steph Your husband.

Yana My husband. Dec.

Steph I didn't know you were married.

Yana Why should you?

Steph Because I've just spent two weeks researching every known fact about Dec. Born Battersea, 1954. St. Joseph's Roman Catholic primary school 1958–65.

Wandsworth grammar school 1965–71. Scholarship to
Pembroke College, Oxford to read English, 1971. First
drugs bust June '72. Second drugs bust November '72.
Involved in series of political actions, sit-ins etcetera. Takes
finals and receives a poor third. Goes to London. Next
heard of running oriental carpet import business. Marries
Oxford girlfriend Susanna Price, 1975. Spends more time
on the continent. Sets up home on houseboat, Amsterdam,
1976. February 1977, houseboat and wife blown up by
bomb believed planted either by IRA or rival drug
smugglers. May '79, warrant issued in London for arrest on
charges of importing cannabis into UK. Eludes arrest.
Rumours circulate of involvement with security services,
IRA, gun-running and terrorism, as well as drugs. 1990,
US Drug Enforcement Agency names Moss as one of its
most wanted men. Moss issues statement denying drugs
activity and accuses DEA and CIA of pursuing vendetta
against him over unspecified activities in connection with
the Iran-Contra scandal. Disappears until traced to private
island in the Aegean. (*Pause.*) No wedding ceremony. No
happy couple smiling for the cameras.

Yana   You think we have a big party so the shitfuck
Americans can come and arrest him. You think we are
stupid?

Steph   No. (*Pause.*)

Yana   So. Again. You want to fuck my husband? (*Beat.*)

Steph   I already have. Years ago.

Yana   When you were childen.

Steph   When I was about your age. Younger even. (*Beat.*)
But I'd like to be closer to him, yes.

Yana   Why? So you can betray him?

Steph   Betray him?

Yana   Of course.

Steph   What for?

Yana For money. What else? (*Beat.*)

Steph I hadn't even thought about that. (*Beat.*) It's funny
. . . I do care about money. I care an awful lot about
money. I never expected to. I mean, when you're young
and having fun and going places and meeting people, you
never expect that you'll find yourself sitting alone, save for
your two cats, in your kitchen at three in the morning with
a feeling in your stomach like . . . like death, actually. All
because the books don't balance. Incomings, outgoings,
direct debits, pension, private health scheme, mortgage
repayments, credit card, income tax, National Insurance . . .
and on and on. (*Beat.*) I often think back to the freedom I
had. (*Beat.*) Does that sound odd? That I don't feel free?

Yana *shrugs.*

I feel like I'm being ungrateful or something. I mean . . . I
have a job I quite like, a nice house . . . (*Beat.*) God, why
do I always say that? I could take you through my entire
world, listing everything down to the smallest detail. And
all of it would be 'good'. Nothing bad or scary in there.
And . . . I feel like I've died. (*Pause.*) But I remember being
alive once. And I remember Dec being there. And he's *still*
there, and I'm here. (*Beat.*) So no, I don't want to fuck
your husband. But I can't bear the pain of not fucking
him.

She holds out her glass. **Yana** *tops it up and takes a swig.*

Yana What do you name them? Your cats?

Steph *smiles.*

Steph Don't laugh . . . Lennon and McCartney. You
know, the Beatles . . .

Yana Sure, I know the Beatles.

Steph I used to worship them. (*Beat.*)

Yana You worship a pop group? (*Beat.*)

Steph, Yes. (*Beat.*) God. (*Beat.*)

Yana   It's not very grown up.

Steph   No. But I was young then. (*Beat.*)

Yana   I was a big fan of Boney M.

Steph   Ah.

Yana   'Ra ra Rasputin, lover of the Russian Queen'.
That was very well liked in my country. Not officially . . .

Steph   Boney M, is that what they sent you? You poor
buggers.

Yana   It was good. Good fun.

Steph   Yeah. (**Steph** *stands unsteadily.*) I am smashed.
D'you think I have a drink problem? My editor does. He's
going to fire me if I don't dry out. (*Beat.*) Should be some
good material in that. (*She wobbles to the table and props herself
up.*) One more for luck.

She takes the bottle from **Yana** *and pours the last of it into her
glass. She drinks, perched on the table and peers around blearily.*

Christ . . . where am I?

Beat. **Yana** *sits beside her.*

Yana   How long have you been with this Murph?

Steph   Murph? Been with? I've only known him a week.
He's new to me. Comes highly recommended . . . 'scuse the
pun. As far as I can tell, he has precisely two interests: sex
and surfing. (*Beat.*) So, you want to fuck my photographer?

Yana   I don't mind.

Steph   Well, that's refreshing. He's awfully good. But
then, they all are these days. At least, the ones *I* meet are.

Yana   You ever make out with chicks?

Steph *bursts out laughing.*

Steph   Where on earth did you get that from? 'Make out
with chicks' indeed. I haven't heard a phrase like that since
. . . God, I dunno . . .

Yana *is stoney-faced.*

I'm sorry, I wasn't taking the piss. No, I don't sleep with women. Why? (*Beat.*) Christ, that wasn't an offer, was it?

Yana   I ask a question. I am curious. (*Beat.*)

Steph   I haven't 'made out with a chick' in a very long time. There was a phase we all went through, that's all. Basically, the blokes liked it.

Yana   You didn't?

Steph   Not fussed either way, really. (*She finishes her drink and stands.*) Right.

Yana   You know ... Dec says you write about people. You ask them questions and tell about their life, yes?

Steph   Sort of.

Yana   Well, I am confusing here, because you are not very interested in other people, I think. Not very curious. Except for yourself. (*Beat.*)

Steph   Darling, I'm a journalist. That's all. (*She goes.*)

Yana *sits at the table and takes her heroin gear out of her bag.*

Fade.

Scene Four

About 3 a.m. The patio is in virtual darkness. From the house, two shadowy figures emerge. They are **Yana** *and* **Murph***. She wears just a T-shirt, he wears just jeans. She leads him by the hand to the middle of the patio, stops and turns to him.*

Murph   What are you doing?

Yana   Shhh. (*She gets a chair from by the table and drops her bag onto it. Then she turns to him and starts unbuttoning his jeans.*)

Murph   Hey the beach was cool but this is living dangerously.

Yana   There is no danger I tell you. Dec takes sleeping
pills or else he cannot sleep.

Murph *looks at her, then pulls her T-shirt up over her head and
drops it on the floor. They kiss. She slowly pulls off his jeans, so he's
wearing just his shorts.*

Murph   I hope you're right.

Yana   I'm always right.

Murph   I guess you get pretty lonely.

Yana   Yeah.

Murph   Dec doesn't let you in on his business? (*Beat.*)

Yana   I am a . . . decoration . . . an ornament.

Murph   So you get bored.

Yana   I die with boredom.

Murph   Uh huh. If you were mine, I'd have you with me
every minute of every day. (*Beat.*) Especially with business
as good as it is.

Yana   I don't know about that . . .

Murph   Do you like what he does?

Yana   I hate it. (*Beat.*) Sometimes I hate *him* . . . I wish I
could leave.

Murph   And can't you?

Yana   I don't know. I must be safe.

Murph   I could make you safe. (*Beat.*)

Yana   How?

Murph   If you really wanted to get away from him . . .

Yana   Yes . . .

Murph   I could protect you.

She laughs.

Yana   Yeah, sure, you're a big strong man. You don't know Dec. He can find anyone.

Murph   Not if you're somewhere safe. Protected. (*Beat.*) I know people more powerful than Dec.

Yana   Who?

Murph   Just people.

Beat. She leads him to the chair and sits astride him.

All you'd have to do is tell us what you know about Dec's business.

She's kissing him.

His partners, contacts . . .

Yana   I know all of them . . .

Murph   And you'll be a thousand miles away. A new identity. A new life?

Yana   America?

Murph   Wherever. We can set you free.

Yana   America. (*She kisses him.*) I dream of America for many years.

Murph   It's yours if you want it.

Yana   I do, I want to be free.

Murph   You won't regret it.

Yana   Who are you?

Murph   I can't tell you, anyway it doesn't matter.

Yana   I can trust you?

Murph   Oh yeah.

Yana   That's good.

Murph   I promise. You won't regret it.

Yana *slips down as if to give him a blow-job. Very slowly, from* *the patio steps, a figure emerges. It is* **Dec**. *He carries his machine gun and a torch. He silently comes up beside them.* **Dec** *suddenly switches on the torch with the beam straight into* **Murph**'s *eyes, and the gun pointed at his face.* **Murph** *opens his eyes and freezes.*

Dec Is that right?

Murph Oh shit . . .

Yana Darling, there you are.

Murph (*terrified*) Christ, man, look . . .

Dec Don't speak, Murph. Not yet. (*Beat.*)

Murph Dec, listen . . .

Dec (*close*) I said don't speak, Murph. Yeah? OK?

Murph *nods.*

Dec *gives* **Yana** *two sets of handcuffs. Through this section she cuffs* **Murph**'s *hands behind his back with one pair, and his ankles with the other pair.*

Have you had weapons training, Murph? (*Beat.*) Yeah?

Murph *shakes his head.*

So you don't know what this is and what it can do? (*He pushes the barrel against* **Murph**'s *face.*) Oh, I forgot, you've been in all those troublespots, haven't you? Seen plenty of heads blown apart. You must have known this was suicide, man.

Murph I'm sorry . . . I know she's your wife, but you know, I mean, she's horny, right?

Dec Murph, I know you didn't come here to fuck my wife. I know you're not just a photographer who likes surfing and chicks. So don't insult my fucking intelligence, OK?

Murph Man, I don't, I really don't know what you're talking about. You got the wrong guy.

Dec *smiles and stands up.*

You gotta believe me. Honest. You got the wrong guy.

Dec Yeah. (*He stares out to where the boat is moored.*) Your friends have gone.

Murph Who?

Dec In the boat. The ones monitoring and taping my calls.

Murph I don't know who you mean . . .

Dec I say 'gone' . . . they've more been kind of disappeared, actually.

Murph I don't know anything about anybody in a boat. (*Pause.*)

Dec What I need to know, Murph, is who you're all working for.

Murph I'm a fucking photographer, for Chrissake . . .

Dec Yeah. So, are you gangsters or the good guys? That's all I need to know. I have to know who's putting the squeeze on, so I can get out of here. The direction I take depends on who you are. So what are you, Murph? Bad guys or government?

Murph Hey, man, government? Me?!

Dec Drug Enforcement Agency, Murph. (*He laughs.*) The Feds.

Murph You're joking, do I look like the Feds?!

Dec *turns and faces him and smiles.* **Murph** *laughs nervously.*

I mean, do I?

Dec *smiles.*

Dec Oh yes.

Murph's *smile fades. Pause.*

Murph Look, what is it you're going to do to me?

Dec Do?

Murph   Well, you've got me mixed up with something I don't know shit about, but you don't believe me. You've got a bloody gun pointed at me . . . I mean, I'm a little nervous here . . . (*Beat.*)

Dec (*suddenly*)   You don't think I'm going to kill you, do you? (*Beat.*) Do you?

Murph   I dunno.

Dec   Rest assured, old son, I won't kill you. Not my style.

Murph   No. Thank Christ for that.

Dec *stares at him.*

Dec   Tell me who you're working for and I'm outa here. I have to know, Murph.

Murph   I can't . . .

Dec *looks at* **Yana**. *She stands and comes over to* **Murph** *and kneels in front of him. She goes down on him.*

Oh, man . . .

Dec *is behind* **Murph**. **Yana** *suddenly bites hard as* **Dec** *clamps his hand over* **Murph***'s mouth, holding his head tight.* **Murph** *tries to scream.* **Yana** *is biting,* **Murph** *is writhing and groaning as* **Dec** *holds his head tight. She stops biting and looks up.* **Murph** *is in agony.*

Dec   Well?

Murph, *distressed, shakes his head. Beat.* **Yana** *bites again. This time* **Murph** *is in intense pain. He stands it for as long as he can, then nods his head madly.* **Dec** *releases his grip slightly.*

Murph   OK, please stop, OK . . . ?

Dec *nods to* **Yana**. *She stops biting. There is blood around her mouth, which she smears across her face with the back of her hand.*

Dec   Sorry about that, but you know how it is.

Murph   Fuck you, man . . .

Dec Yeah. So. (*Pause.*)

Murph DEA.

Dec Yeah . . .

Yana Fucking DEA . . .

Dec You're an agent.

Murph Yeah.

Dec And what are you doing here?

Murph We're coming for you.

Dec When?

Murph Don't know.

Dec Come on, old son. Soon?

Murph No, the back up's not in place. (*Beat.*)

Dec So what are you?

Murph Intelligence.

Dec (*laughing*) Yeah?

Murph (*wryly*) Yeah.

Dec Not very intelligent coming here, when you think about it, was it, Murph?

Murph You take your chances. (*Beat.*) We know you've got a big score coming up . . .

Dec And who told you that?

Murph Lucky guess? (*Beat.*)

Dec Actually Murph, you're a day late. (*Beat.*) Now, gimme a name.

Murph I don't know. (*Beat.*) Look, why don't you run? I can't do anything. Just disappear. Go now. It makes sense.

Dec I can't do that. I have to organise a few things.

Murph   Holding me here, that's another charge. Another five years.

Dec   You shouldn't have come here. It was stupid.

Murph   Yeah, well, I happen to believe in the law.

Dec   Stupid. You think it was worth the risk?

Murph   I dunno . . .

Dec   Murph, you work for the biggest organised crime racket in the world. One way or another, your bosses are responsible for more misery, poverty, exploitation, squalor and death than I could ever be. They want me out because I'm competition. Ideological competition. Because, y'see, and you might think this strange, I believe, really believe in what you only *say* you believe in. Freedom. Pure freedom.

Murph   So you enslave people with drugs . . . (*Beat.*)

Dec   Do you know what alienation is? In the human individual it's when he or she no longer feels connected to the outside world. It's when the outside world seems to operate on a set of rules devised by madmen. It's when the individual feels that it's useless to be 'good' . . . because in this world, good is bad. (*Beat.*) Some people, of course, find ways of living with that, one way or the other. But some can't. Some resist. Any way they can. And it's only when you resist that your life begins to change. The alienation begins to subside. You live by a new set of rules. Rules that, for once, make a kind of sense. And that's all most of us want out of life. (*Beat.*) But then you realise . . . this is life or death, man. This is one critical fucking struggle. And then . . . life and death take on a whole new meaning.

Murph   Did anyone ever suggest to you that you might just be a raving paranoid?

Dec   Oh yes.

Yana   And what about me? Am *I* paranoid?

Murph I dunno . . .

Yana I am born in a crazy country, run by crazy people. Then we had a revolution. We *think* we had a revolution. We think we could kill the craziness and start again. (*Beat.*) And some more crazy people take over. The *same* people. And what happens? Do you help? No. You invest in this crazy country, while we, the people who this country belongs to, we are made to be whores. And you do this all over the world. And then you piss on us with your talk of law and freedom. (*Beat.*) The only freedom I know is to break you and your laws.

Murph Yeah? Well, in my book, your alienation is just egotism. Because there's never enough for people like you, is there? They give you democracy, you want anarchy. They give you freedom, you foul it up with dope. You just want to play in the dirt, like you never grew up.

Dec Oh, do shut up, you silly little man. (**Dec** *flashes his torch into the darkness. A torch flashes back at him.*) D'you believe in God, Murph?

Murph (*beat*) Why?

Dec Just wondered. (*Beat.*)

Murph Yes, actually, I do.

Dec Well, that's nice. (*He takes out a roll of tape and quickly tears off a strip which he sticks over* **Murph**'s *mouth.*) About not killing you . . . I lied. Well, sort of. It's not *my* style, but I have people working for me who have no qualms about it whatsoever. They'll be right up. (*Beat.*) The sun'll be up in a couple of hours. It's going to be another beautiful day.

Yana *goes into the house.* **Murph**, *terrified, gives* **Dec** *an imploring look.* **Dec** *looks at him then goes into the house.* **Murph** *tries to free himself while trying to see round to the steps. As the lights begin an incredibly slow fade, he stares, half resigned, half in disbelief and terror.*

Blackout.

Scene Five

9.30 the next morning. It's bright and sunny. The table is laid for
breakfast. There is a coffee pot, cereals, milk, rolls, jam etc. **Dec** *is*
standing as in Scene One, binoculars to his eyes, staring out to sea.
From the steps, **Louise** *appears. She looks radiant and fresh, her*
hair damp from swimming. She sees **Dec,** *smiles and comes down to*
him. He senses her and looks around. They smile.

Louise   Morning.

Dec   Hello, darling.

They kiss. She puts her arm round his waist. He puts his round her
shoulder.

Louise   You lucky, lucky man.

He smiles.

What are you looking at? (*Beat.*)

Dec   The horizon.

Louise   See anything?

Dec   No. (*Beat.*)

Louise   I walked around the island.

Dec   That's some walk.

Louise   It didn't feel like it. It felt as if time had stopped.

Dec   I know what you mean.

Louise   I had a skinny-dip, too.

Dec   Mmm.

He holds up the binoculars and smiles. She blushes embarrassed. Beat.

Louise   The sky here . . . when you look up at it for a
long time . . . it's like staring at eternity. Strange, isn't it
. . . here we are, on this little rock poking up out of the
sea, and it feels like the safest place I've ever been. One
big wave and we'd be swept away. But there's no terror
here. (*Beat.*) Talking of which, has Spencer surfaced yet?

Dec   I haven't seen him.

Louise   No. (*Beat.*)

Dec   I was, uh, very surprised to hear that you two were still together.

Louise   Yeah, me too.

Dec   Sorry, I didn't mean that to sound the way it did.

Louise   How did it sound? (*Beat.*)

Dec   Gloomy.

Louise   Hmm. Gloomy. Well, that's marriage. (*Beat.*) Is that coffee on the table?

Dec   Yeah, help yourself.

Louise   Decaf?

Dec   No, sorry.

Louise   What the hell. Let's live dangerously. (*She goes to the table and pours a coffee.*) One for you?

Dec   No, thanks. (*He pours himself an orange juice.*) Hey, all that stuff about Spencer nearly being a candidate, last night, is that true?

Louise   Yes, but he was never going to get it. God, imagine being so transparent that even Tory party members can see through you. (*Beat.*)

Dec   And what about his business.

She smiles ruefully.

Louise   Which one? Anglo Properties? Taplow UK Properties? Anglo Taplow Construction? Anglobuild Property Consultants? (*Beat.*) True fact about Spencer: he owns more company names than pairs of underpants. All of a similar level of grubbiness. (*Beat.*) He did very well for a short time in the eighties. But, let's face it, a brain-damaged gerbil with a bank loan could have done very well for a short time in the eighties. He had two or three years of whizzing round, buying places, selling places, harrassing tenants, you know, all the things that make a property developer's life worth living. And then, suddenly, nothing. A lot of waffle about APR, ERM and all that, but in truth he was like the rest of them. He was just terribly, terribly bad at it. Most of our friends bit the dust. Not all. But most. Some were lucky, some were clever. (*Beat.*) Poor Spencer. Neither lucky nor clever. (*Beat.*) Pretty stupid, in fact. (*Beat.*)

Dec   It must be love then.

Beat. She smiles.

Louise   Is that what it looks like?

Dec   I just assumed.

Louise   Love doesn't come into it. Never really has. (*Beat.*) Imagine being in love with Spencer. (*She gives a short, appalled laugh.*)

Dec   So how come?

Louise   Well, according to my therapist –

Dec   Wait a minute, you have a therapist?

Louise   Of course.

Dec   Therapists have therapists?

Louise   Yes. It's an on-going process. You never really arrive, you just keep growing.

Dec   I never knew that.

Louise   Well, now you do . . .

Dec   I suppose it's logical . . .

Louise   Utterly. (*Beat.*) Anyway, according to my therapist, and after a long period of denial, I've come to agree with him . . . I've been hooked on pitying Spencer. Very selfish, really. The worse he got, the more I pitied, and the more I pitied, the more I thought I was getting what I needed. (*Beat.*) The thing is, for a long time, I pretended that he was research. You know, my very own walking case history. Which, in fact, he is. You know I specialise in abuse?

Dec   No, I didn't.

Louise   Well, that's what I do. Not necessarily the horror stories, although I've had a few. No, the people I tend to deal with are adults scarred by negligent parenting. In the main, solid middle class people whose childhoods were marked by the absence of parental love, who consequently suffer what we think of as 'grown up' problems, depression, addiction, various disorders and so on. (*Beat.*) Sorry, you don't want to hear this . . .

Dec   I'm just wondering where marriage to Spencer fits into this.

Louise   Why?

Dec   I'm intrigued . . . (*Beat.*)

Louise   You hate him, don't you?

Dec   No –

Louise   It's all right to say it. (*Beat.*)

Dec   You hate him too, don't you?

Louise   It's not all right for me to say it. (*Pause.*) I do know I pitied him. I mean, look at his upbringing: aloof, distant father; quiet, downtrodden mother. No displays of affection allowed. Sent away to boarding school at the age of seven. (*Beat.*) Seven. (*Beat.*) In a rare, sober moment, he told me about it once. How he felt. It nearly broke my heart. (*Beat.*) Then he was sexually and physically abused by older boys at school, and he in turn abused younger boys. Went to Oxford, failed his exams. Tried to become a businessman. Failed. Tried to become a politician. Failed. Tried to become an alcoholic. Succeeded. (*Beat.*)

Dec   And marriage?

Louise   Failed miserably. (*Beat.*) He's gay, Dec.

Dec   Uh huh.

Louise He can't admit it, and it makes him miserable. (*Beat.*) And I see so many like Spencer. You'd be amazed. The successful ones tend to be fantasists of one sort or another, while the failures are all hooked on something. I think it's one of the reasons there's so much gooey nostalgia, why there's so much sickly hankering after the mythical perfect family these days. They all desperately want to go back and try and make everything all right again. Because, you see, they're in pain, and pain makes people make such a mess of things. (*Pause.*)

Dec You're more understanding than I can be.

Louise So what's your pain, Dec?

Dec (*looking at his watch*) Gosh, is that the time?

She laughs.

Louise I'm writing a book, you know, I've nearly finished. Self-help. A loser's handbook. It's dreadfully down-market, I'm afraid, but that's where the money is, and that's why I'm writing it. I already have an American publisher. So I shall probably amass tons of money and buy myself an island, or a piece of one, buy myself a slice of the sky and sit and contemplate eternity. (*Beat.*) Because . . . and I really believe this . . . I really believe we're beyond help. As a culture, as a species. I actually believe we're doomed. (*Beat.*) And I'm supposed to be one of the healers. That's what I always wanted to help them heal that small child inside. But the child's taken over. He's in control, there's no stopping him. (*Beat.*) If you ask me, I have to say that it's all just too fucked up to be put right. It's just too late.

Dec See, I've never believed that.

Louise Ah, revolutionary optimism.

Dec No, just sheer bloody-mindedness. (*Beat.*) I know what you'll say, but . . . I have this unshakeable hatred. It keeps me going.

Louise And what do you think I'll say to that?

Dec   I imagine you'd say that hatred destroys you from the inside . . . that it takes you over . . .

Louise   Why should I say that? You feel let down, outcast, ignored. I hear that. And I know how it feels. (*Beat.*) Even when you were the golden boy, all those years ago, I could see that this was how you'd end up. (*Beat.*)

Dec   Not such a lucky man after all.

Spencer *comes on. He wears a dressing gown, dark socks and shoes and his Panama hat.*

Spencer   Leave my wife alone, you bloody oik.

Dec   So he finally graces us with his presence. Sleep well?

Spencer   Like a baby. (*To* **Louise**.) Where the bloody hell were you when I woke up?

Louise   I went for a walk and a swim.

Spencer   Oh Christ, communing with nature again. Why must you always be so bloody . . . pure? (*He sits and looks at the breakfast things.*) Is this it, then?

Dec   Is this what?

Spencer   Le petit dejeuner.

Dec   Yes.

Spencer   What, no full monty?

Dec   No what?

Spencer   No Trusthouse Forte-style full English breakfast. Egg, bacon, sausage, mushrooms, tomato, beans, fried slice, strong tea.

Dec   Oh, you mean that crap my dad used to eat.

Spencer   Precisely. *That* crap. It's all the rage, you know.

Dec   We don't bother. It's bad for you.

Spencer   That's the point. Whereas all this stuff, I suppose, is good for one.

Dec   Yes.

Spencer   Good for the bowels, eh? Look after your bowels and your bowels will look after you. That's what they told us at school. Well, bollocks. What have my bowels ever done for me, except let me spectacularly down at moments of crisis?

Louise   Thanks for sharing that with us.

Spencer   Well . . . (*He holds up a roll.*) No chance of slapping a few greasy rashers in this, I suppose?

Dec   There might be some bacon in the kitchen . . .

Spencer   No, no, don't worry . . . (*Beat.*)

Louise   He doesn't want bacon, he wants to make a fuss because he can't have any.

Spencer   Does it never end?

Louise   You engineer things so that you appear deprived. You then feel justified in kicking up a stink.

Spencer   And why not? I *am* deprived. All the things I can't have . . . love, happiness, cooked breakfast. (*Beat.*) OK if I have some coffee, is it?

Louise   Yes, it's fully caffeinated, have as much as you want.

Spencer (*pouring coffee*)   I tell you what would go perfectly with this . . .

Louise   No. I know what you're going to say, and I refuse to participate. I'm going to have a shower. (*She goes into the house.*)

Spencer   God, she hates me so much.

Dec (*beat*)   What was it you wanted with your coffee?

Beat. **Spencer** *looks guilty.*

Spencer   Thing is, I don't know if I do. Do I only want it if she's here? Is it just something to put between us . . .

something to talk about, to talk to each other through?
(*Beat.*) No. Fuck that. I want . . . I *need* a large brandy.

Dec   Help yourself.

Spencer   You don't mind?

Dec   Couldn't give a monkey's.

Spencer   Stout fellow. (*He gets the brandy bottle. He finishes his coffee and pours brandy into the cup.*) This is going to hurt me more than it hurts you . . . (*He swigs, grimaces, then smiles.*) Ah, yes. The good doctor. (*Pause.*) Sorry.

Dec   For what?

Spencer   I wasn't always like this, y'know. (*Beat.*)

Dec   Yes you were. (*Beat.*)

Spencer   That's right. I was. (*He laughs.*) Back when we thought we were immortal . . .

Dec   Don't get nostalgic on me, Spencer. It's much too early.

Spencer   It's much too late. (*Pause. He stares into his cup. Dec starts rolling a joint.*) You, er, really have rather a penchant for that stuff, don't you?

Dec   Yeah.

Spencer   Each to his own.

Dec   I refuse to get high on what's permitted. No fucking politician's going to tell me what I can and can't do with my unconscious, thank you.

Spencer   What, you'd go to war for your right to puff the evil weed?

Dec   I already have.

Spencer *gets up, suddenly energised.*

Spencer   Listen, Dec – mate – let's not beat around the bush, eh? We go too far back for that. So. Straight talk, eh? Listen. I've been there, OK? I've been there big time.

The dizzy heights, mate. At one time, I was worth millions.
No joke, millions. I had properties all over London. It was
fucking great, everywhere you went, places were being
bought, ripped apart, rebuilt, sold on. Prices were sky high.
Just for a time it was truly heaven on earth, and it *worked*.
No one had really believed it before. We'd never gone for
it, you know, like we really *meant* it. But then that all
changed. We were like wild animals who'd been caged up
for eons, prodded at with sticks, half-starved, and then they
threw open the cage doors, and we fucking went. Like the
Mongol hordes we went. And there were no problems, no
arguments like before. For once it *worked*. Anybody
disagreed, anybody piped up with the old bleeding heart,
fairy bollocks, we just laughed in their faces and told them:
'Get real. *Fuck off*!' (*Beat.*) A revolution, Dec. That's what it
was. Glorious. (*Beat.*) But after the revolution came a
revelation. I realised this wasn't enough. I remember I took
myself off somewhere. Savoy Grill, I think, and I blew two
hundred quid on dinner and champagne. But that didn't
do it. So I just went out and bought things. Anything at
all, so long as it cost. (*Beat.*) I'd got what I'd always
wanted, and it *wasn't* what I wanted. I was staring into a
very dark hole, and it was very fucking scary all of a
sudden. (*Beat.*) So I let it all slip. And pretty soon I was
back on the pavement, where, till now, I remain. (*Beat.*)
One consolation though, an awful lot of other people found
themselves there. Oh yes. D'you remember Billy
Robertson? Trinity man, year below us? (**Dec** *nods.*) Mad
Scottish bastard . . . well, he'd done very, very nicely for
himself, doing stuff for the MOD, inside track, y'know . . .
well . . . he only got banged up, didn't he? Fucking prison
sentence. Attempt to defraud, etcetera. Got fifteen months,
poor sod. And *they* stitched him up. *They* dropped him in it.
A sacrificial lamb. (*Beat.*) I went to visit him – nice enough
place they put him in, but still – and I'd just been declared
bankrupt, and anyway, I go to see him, and he's totally
raving. The fellow's possessed with hatred, and he keeps
saying, over and over, 'They lied to me. They fucking well
lied to me!' So I leant across and I said, 'Of course they

did, old son. That's what they *do*'. (*Pause. He pours another brandy.*)

Dec   This . . . revolution . . .

Spencer   Yeah? (*Beat.*)

Dec   Who paid?

Spencer   How d'you mean?

Dec   Well, every revolution creates its dispossessed. Every revolution has its tumbrils, its steady stream of victims for the chop. Somebody had to pay for the fulfilment of your dream.

Spencer   Ah. No, you see, what we did, for the first time, was create wealth where none existed before.

Dec   But you can't do that, not on a grand scale, without somebody paying. (*Beat.*)

Spencer   Oh, Christ, Dec, not the 'workers'? Good grief, I mean, they paid the price for decades of systematic abuse. They were long overdue.

Dec   I see.

Spencer   Yes. Things had to be . . . freed up, before we could get it going. That's modern economics. And that's what I learned. Modern economics is licensed villainy. It's creative theft on a grand scale. The problem is, where it all started to go wrong, they tried to pretend otherwise. So long as everybody *knew* we were operating on the moral level of a knocking shop, things were hunky-dory. But then they decided this all had to be justified. The stupid, sanctimonious bastards. I mean, you don't relieve somebody of their wallet with the aid of a gun, then pick them up, dust them down and say 'by the way, I have a vision of a kinder, gentler Britain where we can all be at ease with ourselves'. No. You stick your boot on their throat and say 'get yourself a gun, you silly bastard!'. (*Beat.*) Which is where you come in, old mate. (*Beat.*)

Dec   I'm not with you.

Spencer   Come on, Dec. I've been around, I know the score. (*He gets close.*) I know what you do. (*Beat.*) And I could be invaluable to you, with the sort of contacts I have. To all intents and purposes, I'm just another businessman. No suspicion attaches to me. Invaluable, that's what I could be to your business.

Dec   Doing what, exactly?

Spencer   Anything. Anything at all.

Dec   Such as?

Spencer   Christ, Dec, you know what I'm saying. Don't be so coy. Look, you're a dope smuggler, everybody knows that. You flog drugs, end of story.

Dec   But that's not what I'm about . . .

Spencer   You must have a turnover of millions. Christ, why didn't I stick with you after Oxford? I could have had my own island by now. (**Dec** *gets up and stares out to sea.* **Spencer** *stands behind him.*) Take me on, Dec. I want in.

Dec   (*venomously*)   You stupid cunt. (**Spencer** *gives a nervous laugh.*) Spencer, I wouldn't trust you to shit without a guidebook. What possible use could I have for a pissed-up invertebrate whose only loyalty is to himself?

Spencer   Be fair, old son . . .

Dec   I'm giving you the benefit of the doubt. Old son. You don't know what I do, you don't know why I do it. All you know is it pays, so you want some. You actually believe you have a right to some of it. (*Beat.*) Don't you ever learn? (*Pause.*)

Spencer   I'm begging . . . (*Beat.*)

Dec   So beg. It's all you're good for. (**Yana** *appears from the steps with carrier bags of fruit and veg.*) Hello, darling here . . . (*He takes the bags from her and puts them on the table. She pours an orange juice.*) How was the market?

Yana .   Crowded, as usual.

Dec My turn tomorrow. (**Dec** *turns and looks at* **Spencer**.)

Spencer I offered. Remember that. (*He goes.* **Yana** *looks at* **Dec**.)

Dec He wants a job. (*She sneers.*) Yeah. (*Beat.*) So what'd Mickey say?

Yana Mickey's gone to Athens.

Dec What?

Yana That's all. (*Beat.*)

Dec Fucking great. (*Beat.*) Well. Let's pack, maybe we'll go to Thailand a little earlier than expected. (*Beat.*)

Yana How close do you think they are?

Dec Too close.

Yana That's what *I* think.

He holds his hand out to her. She puts her hand in his.

Dec Scared?

Yana What's to be scared for?

He smiles.

Dec I'll arrange with George to pick us up in the boat tonight OK? (*She nods. He stands.*) Let's hope that gives us enough time. (*He starts to go.*)

Yana It doesn't matter.

He's gone.

Fade.

Scene Six

The patio, 5 p.m. **Louise** *is sitting on the wall at the back of the patio, knees drawn up, staring at the view.* **Spencer** *comes on, glass in hand, in an intense, drunk state. He wears his suit and hat. He stops and looks at* **Louise**.

Spencer   Oh, for Christ's sake . . . (*She ignores him.*) You're like some dopey bloody schoolgirl. (*Pause.*) Seen the arsehole anywhere?

Louise   Who?

Spencer   You know who

Louise   If I was blessed with a talent for mind-reading, I certainly wouldn't waste it trying to read yours.

Spencer   Ooh, somebody put something sharp in your muesli?

Louise   Just . . . (*Beat.*) Forget it.

Spencer   No, come on, let's have a spat. Make a change . . .

Louise   Spencer, I'm tired . . .

Spencer   Tired? You never bloody *do* anything except gawp at the fucking sky. (*Beat.*)

Louise   I'm tired of *you*.

Spencer   Well what else is bloody new?

Louise   No, I mean *really* tired. As in, exhausted, had enough, kaput. (*Beat.*)

Spencer   Oh, piss off. I mean it, *I've* had enough. You can't treat me like this, I'm not a dog. (*Beat.*) You sit there like some serene bloody Queen of the May, passing judgement on me all the time. I'm sick of it. I deserve to be treated with a little respect. (*Beat.*) Well, don't I? (*She just looks at him.*) Christ, you are so smug. What have you ever done that's so fucking brilliant, eh? When did *you* ever make a million? How many companies have *you* ever run? (*Beat.*) You've done nothing. Big fat zero. All you've ever done is drag me down. Fuck, I'd have been flying now if I hadn't had you hanging round my neck like some giant bloody albatross. Everything that's ever gone wrong for me has been down to you. You've never wanted me to be a success, you never approved when I *was*. You're only happy when I'm on the floor, and that's the simple truth of it. Admit it, you want me to fail, and you always have. (*Beat.*) Come on then, I can't have a spat on my own.

Louise   This isn't a spat. (*Beat.*) When we get home, you're moving out.

Spencer   I'm sorry? *I'm* moving out? Of my own home?

Louise   It's *my* home. Even when you had money you never paid a penny towards it.

Spencer   I had overheads, for Christ's sake! (*Beat.*)

Louise   I've had anything I ever wanted from you years ago. I shouldn't have kept you around like this. I'm sorry.

Spencer (*beat*)   Are you actually being serious?

Louise   Yes.

Spencer   But . . . oh, shit, come on, I love you . . .

Louise   Don't be silly. You don't love me. And I don't love you.

Spencer   But I'm nothing without you.

Louise   You're nothing *with* me. You'll never amount to anything with me. I make it too easy for you not to bother. It's my fault.

Spencer   Thank you. That's a great consolation. (*Beat.*) Well, you don't know what's inside here. (*He touches his chest.*) I'll fucking show *you.*

Louise   Good.

Spencer   No, I mean it.

Louise   *I* mean it. Good. (*Beat.*)

Spencer   I'll show you . . .

Dec *and* **Steph** *appear from the steps.* **Steph** *has a notebook in one hand and a tape recorder in the other.* **Spencer** *turns his back and drinks.*

Steph   Ah, Spencer, Lou, just the people . . . we've been trying to remember the name of that bloke who killed himself, second term d'you remember?

Dec   I'm sure it was Martin something . . .

Louise   What, the one who jumped off Beachy Head?

Steph   That's him.

Louise   Oh, God, that's a tough one.

Steph   Spencer? Come on, he was on your staircase . . .

Spencer   So was Moss.

Dec   Memory like a sieve, me.

Spencer   Well why should *I* bloody remember if he can't?

Steph   It's on the tip of my tongue. I can see his face . . .

Louise   Specs. Wore a cardigan.

Dec   Definitely Martin something . . . (*Beat.*)

Steph   Never mind, I'll get it from the college.

Spencer   Keith. Keith Martin.

Steph   Yes!

Dec   Keith Martin, yeah . . .

Spencer   So why the sudden interest in some twerp who dived off a cliff more than twenty years ago?

Steph   I happen to be doing an interview with Dec. It's part of the story.

Spencer   I don't see why.

Louise   No, you wouldn't.

Steph   You must have known him as well as anybody.

Spencer   He was a complete nonentity. Sorry.

Dec   You were always having run-ins with him,

remember? He was always complaining about the noise.

Spencer   Years ago . . .

Dec   You used to glue up the lock on his door . . .

Steph   You didn't . . .

Spencer   Once . . .

Dec   Invaded his room once, didn't you, with the entire college dining club? Held the guy prisoner for hours while you all got pissed and trashed his room.

Spencer   Pranks, that's all. He took it in good part.

Dec   I don't think he did. I had quite a long talk with him once. He was thinking of leaving, but he was the first in his family to have ever got to Oxford, and he didn't want to let his parents down. And because of all the hassle, he couldn't work, so he was petrified he was going to fail Mods Exams and get sent down . . . (**Spencer** *turns and gives* **Dec** *a vicious look.*) Poor guy. Totally out of his depth. (*Beat.*)

Spencer   What are you trying to say?

Dec ˙   Nothing.

Steph   It's useful background, makes a fascinating counterpoint to Dec's story.

Spencer   Just what are you trying to say, Moss?

Louise   I should have thought that was blinking obvious, even to *you.*

Spencer   You're trying to say I killed him, is that it?

Dec   I'm not trying to say anything. (*Beat.* **Yana** *comes on carrying the mobile phone.*)

Yana   Dec, it's George.

Dec   Oh, right . . . excuse me, everyone . . .

He takes the phone and goes to the top of the steps, turning his back on them, and speaks quietly into the phone.

Spencer (*to* **Steph**)   If you print that stuff, I'll sue. (*Beat.* **Steph** *explodes with laughter.*)

Steph   Don't be so touchy. Anyway, for heaven's sake Spencer, I'm writing about Dec, not you. (*Beat.* **Spencer** *storms off.*) Sorry, Lou.

Louise   What for?

Steph   I didn't mean to upset him.

Louise   Hey, it's open season, feel free.

Dec *turns round and hands the phone back to* **Yana**.

Dec   Eight. OK?

Yana   OK.

Steph   Oh, Yana, did Murph say what time he'd be back from the mainland? (*Beat.*)

Yana   Oh. No. He was going to take pictures, you know . . .

Steph   He'll be in a bar somewhere chatting up some unsuspecting Greek tart, I expect.

Dec   If he's not back tonight, we'll send out a search party.

Steph   He'd better be back by tonight, or it's curtains for Mister Murph.

Yana   OK. (*She goes.*)

Louise *gets up and stretches.*

Louise   I'm going for a walk. See you in a while.

Steph   Bye, Lou. (**Louise** *goes.*) Right.

Dec   I'm all yours.

He perches on the table and starts to roll a joint. She sits and turns on the tape recorder.

Steph   OK. So. After Oxford. There's been a lot of speculation about what exactly you were up to during the time you were in Holland and after. Can we put your story on the record?

Dec   Yeah. The problem is I got involved with a lot of people whose whole existence is based on not telling the truth. They live in a world where the only reality is knowing who your enemy is. I didn't realise until too late that that was how it was.

Steph   So who were these people? (*Beat.*)

Dec   MI5. Drug dealers. Arms dealers. Men with exotic nicknames and even more exotic girlfriends. A crazy scene, basically.

Steph   And what were you doing in all this? Who were you working for?

Dec   To start with, me. I was making a good living out of smuggling dope into Britain. Nothing too grand, you know. The odd shipment here, the odd shipment there. But it was strictly small time. (*Beat.*) Until Osborne got hold of me.

Steph   Osborne?

Dec   Harry Osborne, MI6, Balliol man.

Steph   I remember. Long sideburns, waistcoat . . .

Dec   Yeah. He recruited me to keep an eye on some of the guys in the network who were into arms and explosives.

Steph   You were recruited?

Dec   Yeah.

Steph   That's incredible.

Dec   But true, I swear.

Steph   So if I get onto this Osborne guy, he'll confirm that?

Dec   The first thing they tell you: get into any trouble and we disown you, never heard of you. Which is exactly what happened. When the warrant was issued for my arrest, I got onto them and said, you know, you've got to get this torn up. I mean, I'm working for you.

Steph And what did they say?

Dec Dec who?

Steph Just like that?

Dec Just like that. (*Beat.*)

Steph I'll have to run this by the paper's spook expert.

Dec Do. I wasn't the only one. They've been fighting a very dirty war for a very long time. And Osborne's still there, somewhere. (*Beat.*)

Steph So what did you do? When they dumped you?

Dec I switched. I joined the bad guys, full time.

Steph The IRA?

Dec Well . . . at that time, there were three Republican organisations: the Provos, the Officials and the INLA. Then there were the hangers-on, the guys who were working for whoever paid them. It was all very confused. These guys were just as likely to kill each other as kill Brits. So it was a question of maintaining a fine balance, not getting too closely involved with any one group.

Steph But . . . let's get this clear . . . was there any ideological commitment on your part to Irish Republicanism?

Dec I'm half Irish.

Steph Yes. So was there? (*Beat.*)

Dec Sure. (*Beat.*) Think back to what it was like in those days. Lots of us believed it was possible to change society through confrontation. And creating that change was our one aim. Many, many people thought the only alternative was creeping fascism. (*Beat.*) Every generation needs its rubble. Every generation has to level what exists in order to creat the world they want to live in. That's what the other side's been doing for the last fifteen years back home. God when I was back last time I couldn't believe what they'd done.

Steph   Such as.

Dec   I've always believed that the very best of working class culture was our best hope. Unfortunately the Right know this as well, so they turned working class culture into a consumer product. They've sold back to the working class a bogus version of their own reality, and fooled them into thinking that that gives them a power they never had before. And what do they sell them back? All the crap. All the things the middle class most fear and secretly envy, aggression, philistinism, crudity, booze-culture. And all the good stuff's gone down the drain. Instead of community, fear – hopelessness. (*Beat.*) They let the demons loose.

Steph   (*beat*)   Listen, I'm ashamed to say it, and I regret it every day . . . but I voted for them last time. It was pure panic. Christ, I'm an intelligent person, I knew all the arguments . . . but when it came to it, I was scared. They appealed to some dreadful, instinctive fear in me, and I put my cross next to their man. (*Beat.*) I'm ashamed.

Dec   Big deal. The dear old British middle classes, eh? Well-informed, know all the arguments, weigh everything in the balance . . . and then they vote simply for their own self-interest. All those reams of newsprint devoted to Britain's failure . . . who failed who? Well, it's you, the middle classes who failed Britain, with your fear of anything that might disrupt your mediaeval little souls. You have no ideas, no culture, no imagination for Christ's sake. All those things scare you witless. You've got a vote and you give it to whoever promises to leave you alone and hammer the other guy. And then you complain when they turn out to be what anybody with half a brain cell always knew they were: liars. You don't want to know anything beyond your garden gate. Beam the world in by satellite by all means, but don't, dear God, let it affect *us*. And if they want to turn the country into an embarrassing little theme park, you'll cheer them on, just so long as there's a job for you there flogging ice creams or plastic knick-knacks. (*Beat.*) You've no need to be ashamed. You got what you wanted. (*Beat.*)

Steph   Well, that's one way of looking at it . . .

Dec   It's a game for you. Trivial pursuit on a bigger board. Corporate Britain: a silly little depressed imitation of countries who've already done it better. (*Beat.*)

Steph   I might take this more to heart if it didn't come from a man who owes his living to other people's misery and addiction.

Dec *laughs.*

Dec   Yeah, all those desperate dope smokers, mugging old ladies and dying in the streets. (*Beat.*) You don't believe that shit.

Steph   I know drugs kill.

Dec   Hard drugs. But so does tobacco, pollution, junk food, booze. (*Beat.*) Drugs are a symptom, not the cause. The cause is a culture that is unnatural, that forces people to look for ways out rather than ways in. Sensible people run away from chaos. Only perverts thrive on it. But one day, when it's all crumbled, when everything's up for grabs, maybe there'll be enough people with the consciousness to build something better. (*Beat.*)

Steph   You don't believe that shit. (*He smiles.*) Can we talk about Susanna?

Dec   Why?

Steph   I think it would be of interest.

Dec   Not much to say. She's dead.

Steph   But do you know who was responsible. (*He shrugs.*) Don't you care?

Dec   What's the point?

Steph   You seem to care about everything else. I should have thought it would be a matter of some importance to find out who murdered your wife. (*Beat.*)

Dec   Is this going to be a stitch-up? Is this some kind of revenge?

Steph   Don't be so idiotic.

Dec   You know, I don't think you like me very much.

Steph   Of course I do.

Dec   I think not. (*Beat.*)

Steph   I used to love you. (*Beat.*)

Dec   Not a word I ever use.

Steph   Why not?

Dec   It's a waste of time. To be able to love, you have to be able to trust completely. And tell me, Steph, who do *you* trust that much? (*Beat.*)

Steph   I could have had your baby. (*Beat.*)

Dec   So could half of Oxford.

Steph   No, I mean . . . I could have had your baby. (*Beat.*) You won't remember, but I had some time off with glandular fever. Well, it wasn't glandular fever. I was aborting your baby. *And* they buggered my tubes up in the process. (*Pause.*)

Dec   So that's why you came here. (*He gets up.*) Susanna left me. She was screwing some German guy. She moved out . . . (*Beat.*) I'd upset some people over a deal. I was warned they were going to total the houseboat with me in it. (*Beat.*) Then Susanna called, said she needed to get her things from the board. I said, sure I'm away for a couple of days. (*Beat.*) So she went to pick up her things. And the tip-off was accurate.

Steph (*shaken*)   You . . . you mean you told her . . . and you knew . . . ?

Dec Mmm.

Steph You told her to go to the boat . . . and you knew there was a bomb on board?

Dec I had a shrewd idea. (*Beat.*) Neat, eh?

Steph That's monstrous.

Dec I suppose so.

Steph I mean . . . monstrous . . .

Dec I sort of aborted her, in a way.

Steph That's not fair. There's no comparison.

Dec Not everyone would agree.

Steph You let a living person die for no reason . . .

Dec I loved her. I trusted her completely. The one person in my life, ever . . . (*Beat.*)

Steph I feel sick.

Dec You shouldn't drink so much.

Steph Go to hell.

Dec It'll pass, I'm sure.

She stands.

Steph I feel I don't know you at all.

Dec It's impossible to know anybody else. In fact, it's very selfish to presume that we ever can.

Yana *comes on.*

Take me and Yana. We don't bother with any of that stuff.

Yana What stuff?

Dec Love.

Yana *puts two fingers in her mouth and mimes throwing up.*

See? (*Beat.*) I have this theory. The reason we're all so

fucked up is because of pop music. What's the theme of all the best pop music? Lurve. It's all about a retarded adolescent epiphany where suddenly somebody, in reality our own selves, but we pretend it's another person, becomes so important to us that the world seems to stop. We experience a perfect feeling of self, of our individual importance. (*Beat.*) Well ... if you make the chasing of that moment one of the pivotal experiences of the culture, you're going to end up with a lot of disappointed, not to mention emotionally crippled, people running around. We become eternally juvenile and incapable of adult emotional behaviour. (*Beat.*) Well, it's just a theory.

Steph   What *are* you?

Dec   Good question. Maybe your spiffing little article will provide us with an answer. (*Beat.*)

Steph   You've broken my heart. Again. (*She goes off.*)

Dec   Anybody call?

Yana   No.

Dec   Fuck, George should have called. This is bad. I don't like it.

Yana   What's to not like?

Dec   I feel set up. I feel trapped.

Yana   So untrap yourself.

She turns and tosses him her bag. He looks at her. She goes off down the steps. **Dec** *sits on the table with the bag.*

Fade.

Scene Seven

The patio about eight o'clock. **Steph** *is standing staring out to sea.* **Spencer** *and* **Louise** *are sat at the table.* **Spencer** *looks vague, glass in hand;* **Louise**, *unusually for her, drinking a glass of wine. The atmosphere is very down, very tense.*

Steph   Where *is* he? (*Beat.*) I don't suppose there'll be any boats coming across in the dark, so he'll be stranded over there. (*Beat.*) Bastard.

Louise *looks at the sky.*

Louise   Is that a helicopter?

Steph   Where?

Louise (*pointing*)   There.

Steph   Can't see. Anyway, I don't think he'd be coming back in a helicopter.

Louise   I didn't mean that. I was just pointing it out.

Spencer   It's probably just some rich bastard flying home to his island. (*Pause.*)

Steph   It's just . . . his plane tickets are here and everything. All his gear. What if he's not back when we leave tomorrow?

Louise   He'll turn up, Steph. (*Beat.*)

Steph   Shit. I'm lonely.

Beat. **Louise** *gets up and comes and puts her arm around* **Steph**.

Louise   It's OK.

Steph   I wish I could go now. Forget I ever knew Dec Moss.

Louise   Why? (*Beat.*)

Steph   God, what happened to it all?

Louise   What's brought this on?

Steph   I need a drink.

Louise   You don't need a drink.

Steph   I *need, need, need,* a drink. (*Beat.*)

Louise   OK. (**Louise** *pours* **Steph** *a brandy and herself a wine.*)

Spencer Hitting the bottle, are we darling?

Louise I'm having a glass of wine in a civilised fashion. I'm not going to make an exhibition of myself, or fall over or do any of the things which inevitably occur whenever *you* get within spitting distance of alcohol.

Spencer Pity. I'd like to see you sloshed.

Louise I know you would. That's why it'll never happen. (*She takes* **Steph** *her drink.*)

Steph Thanks. (*They drink.*) You carry this person around inside you for years . . . you think you know somebody . . .

Spencer Quite.

Louise Look at him. Thinks he's Jimminy Cricket. Are you going to sit dropping gnomic utterances into the conversation all night?

Spencer I might.

Louise God.

Yana *comes on. She goes to the table and sits down without speaking. She looks at her watch and pours a glass of wine. Uneasy pause.*

Spencer Is the master not going to appear this evening.

Yana What?

Spencer Is Mr Moss going to grace us with his presence at some point?

Yana I'm not understanding. You speak like a foreigner.

Spencer Where's Dec?

Yana How in the fuck should *I* know?

Spencer I thought you were married to him.

Yana So what? We don't go everywhere holding hands.

Spencer No, but I just thought you might know where he is.

Yana   Of course I know where he is. He's inside.

Spencer   Yes, but . . . oh, what's the point.

Yana   What's the point? What's the point? Why don't you ever shut your mouth?

Spencer   I beg your pardon?

Yana   Why must you always keep talking? Nobody listens. Look. (*She points to* **Steph** *and* **Louise**.) They don't listen to you. You think *I* listen to you?

Spencer   I couldn't care less.

Yana   Yes. You do. Or why do you talk all the time? You want that we should listen, when all you say is nothing.

Spencer   Look, you little bitch –

Louise   Spencer. Don't. (*Pause.*)

Yana   Why do you all come here? What do you want? You want to remember the old times? You want to get your hands on Dec? Why? (*Beat.*) We are not like you. You don't understand us. Go home. Go back to your little country. Go home and die.

Dec *comes on. He wears a bomber jacket and jeans and carries two large holdalls which he drops to the floor.*

Spencer   Going somewhere?

Dec   That's right. (*He takes the phone out of his pocket and dials.*)

Louise   Where are you going? What's happening?

Dec   Change of plan. Nothing to worry about. Often happens in my business. (*The phone isn't being answered.*) Come on . . .

Steph   What about us?

Dec   You can look after yourselves.

Steph   Thanks a bunch.

Dec You've got what you came for. (*The phone is still ringing.*) Come on, George . . . ! (*Beat.*)

Spencer Can you raise my broker on that thing? I feel like a flutter.

Dec *puts the phone in his pocket.*

Louise Are you seriously leaving?

Dec Yes. (*Beat.*) Lou, I'm sorry, things have, uh . . .

Steph They're catching up with you, aren't they?

Dec Are they?

Steph You are crapping yourself. You're scared.

Dec *stares at her.*

Dec I just don't want them to win. That's all.

Steph God, how bloody seedy . . .

Dec Look, Steph, you've never taken a risk in your entire fucking life. Mine has been one long risk. And that means that sometimes it gets worse than seedy. A lot worse. But don't worry, we're out of here as soon as our transport arrives.

Spencer Oh, it was yours, was it? I might have guessed.

Dec What was?

Spencer Don't be shy old man. No shame in owning a helicopter.

Dec What are you talking about?

Louise There was a helicopter circling round earlier.

Dec Where?

Louise In the sky. Where else?

Dec What did it look like?

Louise Well, like a helicopter.

Dec (*to* **Yana**) We're fucked, honey. Sorry.

Beat. **Dec** *looks at* **Yana**. *He takes a deep breath then turns quickly and goes into the house. Through the next section, without being noticed,* **Yana** *takes a hypodermic syringe out of her bag and injects herself in the arm under the table.*

Spencer   What the fuck is going on?

Steph   I think they're in trouble.

Louise   Well, I hope that doesn't mean *we* are.

Spencer   I hardly think so. It must be the police.

Steph   Oh my God . . .

Spencer   You'd certainly have a story.

Dec *rushes back on, carrying the machine gun and binoculars.*

Steph   What the hell are you doing with that?

Spencer   I'd say it's probably the police.

Dec   Yana, see if you can raise George on that. (*He throws the phone onto the table in front of her. She picks it up and feebly tries to dial the number.*) I think you lot had better go inside.

Steph   Not until you tell us what's happening. (*Beat.*)

Dec   They're coming for me.

Steph   Who?

Dec   The Drug Enforcement Agency, darling. It's who your boy Murph was working for.

Steph   Are you completely bonkers?

Spencer   How do you know he was working for them?

Dec   He told me. (*Beat.*)

Steph   When?

Dec   Who cares, look . . .

Steph   Where is he? Where's Murph?

Dec   I don't know. (**Dec** *scans the horizon.*)

Steph   What do you mean, you don't know? (*Beat.*) Dec!?

Dec   I DON'T FUCKING KNOW! OK?! (*He fixes the binoculars on a point on the shore.*) Fuck, they're here. Yana, come on.

Yana *is sitting, staring blearily straight ahead, her arms outstretched on the table in front of her.*

We've got to run.

Spencer   I don't think she can even walk . . .

Dec *goes to her. He strokes her hair.*

Dec   Yana? Baby? (*He sees the syringe in her bag. He studies the remaining liquid in it then drops it back in the bag. He stares.*)

Louise   Please, Dec, what's going on?

Yana*'s eyes close as* **Dec** *perches on the table beside her and feels the pulse in her neck. Her head starts to droop. He puts the gun on the table and cradles her head in his hands.* **Spencer** *comes over.*

Spencer   What is it? What's the matter with her? (*Beat.*)

Dec   Pure heroin.

Louise   Can't you do something?

Dec   No.

Pause. Suddenly, **Spencer** *picks up the machine gun and points it at* **Dec**.

Spencer   Sorry, Moss.

Dec *stares at him. A long nervous pause.*

Dec   What are you doing?

Spencer   I'm sort of arresting you. (**Dec** *starts to move towards him.* **Spencer** *raises the gun.*) Don't, there's a good chap.

Dec   I'm assuming you know how to work that?

Spencer   'Fraid so. (**Dec** *lets* **Yana***'s head drop on the table.*) Right. Let's do this properly. Don't want them mistaking me for you. Hande hoch, there's a good chap. (**Dec** *raises his hands.*)

Dec   Is this initiative? Or are you on the payroll?

Spencer   I'm not strictly speaking on the payroll . . . (*Beat.*) You remember Harry Osborne.

Dec *smiles.*

Dec   Yes, I remember Harry.

Spencer   Nice man. Bought me lunch at the Carlton Club last week. We had a little chat. I did offer my services to *you*, remember. And I'm sure you'd have paid far more handsomely than HMG.

Dec   You'd have turned me in sooner or later.

Spencer   Yes probably a fair assumption.

Dec *nods.*

Spencer   Isn't this fucking splendid?

Dec   So. This is how it ends. Boy, with friends like you . . .

Steph   How dare you? You're nothing but a murderer.

Dec (*wearily*)   Oh, Steph, really. You spend your entire life in complete ignorance of even the most basic moral questions until something occurs around which you can circle the wagons and make a last stand. (*Beat.*) That's your problem. Morality for you is always a last resort.

Louise   And with you it's a fetish.

Dec *looks up at her.*

Dec   At least I know where I stand.

Spencer   In the dock, old boy.

Dec   Yes, to be tried by the likes of you. Ha bloody ha.

Louise   If you despise us so much, why do you care. (*Beat.*)

Dec   I'll think about that. I'll probably have plenty of time.

Steph   Your wife lying there half dead and you couldn't care less . . .

Dec   Steph, don't presume to know what I'm feeling. (*Beat.*) It happens to be what she wanted. You won't understand that. And you won't respect her for it. Because you're cowards. You can't bear the thought that somebody could do something you wouldn't have the guts to do. And do it right in front of you. It makes you feel small.

Sound of the helicopter approaching. They watch it coming nearer.

Dec   The cavalry! (*He laughs.*)

The helicopter gets louder and a searchlight sweeps the patio.

Spencer   Absolutely fucking great.

Spencer *stands and waves his hat.* **Steph** *and* **Louise** *cling to each other as the wind from the helicopter blows around them. They all cower slightly in the blast, except for* **Dec**.

Fade.